MODERN METHODS FOR MUSICOLOGY

Digital Research in the Arts and Humanities

Series Editors
Marilyn Deegan, Lorna Hughes and Harold Short

Digital technologies are becoming increasingly important to arts and humanities research and are expanding the horizons of our working methods. This important series will cover a wide range of disciplines with each volume focusing on a particular area, identifying the ways in which technology impacts specific subjects. The aim is to provide an authoritative reflection of the 'state of the art' in the application of computing and technology. The series will be critical reading for experts in digital humanities and technology issues but will also be of wide interest to all scholars working in humanities and arts research.

Modern Methods for Musicology

Prospects, Proposals, and Realities

Edited by

TIM CRAWFORD
Goldsmiths, University of London, UK

LORNA GIBSON
University College London, UK

ASHGATE

Published by
Ashgate Publishing Limited
Wey Court East
Union Road
Farnham
Surrey, GU9 7PT
England

Ashgate Publishing Company
Suite 420
101 Cherry Street
Burlington
VT 05401-4405
USA

www.ashgate.com

British Library Cataloguing in Publication Data
Modern methods for musicology : prospects, proposals, and
    realities. - (Digital research in the arts and humanities)
    1. Musicology - Data processing
    I. Crawford, Tim II. Gibson, Lorna, 1977-
    780.2'85

Library of Congress Cataloging-in-Publication Data
Modern methods for musicology : prospects, proposals, and realities / [edited] by Tim Crawford and Lorna Gibson.
    p. cm. -- (Digital research in the arts and humanities)
    Revised versions of conference proceedings, Expert Seminar in Music, held at Royal Holloway, University of London, Mar. 3, 2006.
    Includes bibliographical references and index.
    ISBN 978-0-7546-7302-6 -- ISBN 978-0-7546-8175-5 (ebook) 1. Musicology--Data processing--Congresses. 2. Information storage and retrieval systems--Music--Congresses. I. Crawford, Tim. II. Gibson, Lorna, 1977-

    ML3797.1.M64 2008
    780.72--dc22

2009001728

ISBN   978 0 7546 7302 6
eISBN   978 0 7546 8175 5

Mixed Sources
Product group from well-managed forests and other controlled sources
www.fsc.org Cert no. SA-COC-1565
© 1996 Forest Stewardship Council
FSC

Printed and bound in Great Britain
by MPG Books Group, UK

Contents

List of Illustrations

Figures

Examples

Tables

List of Plates

Notes on Contributors

Michael Casey is Professor of Music and director of the graduate program in Digital Musics at Dartmouth College, USA, and visiting Professor of Computer Science at Goldsmiths, University of London, UK. He received his Ph.D. from the MIT Media Laboratory in 1998 and has since authored numerous articles in the fields of music information retrieval, statistical audio analysis/synthesis, and audio-visual signal processing. His recent activities include forming the OMRAS2 (Online Music Recognition and Searching) group at Goldsmiths, for which he served as Principal Investigator, and authoring AudioDB: an open-source, scalable audio-similarity software application that scales to searching through millions of recordings at interactive time-scales. Michael leads AudioDB's international consortium of software developers at Dartmouth College, Goldsmiths, and Yahoo! Inc., USA.

Tim Crawford worked for 15 years as a professional musician before joining the Music Department at King's College in 1989. As a musicologist, he has an international reputation as an expert in the field of lute music, and is the current editor of the *Complete Works* of S.L. Weiss for *Das Erbe deutscher Musik* (Bärenreiter). In the field of Music Information Retrieval (MIR), he was the co-author and coordinator of the US-UK project, OMRAS (Online Musical Recognition and Searching), and currently works on its successor, OMRAS2, in the ISMS group at Goldsmiths, University of London, where he is currently Senior Lecturer in Computational Musicology. He has been active in the setting up of ISMIR, the first regular conference series devoted to MIR (annual since 2000), acting as Program Chair (2002) and Joint General Chair (2005). For the duration of the AHRC Research Methods Network he was a member of its Academic Advisory Board.

Nicolas Donin, a musicologist, is Head of the IRCAM Analysis of Musical Practices research group, see <http://apm.ircam.fr>. His research centres on the history and practices of analysis and attentive listening since the end of the nineteenth century, and on the analysis of performance practice. He also works in collaboration with Jacques Theureau (IRCAM-CNRS) on cognitive anthropology of music composition.

Celia Duffy is Director of Academic Development at the Royal Scottish Academy of Music and Drama (RSAMD). Formerly as Head of Research she led the team responsible for development and management of research, consultancy and knowledge transfer activities and designed the RSAMD's innovative practice-based research programmes. Her career experience ranges from lecturing in music at Goldsmiths College to commercial software design and project management and new applications of ICT in higher education. Celia sits on a number of national steering and consultative groups. Her research interest in utilizing new technology in learning, teaching and research in the performing arts combines with much practical experience of working with support and funding agencies.

Michael Fingerhut, a trained mathematician and computer scientist, is the director of the IRCAM Multimedia Library, a musical and scientific hybrid (physical and digital) library which he founded in 1995. He is the editor of the newsletter of IAML (International Association of Music Libraries, Archives and Documentation Centres) and member of the Steering Committee of ISMIR (the yearly international conference on music information retrieval) and of the research commission of Enssib (the French national school of Library and Information Systems). His main interests lie in the design and development of federated access to heterogeneous music information systems.

Lorna Gibson completed her PhD in Music at Royal Holloway, University of London. Prior to this, she studied for a MA in Musicology, and BA Hons in Music at Southampton University. During her time at the AHRC ICT Methods Network, she was involved in the centre's music activities and developed her interest in music and technology. In addition to humanities computing, other interests include women's history, and British musical culture. Recent publications include *Beyond Jerusalem; Music in the Women's Institute, 1919-1969* (Ashgate 2008), 'Conducting and Empowerment: Music-Making in the Women's Institute during the Inter-War Years' in *Women in Europe between the Wars: Politics, Culture and Society* ed. Angela Kershaw and Angela Kimyongur (Ashgate, 2007), and 'The Women's Institute and Jerusalem's suffrage past' in *Women's History Review* (2006). She currently works at University College London.

Werner Goebl is a post-doctoral fellow at the Department of Psychology at McGill University in Montreal, Canada under the auspices of Caroline Palmer. He holds both a Masters in piano performance (Vienna Music University) and in Systematic Musicology (University of Vienna). He obtained his PhD at the University of Graz with Richard Parncutt. Over a period of six years, he worked in Gerhard Widmer's research group at the Austrian Research Institute for Artificial Intelligence in Vienna. His work addresses aspects of expressive performance from analysis to visualization as well as aspects of piano acoustics. For his current research on movement analysis and motor control in piano performance at McGill, he received a prestigious Erwin Schrödinger Fellowship from the Austrian Science Fund.

David M. Howard holds a first class honours BSc degree in Electrical and Electronic Engineering and a PhD in Human Communication. He currently holds a Personal Chair in Music Technology in the Department of Electronics at the University of

York. His research interests include the analysis and synthesis of singing, music and speech. He currently holds an EPSRC-funded Senior Media Fellowship to popularize science, engineering and technology. As part of this work, he co-presented a BBC4 programme on the castrato voice in 2006 and was presenter for the BBC4 programme *Voice* in 2008. David plays the organ, sings as a Deputy Tenor Songman at York Minster and directs a 12-strong a capella group, the Beningbrough Singers, from its tenor line.

Adam T. Lindsay is a Research Fellow in Lancaster University's Lancaster Institure for the Contemporary Arts (LICA) and Computing Departments. He gained bachelor's degrees in cognitive science and music at the Massachusetts Institute of Technology, and then completed a Masters degree at the MIT Media Lab concentrating on music cognition. He then spent three and a half years at Starlab NV/SA in Brussels leading research in intelligent multimedia. This led to his very active role in shaping the MPEG-7 standard, most notably as a co-editor of both its Audio and Systems parts. At Lancaster University, he pursues research related to multimedia content and description. His PhD on multimedia description and transformation is in progress.

Alan Marsden is a Senior Lecturer in Music at Lancaster University and editor of the *Journal of New Music Research*, the leading journal in the field of systematic and scientific approaches to the study of music. His study at undergraduate and postgraduate levels, at the universities of Southampton and Cambridge, concentrated on music analysis, and it was while a doctoral student that he first developed an interest in the use of computers in music research. As a Research Fellow at Lancaster University, he pursued work on the modelling of music theory by computer with Anthony Pople. Early work in organizing conferences on the topic of computers in music research led in 1992 to the publication of *Computer Models and Representations in Music*, edited by Alan Marsden and Anthony Pople. He has continued to work in the field of computational music theory as a lecturer at Queen's University Belfast and now at Lancaster. He has contributed chapters to volumes edited by Eero Tarasti, Terry Coppock, Eduardo Miranda and others, and has published articles in *Computers and the Humanities*, *Contemporary Music Review* and other journals. His book *Representing Musical Time: A Temporal-Logic Approach*, published in 2000 by Swets & Zeitlinger, has become the standard reference work for projects involving computational representation of rhythm. He is currently working on the automatic derivation of musical structure by computer in the manner of Schenkerian Analysis.

David Meredith is an Assistant Professor in the Department of Media Technology at Aalborg University. He has used computational methods to analyse musical structure and model music cognition since graduating in music from Cambridge University in 1989. From 1999 to 2006 he was a Research Fellow, first at City University and then at Goldsmiths College, University of London, developing new algorithms for pitch spelling and for pattern matching and pattern discovery in multidimensional point sets. His doctoral dissertation (Oxford University, 2007) is the most comprehensive study to date on pitch-spelling algorithms. From 2002 to 2005 he taught courses on music perception and cognition at City University and, from 2006 to 2007, he was a lecturer in the Computing Department at Goldsmiths, where he taught software engineering and web technologies. He then worked as a software engineer for Taptu Ltd in Cambridge before moving to Aalborg at the beginning of 2009.

Gerhard Widmer is Professor and Head of the Department of Computational Perception at the Johannes Kepler University in Linz, Austria, and also the founder and Head of the Intelligent Music Processing and Machine Learning Group at the Austrian Research Institute for Artificial Intelligence in Vienna. He studied computer science at the University of Technology, Vienna, and computer science and music at the University of Wisconsin, Madison, USA. He has been one of the pioneers in international research in the intersection of Artificial Intelligence and Music. He has been invited keynote speaker at numerous major international conferences, and has received various scientific honours and awards. In 1998, he was the recipient of one of Austria's highest-funded research awards (the 'START Prize') for his research on Artificial Intelligence and Musical Expression.

Frans Wiering received a PhD in musicology from the University of Amsterdam (Netherlands) for his thesis *The Language of the Modes: Studies in the History of Polyphonic Modality* (1995, published by Routledge, 2001). Since the late 1980s, he has been researching computer applications in musicology. He is the founder of the Thesaurus musicarum italicarum (<http://www.euromusicology.org>), a corpus of online music treatises by Gioseffo Zarlino and his contemporaries. His present research is in digital scholarly publishing of music and music information retrieval. He was a Visiting Scholar at Stanford University and a Visiting Fellow at Goldsmiths College, University of London. He is currently a lecturer at the Department of Information and Computing Sciences of Utrecht University (Netherlands).

Geraint A. Wiggins studied Mathematics and Computer Science at Corpus Christi College, Cambridge, and holds PhDs in Artificial Intelligence and in Musical Composition, from the University of Edinburgh. He is Professor of Computational Creativity in the Department of Computing at Goldsmiths, University of London, where he leads the Intelligent Sound and Music Systems (ISMS) group. He is Associate Editor (English) of *Musicae Scientiae*, the journal of the European Society for the Cognitive Sciences of Music, and a consulting editor of *Music Perception*.

Series Preface

Modern Methods for Musicology is the fourth title in the *Digital Research in the Arts and Humanities* series.

Each of the titles in this series comprises a critical examination of the application of advanced ICT methods in the arts and humanities. That is, the application of formal computationally based methods, in discrete but often interlinked areas of arts and humanities research. Usually developed from Expert Seminars, one of the key activities supported by the Methods Network, these volumes focus on the impact of new technologies in academic research and address issues of fundamental importance to researchers employing advanced methods.

Although generally concerned with particular discipline areas, tools or methods, each title in the series is intended to be broadly accessible to the arts and humanities community as a whole. Individual volumes not only stand alone as guides but collectively form a suite of textbooks reflecting the 'state of the art' in the application of advanced ICT methods within and across arts and humanities disciplines. Each is an important statement of current research at the time of publication, an authoritative voice in the field of digital arts and humanities scholarship.

These publications are the legacy of the AHRC ICT Methods Network and will serve to promote and support the ongoing and increasing recognition of the impact on and vital significance to research of advanced arts and humanities computing methods. The volumes will provide clear evidence of the value of such methods, illustrate methodologies of use and highlight current communities of practice.

Marilyn Deegan, Lorna Hughes, Harold Short
Series Editors
AHRC ICT Methods Network
Centre for Computing in the Humanities
King's College London
2009

About the AHRC ICT Methods Network

The aims of the AHRC ICT Methods Network were to promote, support and develop the use of advanced ICT methods in arts and humanities research and to support the cross-disciplinary network of practitioners from institutions around the UK. It was a multi-disciplinary partnership providing a national forum for the exchange and dissemination of expertise in the use of ICT for arts and humanities research. The Methods Network was funded under the AHRC ICT Programme from 2005 to 2008.

The Methods Network Administrative Centre was based at the Centre for Computing in the Humanities (CCH), King's College London. It coordinated and supported all Methods Network activities and publications, as well as developing outreach to, and collaboration with, other centres of excellence in the UK. The Methods Network was co-directed by Harold Short, Director of CCH, and Marilyn Deegan, Director of Research Development, at CCH, in partnership with Associate Directors: Mark Greengrass, University of Sheffield; Sandra Kemp, Royal College of Art; Andrew Wathey, Northumbria University; Sheila Anderson, Arts and Humanities Data Service (AHDS) (2006–2008); and Tony McEnery, University of Lancaster (2005–2006).

The project website (<http://www.methodsnetwork.ac.uk>) provides access to all Methods Network materials and outputs. In the final year of the project a community site, 'Digital Arts & Humanities' (http://www.arts-humanities.net>) was initiated as a means to sustain community building and outreach in the field of digital arts and humanities scholarship beyond the Methods Network's funding period.

Preface

The rapid evolution of technology in recent decades has had a profound impact not only on our daily lives, but also on almost every field of academic endeavour. Musicology is no exception, the power and unprecedented availability of modern computers having endowed researchers with the ability to discover and analyse a wide range of musical phenomena on a scale previously inconceivable.

This book is unique in presenting a snapshot of the current frontier of technologically inspired musicological innovation, on topics spanning content-based sound searching/retrieval, sound and content analysis, markup and text encoding, audio resource sharing, and music recognition. This harmonization of the arts and sciences brings with it a new appreciation and perspective of musical works, opens the frontiers of creativity, and dramatically increases accessibility of musical works previously available only to the privileged few.

We hope that this book will stimulate further collaboration between computer scientists and musicologists, as the boundaries of knowledge continue to be pushed back on this joint voyage of discovery. More broadly, the series of which this book forms part aims to provide an authoritative reflection of the 'state of the art' in the application of computing and technology spanning a wide range of fields. It is hoped the entire series will be critical reading for experts in digital humanities and technology issues and also of interest to all scholars working in humanities and arts research.

Tim Crawford
Lorna Gibson

List of Abbreviations

ABRSM	Associated Board of the Royal Schools of Music
ADT	Abstract Data Type
AES	Audio Engineering Society
AHDS	Arts and Humanities Data Service
AHRC	Arts and Humanities Research Council
API	Application Program Interface
BMJE	British Journal of Music Education
BRAHMS	Base Relationnelle d'Articles Hypertextes sur la Musique du 20e Siècle
CHARM AHRC	Research Centre for the History and Analysis of Recorded Music
CLAM	C++ Library for Audio and Music
CMME	Corpus Mensurabilis Musicae Electronicum
CMN	Common Music Notation
CQ	larynx Closed Quotient
DIAMM	Digital Image Archive of Medieval Music
DRH	Digital Resources in the Humanities
DRHA	Digital Resources in the Humanities and Arts
DRM	Digital Rights Management
DTW	Dynamic Time-Warped
EAD	Encoded Archival Description
EARS	ElectroAcoustic Resource Site
EASAIER	Enabling Access to Sound Archives through Integration, Enrichment and Retrieval
ECML	European Conference on Machine Learning
ECOLM	Electronic Corpus of Lute Music
ELIA	European League of Institutes of the Arts
EMG	Electromyography
$f0$	fundamental frequency
HOTBED	Handing On Tradition By Electronic Dissemination
HH-MM	Hierarchical Hidden Markov Models
ICAD	International Community for Auditory Display
ICMC	International Computer Music Conference
ICT	Information and Communications Technology
IJCAI	International Joint Conference on Artificial Intelligence
IMUTUS	Interactive Music Tuition System
IRCAM	Institut de Recherche et Coordination Acoustique/Musique

ISO	International Organization for Standardization
JISC	Joint Information Systems Committee
JNMR	Journal of New Music Research
LFCC	Log Frequency Cepstral Coefficients
LSH	locality sensitive hashing
LTAS	Long Term Average Spectrum
MATCH	Music Alignment Tool Chest
MDS	Multimedia Description Schemes
MEI	Music Encoding Initiative
METS	Metadata Encoding & Transmission Standard
MFCC	mel-frequency cepstral coefficients
MIDI	Musical Instruments Digital Interface
MIR	Music Information Retrieval
MPEG	Moving Picture Experts Group
MUCOSA	Music Content Semantic Annotator
n-ISM	Network for Interdisciplinary Studies in Science, Technology, and Music
NIME	New Interfaces for Musical Expression
OAI-PMH	Open Archive Initiative Protocol for Metadata Harvesting
OCVE	Online Chopin Variorum Edition
ÖFAI	Austrian Reseach Institute for Artificial Intelligence
OSIS	Operating System Independent Software
PCP	pitch class profile
PDF	Portable Document Format
PRIMO	Practice-as-Research in Music Online
RFID	Radio Frequency IDentification
RSAMD	Royal Scottish Academy of Music and Drama
SDX	System for Documentation in XML
SGML	Standard Generalized Markup Language
SINGAD	SINGing Assessment and Development
SMDL	Standard Music Description Language
SMIL	Synchronized Multimedia Integration Language
TabXML	TABcode XML
TEI	Text Encoding Initiative
URL	Uniform Resource Locator
XML	eXtensible Markup Language
XSLT	eXtensible Stylesheet Language Transformation

Chapter 1

Introduction

David Meredith

This collection of papers is based on revised versions of presentations made at a day-long Expert Seminar in Music held at Royal Holloway, University of London, on Friday 3 March 2006. This seminar, hosted by Tim Crawford and Andrew Wathey and funded by the AHRC ICT Methods Network, was entitled 'Modern Methods for Musicology: Prospects, Proposals and Realities'. The main purpose of the seminar was to explore the ways in which Information and Communication Technology (ICT) can be used to enhance research, teaching and learning in musicology. Since the Expert Seminar in March 2006, the papers have been revised in the light of discussions, and two further contributions added.

In his introductory address, Tim Crawford explained that, when conceiving the Seminar, he intended the term 'musicology' to be understood to include fields such as music theory, analysis and performance analysis as well as traditional historical musicology. The original intention was to exclude consideration of composition on the grounds that ICT has already been much more extensively and fruitfully applied in this area than it has in other fields of musical study. Nevertheless, some consideration was given to the ways in which ICT can be used in creative music practice (i.e. performance and composition, see Duffy, Chapter 6, this volume). This book, which is the direct result of the expert seminar, therefore provides both a picture of the *realities* of how ICT is currently being used in musicology as well as *prospects* and *proposals* for how it could be fruitfully used in the future.

The chapters that follow cover a diverse range of topics that reflect the breadth and multidisciplinarity of the field. Wiggins focuses on the problem of representing musical knowledge so that it can be effectively processed using computers. Wiering highlights the limitations of traditional book-based critical editions and proposes their replacement with multidimensional digital editions in which relationships between digitized source materials are represented by a network of hyperlinks. Fingerhut and Donin describe software tools developed at IRCAM that can be used to facilitate and enhance musicological study. Howard discusses the various ways in which computers have been used in singing for voice training, analysis and research. Duffy presents a preliminary map of how ICT is currently used within creative music practice. Goebl and Widmer provide an up-to-date overview of computational tools and models for analysing and understanding expressive performance. Lindsay describes an on-going project (now complete) to identify user needs and existing technology for processing time-based audio-visual media. Casey focuses on tools for structural analysis and information retrieval in musical audio. Finally, Marsden suggests that there is still a wide 'gulf' between those musicologists who use traditional methods and those who use the computer as their chief research tool, and proposes ways in which this gulf might be bridged.

During the seminar in which the present volume originated, there were two extended open discussions that focused in particular on the following four themes:

- The computational representation of musical information and knowledge and, in particular, the dichotomy between symbolic and audio music representations.
- Visualizing musical information and the design of appropriate interfaces for music processing software.
- The need for greater transdisciplinary awareness and collaboration among technologists and musicologists.
- The ways in which the use of ICT is transforming musicological practice and whether this transformation should be sudden or gradual.

These issues also occur time and again in the chapters that follow. I shall therefore now present a reasonably detailed account of the discussions that took place at the Expert Seminar, which, I hope, will provide a more engaging introduction to the chapters that follow than a blow-by-blow summary of the rest of this book. A complete report on the Expert Seminar is available online.[1]

An account of the discussions held at the Expert Seminar

One of the main topics debated in the discussion sessions at the Expert Seminar was the computational representation of musical information and knowledge and, in particular, the dichotomy between symbolic and audio music representations. It was proposed that a clear distinction should be made between the implementational details of how musical data is encoded (e.g. the design of file formats) and the design of representational systems (e.g. abstract data types) that support the logical and mathematical properties of musical materials (see Wiggins, Chapter 2, this volume).

Following on from this discussion, it was also suggested that, in the design of music software systems (or, indeed, *any* software system), the way in which a concept is implemented within a system should be properly hidden from the user and encapsulated within an interface that allows access only to appropriate parts of the implementation. There followed some debate as to whether MusicXML

---

1 D. Meredith, 'Rapporteur's Report' on AHRC ICT Methods Network Expert Seminar on 'Modern Methods for Musicology: Prospects, Proposals and Realities', Royal Holloway, University of London, 3 March 2006. Available online at <http://www.methodsnetwork. ac.uk/redist/pdf/es2rappreport.pdf>, accessed 21 April 2009.

(<http://www.recordare.com/xml.html>, accessed 21 April 2009) could become a universal format for exchanging musical information. However, the practical viability of the whole notion of a universally accepted music data file format was questioned and it was suggested that any data structure for music should be designed with specific test applications in mind. It was then proposed that probabilistic and machine-learning techniques had to be employed in order to represent properly the multiplicity of models employed by musicians and musicologists (e.g. the various different ways in which key is determined). It was observed that different 'musical surfaces' are required for different applications; a musical surface being a description of a passage at the most detailed level necessary for a particular application. The sonic, notational and perceptual manifestations of a musical work are therefore simply different musical surfaces giving different perspectives on the Platonic, unattainable compositional idea of a musical work (see Wiggins, Chapter 2, this volume).

There was a lively discussion about just how successful, or complete, Western staff notation (CMN) is at representing music. It was pointed out that, for example, the physical 'sound' of a specific performance and the 'intention' of a composer are not well served by CMN, which should only be regarded as one – albeit very useful – choice among an indefinite number of possible musical surfaces. A notated score can provide a convenient common point of reference for performers and musicologists, as can the graphical representations produced by certain analytical techniques such as that of Schenker.[2] However, it may be that musicology has been concerned too much with the explanation of the structures of scores and too little with the active perception and cognition of music. In particular, representational systems should be designed to handle not just notes but also perceptual entities such as voices (or, more generally, streams), chords, phrases (or, more generally, groups) and so on.

The presentations given at the seminar could be neatly divided into those concerned primarily with music at the symbolic level and those focused primarily on sub-symbolic, audio processing. However, ideally we should be able to map seamlessly and transparently between representations at different levels of structure (i.e., between musical sounds, notes and perceptual entities such as groups, streams and chords). Moreover, there no longer seems to be such a clear dichotomy between the symbolic and audio domains, as we are beginning to use similar techniques (e.g. chromagrams) on both types of data.[3]

A second important topic discussed was the design of appropriate interfaces for music processing software and the visualization of musical information. A major difficulty lies in providing technologically-naïve users access to the power of a system when there is complex underlying technology. For example, the

---

2 H. Schenker, *Free Composition (Der freie Satz)*, ed. and trans. E. Oster (New York: Schirmer, 1979).

3 See, for example, C.L. Krumhansl, *Cognitive Foundations of Musical Pitch* (New York and Oxford: Oxford University Press, 1990); Casey, Chapter 9, this volume.

HUMDRUM tool kit[4] (see <http://www.music-cog.ohio-state.edu/Humdrum/>, accessed 21 April 2009) is undoubtedly a powerful music processing system, but the bare-bones nature of its interface means that it can only be used by those who are familiar with writing UNIX shell scripts – not a skill that one expects of a typical musicologist. A software interface needs to be *graded* so that beginners can easily perform typical, common tasks and gradually become able to perform more complex tasks as they become more familiar with the system.

The third main topic considered was the need for greater transdisciplinary awareness and collaboration among technologists and musicologists. It was observed that there is now a new generation of people who have high-level skills in both music and technology and who are therefore not locked into traditional disciplines. It might therefore only be a matter of time before the problem of interdisciplinarity in our field disappears for good. Concerns were raised over the danger of technologically-naïve (but, possibly, musically sophisticated) users making false conclusions from (or attaching too much significance to) the output generated by analytical software tools. It was suggested that therefore users in the field could no longer be excused for being technologically-naïve. Musicologists must at least be able to frame questions in a way that is comprehensible to a computer scientist so that useful new tools can be developed. Several examples were cited of music practitioners obtaining useful results by misusing software tools. However, in the longer term, it is clear that a certain degree of focused training in particularly relevant technologies should be compulsory within musicological education. It also seems clear that musicology needs to become a less isolated activity and that a new culture of inter- and intradisciplinary collaboration needs to be nurtured within it. This is already being promoted by the research councils who are funding projects that employ both computer scientists and musicologists. However, it was noted that musicians and musicologists still seem to be somewhat under-represented within the Music Information Retrieval (MIR) community.

The final general topic debated during the discussion sessions at the seminar was the ways in which the use of ICT is transforming musicological practice and whether this transformation should be sudden or gradual. The use of computing technology transforms the nature of musicology because it is so different from traditional methods. However, some would argue that, if such change is to be sustainable in the long term, it needs to be effected gradually. Lessons can be learned from the field of text analysis, where computer-based researchers wrote themselves out of their communities by working too far outside traditional methods for their colleagues to be able to make use of their results. Those using traditional techniques need to be able to evaluate the work of those using newer methodologies.

---

4 D. Huron, 'Humdrum and Kern: Selective Feature Encoding', in E. Selfridge-Field (ed.), *Beyond MIDI: The Handbook of Musical Codes* (Cambridge, MA: MIT Press, 1997), pp. 375–401.

Nevertheless, it is neither possible nor desirable to prevent technology from being used, not merely to assist with tasks that can already be done by humans, but to do entirely new things that were impossible without it. And there are large, well-established and flourishing communities of researchers, such as those who attend conferences such as ICMC (<http://www.computermusic.org/page/23>, accessed 21 April 2009), ISMIR (<http://www.ismir.net>) and NIME (<http://itp.nyu.edu/nime/2007/>, both accessed 21 April 2009), that actively seek out and extend the limits of what can be achieved in music with technology.

Closing remarks

One of the major themes and conclusions that emerged throughout the course of the Expert Seminar is that the traditional dichotomy between symbolic and audio music representations in music informatics is dissolving, with similar techniques being used on both types of data. It has become clear that representation systems for music must be able to cope, not just with notes, but also with the detailed structure of musical sounds, the composer's intent, and other higher-level structures such as streams, groups and chords. Furthermore, it must become possible to map transparently between representations at these different structural levels. On the other hand, it would be a mistake to attempt to develop universal representational systems without having specific test applications in mind.

There is also evidence that considerably more effort and interdisciplinary coordination need to be applied to the design of appropriate software interfaces and methods of visualizing music information. Technologically-naïve but musically sophisticated users should be able to access the full power of a system by means of a graded interface that can be customized for use by both beginning and advanced users. Representations should support a multiplicity of views on the data and allow for multiple methods to be applied. New web and database technologies should be exploited to produce multidimensional networked online archives containing both visual and audio digital musical materials.

It is also clear that important issues arise from the interdisciplinary nature of the field of computational musicology. There is a great need for increased transdisciplinary awareness: technologists need to be more in touch with what is required by music professionals and music professionals need to have a better understanding of what is technologically feasible. This suggests that training in relevant technology should be more central in music education, and professional users of ICT should be properly trained in its use. It also seems that, gradually, the 'lone-scholar' culture in musicological research should be replaced with a more collaborative culture like the one that is typical in scientific disciplines.

Finally, the Expert Seminar highlighted the debate that is ongoing about how best computing technology can transform musicological practice. In my view, this is not an issue that is worthy of debate: the way that the use of technology within musicology evolves is limited only by the imagination and courage of musicologists and will be determined by what musicologists actually do with the technology. There seems little doubt that a more open-minded attitude and willingness to collaborate with experts in other fields will accelerate the development of ICT use within musicology in exciting new directions.

The chapters that follow explore these and other important issues in depth. This book will therefore provide a valuable resource to technologists, musicologists, musicians and music educators, facilitating the identification of worthwhile goals to be achieved using technology and effective interdisciplinary collaboration.

Chapter 2

Computer Representation of Music in the Research Environment

Geraint A. Wiggins

1. Introduction

Music representation systems have been a part of human culture for millennia. The primary purpose of early music representation systems (that is, from ancient times until the beginning of musicology in the eighteenth century) was to record music for the purpose of reproduction by performers other than the composer and/or as *aides memoire* to the composer. With the advent of academic study of music, music notation became more than performance instructions, providing data for research and teaching. At the end of the nineteenth century, audio recording became possible, supplying a new, much more detailed representation of the musical signal – though it lacked the structural information made explicit in the (modern) score.[1] In the mid-twentieth century, computers were applied to the analysis of both score and audio data, producing a plethora of new data, which then had to be stored. Typically, this data was (and is) produced piecemeal across the world, as the output of many separate projects, and was (and is) often represented for storage in ways which were (and are) not general and therefore not interoperable;[2] nor were (and are) they intended to be so, interoperability not being the aim of the research. In the late 1980s and early 1990s,[3] there were several attempts to produce symbolic representations for music,[4] and some research on the philosophy

1 G.A. Wiggins, E. Miranda, A. Smaill and M. Harris, 'A Framework for the Evaluation of Music Representation Systems', *Computer Music Journal*, 17/3 (1993): 31–42. Also available as Edinburgh DAI Research Paper no. 658.

2 Interoperability is the property of computer systems that enables them to exchange data or processes seamlessly.

3 And in fact much earlier than this (e.g. R.F. Erickson, 'The DARMS Project: A Status Report', *Computing and the Humanities*, 9/6 (1975): 291–8), though the early attempts were marred by the relatively limited computer science available at the time.

4 D. Lewin, *Generalized Musical Intervals and Transformations* (New Haven and London: Yale University Press, 1987); M. Balaban, 'Music Structures: Interleaving the Temporal and Hierarchical Aspects in Music', in O. Laske, M. Balaban and K. Ebcioğlu (eds), *Understanding Music with A: Perspectives on Music Cognition* (Cambridge, MA: MIT Press, 1992), pp. 110–39; M. Chemillier and D. Timis, 'Towards a Theory of Formal

and underlying mathematics of such representations.[5] However, no conclusive consensus on generally appropriate features for music representation was reached. More recently, approaches have been developed which do model music more fully, albeit focusing on particular extant representations of music, such as staff notation, and usually only partly or indirectly addressing more difficult issues such as timbre, nor including well-behaved inference from the data represented – for example, MEI,[6] MusicXML,[7] MPEG7 Notation[8] and MPEG4 Structured Audio.[9]

Very recently, two attempts have been made to represent music in ways which clearly conform to the principles of knowledge representation developed in the artificial intelligence (AI) community in the 1960s and 1970s,[10] in that their specifications explicitly include inference systems:[11] a temporal logic[12] for music[13] and Leibnitz; a general ontology[14] for the representation of music.[15] This inferential

---

Musical Languages', in C. Lischka and J. Fritsch (eds), *Proceedings of the 14th International Computer Music Conference* (1988), pp. 175–83.

5 D. Lewin, *Generalized Musical Intervals and Transformations*; G.A. Wiggins, M. Harris, and A. Smaill, 'Representing Music for Analysis and Composition', in M. Balaban, K. Ebcioğlu, O. Laske, C. Lischka and L. Sorisio (eds), *Proceedings of the 2nd IJCAI AI/Music Workshop*, Detroit, Michigan (1989), pp. 63–71. Also available as Edinburgh DAI Research Paper no. 504; Wiggins et al., 'A Framework for the Evaluation of Music Representation Systems'.

6 P. Roland, 'Design Patterns in XML Music Representation', in *Proceedings of ISMIR 2003*, Baltimore, Maryland, 2003. Available online at <http://www.ismir.net>, accessed 21 April 2009.

7 Recordare, 'MusicXML Definition, v. 1.1 (2005). Available online at <http://www.recordare.com/xml.html>.

8 G. Zoia, P. Nesi, J. Barthelemy et al., 'Proposal for Music Notation Modelling and Its Integration within MPEG-4 and MPEG-7' (2003). ISO/IEC JTCI/SC29/WG11.

9 J. Lazzaro, and J. Wawrzynek, *The MPEG-4 Structured Audio Book* (1999). Available online at <http://www.cs.berkeley.edu/~lazzaro/sa/book/index.html>, accessed 21 April 2009.

10 R.J. Brachman and H.J. Levesque (eds), *Readings in Knowledge Representation* (Los Altos, CA: Morgan Kaufmann, 1985).

11 An inference system is a mathematical theory that may or may not be implemented as a computer program, which allows the production of new facts from existing ones in ways that are provably correct with respect to some criterion of internal consistency (which serves to mean 'truth').

12 Temporal logic is an inference system which is focused on reasoning about time.

13 A. Marsden, *Representing Musical Time: A Temporal-logic Approach* (Lisse: Swets & Zeitlinger, 2000).

14 In this technical context, an ontology is a set of labels for objects and concepts linked with a language for expressing and reasoning about essential relationships between them.

15 S. Abdallah, Y. Raimond and M. Sandler, 'An Ontology-based Approach to Information Management for Music Analysis Systems', in *Proceedings of the 120th AES Convention, Toulouse, France*, 2006.

aspect of knowledge representation is fundamentally important: a computer encoding of data is meaningless without a method for interpreting it, and if that method is buried in the implementation of a program, it is formally opaque, prone to error and generally inaccessible, all of which features are undesirable.

In this chapter, I set out the requirements for what is intended to be a truly general computer representation for music, at the abstract level. I base my proposal on the CHARM system,[16] aiming to be able to represent a very broad range of musical knowledge at widely differing, but interrelated, levels of detail, from spectrum through to perceptual construct, from waveform through to notated score, and from different viewpoints, which allow the annotation of relationships between, for example, notation, performance, audio and perception. The system is presented not as a working, implemented database, but as a specification for a notionally complete representation system, so that other more specific systems may use it as a reference, thereby improving the prospects for interoperability between such systems. Only thus is there hope that interoperability between the various systems developed throughout the digital music research world may be facilitated.

I begin by clarifying the difference between *knowledge representation*, with which we are concerned, and *data encoding*, with which we are not. Next, I outline the notion of *data abstraction*, which is key to the utility of my proposal, and, I claim, to the representation of music in general. I then present and motivate the key features of the knowledge representation system that I suggest must underlie any computer-based intelligent music system.

2. What this chapter is not about

It is important, when considering knowledge engineering, to understand the difference between encoding of data, at the engineering level of building a computer system, and representation of knowledge, at the theoretical level of describing the operation of a phenomenon (in this case, music) that is being modelled. These two things are quite separable, both theoretically and practically, and the former is of no interest to us here. This sets the current exercise apart from much of the work presented by, for example, Selfridge-Field.[17]

To illustrate this point *in extremis*, we have no interest, for the purposes of this chapter, in how many bits of computer memory are required to store a piece of information; rather, we are interested only in the knowledge stored and its

---

16 Wiggins et al., 'Representing Music for Analysis and Composition'; Wiggins et al., 'A Framework for the Evaluation of Music Representation Systems'; A. Smaill, G.A. Wiggins and M. Harris, 'Hierarchical Music Representation for Analysis and Composition', *Computers and the Humanities*, 27 (1993): 7–17. Also available as Edinburgh DAI Research Paper no. 511.

17 E. Selfridge-Field, *Beyond MIDI: The Handbook of Musical Codes* (Cambridge, MA: MIT Press, 1997).

meaning: how complete it is, how accessible and manipulable it is, what can be inferred from it and how efficiently, in the sense of computational complexity, such inferences can be made. Anything below this level of abstraction is viewed as implementation detail, and as such is not relevant to the subject of this chapter (though it is, of course, important when we come to implementation itself).

3. Data abstraction

The primary purpose of computer systems is to manipulate data. However, data can be presented in different ways – even the *same* data can be presented in different ways. The consequence of this is that as applications are developed (by different people in different places) to serve related purposes (for example, different aspects of music analysis) related and even identical data can be expressed in different, non-interoperable encodings, and, very often, these encodings are built in to the software, so that one researcher's software can be used only on their particular choice of data encoding.

Data abstraction is a means to circumvent this problem. The idea is to identify and make explicit the properties of the data which are specifically relevant to a particular task or situation to be addressed by a program, and then supply library functions[18] that will allow the program to manipulate that data *without explicit reference to its actual syntax*. This means that other data, represented in other ways, can then be used with the same program, conditional only upon the supply of appropriate library functions for that other data representation.

To put this in context, consider the example given in a paper published in the early 1990s.[19] First, we represented *Syrinx* by Debussy in a rich representation using the words of the UK version of common music notation (CMN): crotchet, quaver and so on; and a full equal-tempered chromatic representation of pitch: A, G, E and so on.[20] Next, we built a library of software functions for comparing, adding, subtracting, multiplying and supplying constants for data represented in this language. Then we built a program to carry out a procedure of *paradigmatic analysis* as defined by Ruwet,[21] using the library defined over the data. The program was then used to produce an analysis of the piece similar to that of Nattiez.[22]

---

18 Library functions are ready-made pieces of code supplied to programmers for their use in producing their own programs.

19 Smaill et al. 'Hierarchical Music Representation'.

20 This example is specified in terms of the familiar, if vaguely specified, notion of 'notes'. However, the principles exemplified here can apply to more subtle and complex musical concepts; it should not be assumed that these authors or others in the field naïvely supposed that music was nothing but 'notes'. We return to this issue in section 4.2.

21 N. Ruwet, *Language, musique, poésie* (Paris: Editions du Seuil, 1972).

22 J.-J. Nattiez, *Fondements d'une sémiologie de la musique* (Paris: Union Générale d'Editions, 1975).

(a)

(b)

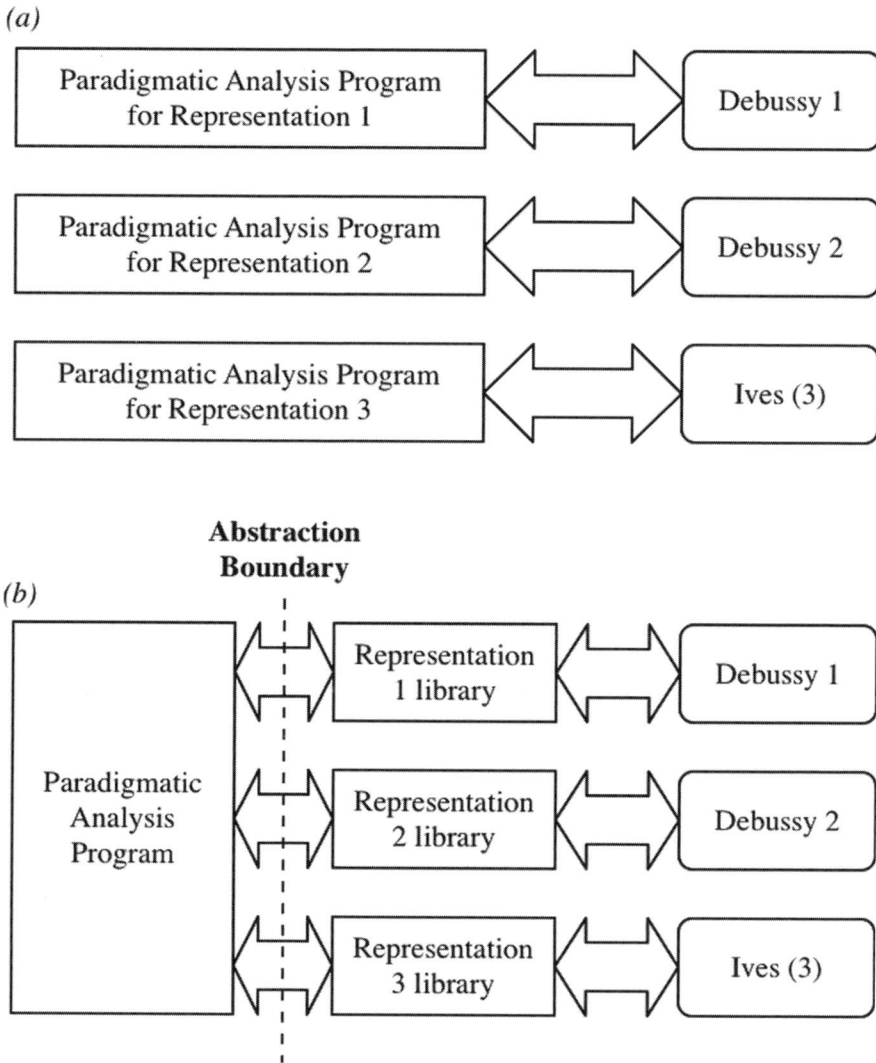

Figure 2.1   **Graphical representation of (a) the naïve construction of three separate programs, one for each representation, compared with (b) Smaill et al.'s approach**

The difference between this and the more conventional approach to programming is the existence of the library, mediating between the analysis program and the data. However, so far, little is gained, except a more intellectually complete representation.

The next thing we did was to produce another representation of the same data using integers to represent both pitch and time values of the piece, along with another library, supplying the same operations as above for this new representation. The analysis program was then run on the new representation, using the new library, but *without any change to the analysis program itself.* The analysis resulting from this was compared with the original, and found to be identical. Thus, the program was shown to be operable over an alternative representation encoding the necessary *musical* features of the data, notwithstanding the detail of the computer encoding.

Finally, to demonstrate the power of the simple abstraction used, we represented a piece of music in a completely different pitch system using integers, in a way similar to the second representation above. This piece of music was the first of the *Three Pieces for Two Quarter-tone Pianos* by Charles Ives; as the title suggests, these pieces are written for a scale with 24 divisions per octave instead of the more familiar 12. Notwithstanding the fact that the pieces are in this very different pitch vocabulary, the paradigmatic analysis approach is in principle applicable to it; we were able to run our analysis program on the new data, again *without changing the program.* All that was necessary was the implementation of a library containing functions for the *musically relevant* operations on the data in terms of which the analysis program was specified. The theoretical line drawn between the operations of the analysis process and those which define the data types is called the *abstraction boundary.* A key issue in the design of such a system is the selection of the correct abstraction boundary. This approach, which is illustrated in Figure 2.1, is a simple demonstration of how carefully planned data abstraction may allow data and program sharing, and thus facilitate research in any computer-based field. Music is no exception.

However, properly planned data abstraction is much more than just good engineering. It is also a theoretical practice that can elucidate the nature of our data and the operations we apply to it. It is this latter motivation which gives rise to the current discussion. In particular, an abstraction boundary specified at the level of concepts and language naturally used in the process embodied in the program (in our example, music analysis) will generally be best (though these concepts sometimes need to be deconstructed and expressed in terms of smaller, lower-level ones). To clarify: it is more useful to let a music program use functions with names like 'transpose pitch' rather than functions with names like 'add integer', because doing so is more meaningful in terms of the task in hand, and therefore more meaningful to the intended user. At this point, it also becomes clear, at least to programmers, that there is a strong relationship between these abstract data types (ADTs) and the usually less precisely specified application program interfaces (APIs) with which software engineers are familiar.

4. Key features of music representation systems

While careful abstraction at appropriate levels contributes to general good design of knowledge representations, a knowledge representation for music requires much more than that. The key requirements are listed in the following subsections. Though I do not claim that this list is exhaustive for all musical applications, I believe that it is usefully representative in terms of the mode of thinking which is most appropriate.

4.1 Information content

Wiggins et al.[23] give two orthogonal[24] dimensions on which a representation system for music may be placed, with the intention that the generality and utility of the system will increase as both dimensions are maximized.

Expressive completeness is the extent to which the original content of the music represented may be retrieved and/or recreated from the represented knowledge. For example, an audio signal is a very expressively complete representation of a given performance of some music; but a piano-roll cut of the same performance is less so, because exact timbral information is thrown away;[25] a transcribed (CMN) score is less expressively complete still because exact timing information is thrown away.

Structural generality is the extent to which information about musical structure (in whatever sense and at whatever level) may be stored in the representation. For example, an audio signal is minimally structurally general: significant work must be done to isolate, for example, individual notes; but a piano-roll of the same performance explicitly contains the information about which notes composed the sound, even though the detailed timbral information is thrown away; a transcribed CMN score is more structurally general still because it can contain expression markings, repeats, dynamic markings and so on.

In the examples above, expressive completeness and structural generality are more or less mutually inverse. However, this is not generally the case, as exemplified by Wiggins et al.[26] In designing music representations, the aim should be to increase scope for both expressive completeness and structural generality as far as possible.

4.2 Focusing on a musical surface

Nattiez[27] introduces a notion of *musical surface* that is similar to the concept of abstraction boundary introduced above. The idea is that, for a given musical

---

23 Wiggins et al., 'A Framework for the Evaluation of Music Representation Systems'.

24 Orthogonal is a property of pairs of geometrical structures: they are, in some sense, at right angles to each other. This is extended in common scientific parlance to mean 'mathematically independent'.

25 Even if the performance was made from the same roll this is still true: the acoustics of the room in which the performance was given are lost.

26 Wiggins et al., 'A Framework for the Evaluation of Music Representation Systems'.

27 Nattiez, *Fondements d'une sémiologie de la musique*.

task, there is a 'lowest level of interest' – that is, a level of detail below which further detail is unimportant. For example, in Nattiez's paradigmatic analysis of Debussy's *Syrinx*, he chooses the musical surface of *notes*, which is most natural to the chosen analysis technique. Other examples of musical surface might be spectra, chords or even large sections of musical works, if one were interested, for example, in large-scale structural analysis.

In any general music representation system, it will be useful to have an explicit notion of musical surface, because, as explained below, we need to represent many different levels hierarchically, and it will be convenient to be able to group all the entities appearing on a given musical surface together (and hence to ignore lower levels of detail); explicit annotation will be useful because the location of the musical surface will not necessarily be otherwise inferable from the represented knowledge. However, it is important to understand that the musical surface is only the *lowest* level of interest in the musical structures in a fully structurally general representation; that is, the structural information above the surface is still visible and available for reasoning.

4.3 Multiple hierarchies

This last remark implies an important point made by several researchers, including Lerdahl and Jackendoff,[28] Balaban,[29] Smaill et al.[30] and Marsden,[31] and which is implicit in the vast majority of music analysis: musical knowledge is *hierarchical*. A further refinement of this, emphasized by Smaill et al. and Lerdahl and Jackendoff, is that musical knowledge is *multiply hierarchical*, in the sense that many different hierarchies may be constructed simultaneously on any given musical surface. For example, consider a typical hymn or chorale harmonization, based on the musical surface of notes. In general, this may be thought of in several ways: it is a collection of notes; it is a collection of vocal parts, each of which may be a collection of notes or a collection of verse parts, each of which in itself may be a collection of notes; it is a collection of chords, some of which may be grouped into cadences; and so on. These multiple hierarchies may be arbitrarily complex and arbitrarily intertwined; however, for a given non-partitioned set of data at the musical surface, they must all join at some (possibly very abstract) top point. Roughly speaking, one might characterize the information contained in such hierarchies as *syntactic*; Smaill et al. name them *constituent hierarchies* for this reason. Constituent hierarchies are characterised by the ⊆ (non-strict subset) relation. Constituent hierarchies must carry formal and textual descriptions of the relationships they denote.

---

28 F. Lerdahl and R. Jackendoff, *A Generative Theory of Tonal Music* (Cambridge, MA: MIT Press, 1983).

29 Balaban, 'Music Structures: Interleaving the Temporal and Hierarchical Aspects in Music'.

30 Smaill et al., 'Hierarchical Music Representation'.

31 Marsden, *Representing Musical Time*.

4.4 Non-hierarchical relations

However, there may be (and, I claim, always are) annotations on these hierarchical structures which are not part of the constituent hierarchy. These annotations describe relationships between parts of the hierarchies that are based not purely on structural inclusion, but on more subtle musical relationships such as similarity. Some researchers view these relationships as taking the place of linguistic semantics in music; here, I label them more neutrally as *referential*. Referential relations may be hierarchical, and possibly even cyclic; however, for efficiency of computation, we require that they form a directed graph, whose nodes are nodes in the constituent hierarchy. Like constituent hierarchies, referential relation annotations should carry formal and textual descriptions of the relationship they denote, so that information does not need to be repeatedly computed.

4.5 Description language(s)

This in turn implies the need for a formal description language, with appropriate primitives and combination operators for describing relationships within and between musical surfaces. This language must be itself extensible, so as to allow the definition of new types of surface and their predications, and, indeed, new predications on existing surfaces; however, the extensibility must be conservative with respect to the soundness[32] and completeness[33] properties of the language. The design of such a language is a major task, and will form a significant part of any project in this area.

Because of the complexity of any system implementing all the features described here, an important part of the language will be projection operators,[34] to extract particular dimensions or combinations of the representation for study in themselves. This will allow inclusion of constructions such as *viewpoints*.[35]

---

32 Soundness is the property of an inference system which guarantees that no new information can be derived which would lead to internal inconsistency in the system (i.e. only things which are 'true' can be deduced).

33 Completeness is the property of an inference system which guarantees that anything that is consistent in the system can be derived (i.e. all things that are 'true' can be inferred).

34 Projection is the mathematical operation of finding the image, in one space, of an object expressed in another space. For example, a shadow on a flat surface is a two-dimensional projection of a three-dimensional object.

35 D. Conklin and I.H. Witten, 'Multiple Viewpoint Systems for Music Prediction', *JNMR*, 24 (1995): 51–73; D. Conklin and C. Anagnostopolou, 'Representation and Discovery of Multiple Viewpoint Patterns', in *Proceedings of the 2001 International Computer Music Conference*, ICMA, October 2001.

4.6 Multiple domains of representation

Babbitt[36] presents a view of music representation in which representations are in either the *acoustic* (or physical), the *auditory* (or perceived) or the *graphemic* (or notated) domain. I follow this view here, taking the philosophical stance that the mysterious thing that is music is actually something abstract and intangible, but described by all three of these representations, in a sense something like that of the Platonic ideal.[37] Therefore, it will be necessary to label each constituent and entity in the representation system with the name of the domain in which it exists, and to include a distinguished *coreference* relation in the representation system, which will allow us to specify explicitly that two constituents in different domains refer to the same (abstract, musical) thing.

It should be noted that there is a relationship, or at least an analogy, between the idea of Babbitt's domains and the projections introduced in the section above. It is perhaps helpful to think of each of the domains as a projection of the 'whole musical object', which is itself not directly available.

I conjecture that there are probably more useful domains than the three in Babbitt's list. For example, it is not clear where, in this trinity, a composer's *intention* would be best represented; maybe this is a domain in itself, or maybe it is a relationship between (Babbitt's) domains – or maybe the answer to this question depends on which composer one is discussing.

4.7 Inference and operations

Introducing a notion of coreference, as above, leads naturally to the question of identity between represented entities. It is not adequate here to rely on what is usually thought of as Leibnitz identity,[38] in which objects are identical if and only if their properties are identical, because non-identical objects can be rendered apparently (but spuriously) identical through projection on to a lower-dimensional representation.[39] Therefore, each entity that is represented using the system must have a unique identifier, through which it may be named explicitly. Identity of identifier is then strictly equivalent to identity of identified, by definition. Identity, then, is not a semantic operation, but a syntactic one: two mentioned entities are identical if their syntactic identifiers are the same, and not otherwise.

---

36 M. Babbitt, 'The Use of Computers in Musicological Research', *Perspectives of New Music*, 3/2 (1965): 74–83. Available online at <http://www.jstor.org/>, accessed 21 April 2009.

37 Plato, *The Republic*, trans. J.L. Davies and D.J. Vaughan (Ware: Wordsworth Editions, 1997).

38 Audi, R. (ed.), *The Cambridge Dictionary of Philosophy*, 2nd edn (Cambridge: Cambridge University Press, 1999), p. 416.

39 For example, a blue cube and a red cube held in the same orientation are indistinguishable by comparison only of their shadows.

As such, coreference takes on the status of a common-usage 'identity' function: we might say that the performed note (acoustic domain) we have just heard (auditory domain) *is* a particular note on a stave (graphemic domain); in the view espoused in this and the previous sections, this actually means the three domain-specific representations *corefer* to the abstract musical entity that is a note in the context of the piece being performed.

None of the above discussion impinges upon the equality theories[40] of the various features used to describe the music. For example, comparing the locations of two notes on a page modelled as a geometrical plane (graphemic domain) can be done with the familiar Euclidian geometrical comparators.

4.8 Continuous features

Much past work in music representation has chosen a musical surface that avoids the difficult area of symbolic representation of values which vary continuously in time. For example, a portamento in CMN is commonly notated as a straight line between one note and another – but this may be performed in many different ways by different performers, and the majority of systems do not attempt to describe it precisely.

The continuity is difficult to handle for several reasons, but most formally because the meaning of equality between time-variant values is difficult to define. Suppose, for example, that we represent the pitch of two performances of a portamento, as above. The first dilemma is: should we consider equality at the level of 'a portamento between a given two notes' or at level of 'the actual pitches on a millisecond-by-millisecond basis'? If the former, then it is necessary in general to be able to infer the CMN form from the performance, or at least to store it in conjunction with the performance representation – in general, this is currently unachievable. If the latter, then other problems arise: first the tempi of the two performances are probably not identical, so the question arises of how we deal with any disparity in time: should we normalize the two to the same length; and if we normalize, should we normalize with respect to real time or with respect to musical beat (if there is one)? And so on ... An orthogonal issue is the representation of the performance itself. If we use a continuous function to model the portamenti, then intensional equality[41] between the two specifications is (at least in general) undecidable.[42] This problem can be overcome by sampling the

---

40 An equality theory for a given type of data is the set of operations by which equality between items of that type of data may be affirmed or denied.

41 Intensional equality is equality determined only in terms of functions describing the objects compared, and not by comparing their actual values.

42 Decidability is the property of a predicate which guarantees that an effective procedure can be given to affirm or deny that predicate for well-formed input data. An undecidable predicate is one for which it is provably impossible to give such a procedure. Broadly, the concept of decidability is exemplified by the Halting Problem (A. Turing, 'On

continuous values, and representing them extensionally,[43] as an array of discrete ones. At this point it becomes easy to compare the portamenti, on a value-by-value basis; however, the meaning of equality still needs to account for issues such as quantization error, introduced by the sampling (which, of course, may be exacerbated by prior audio processing in any case).

It seems unlikely, in the face of these questions, which may well receive context-dependent answers, that any one notion of equality will serve for all purposes. It is therefore necessary to admit the definition of specialized, context-dependent equality theories for these continuous and discrete quantities, which occur throughout musical performance. This can be neatly achieved through the use of ADTs.

4.9 Representing uncertainty

Any formal system used for the purposes of humanities research is likely to need the ability to represent uncertainty explicitly, and music is no exception. Examples of uncertainty arise in many ways, of which the following are but a few:

- In the graphemic domain, the provenance of a source may be uncertain, or editions may not be definitely attributed, or the ink on a page may be smudged. Composers may also deliberately notate chance operations in scores, and this must be represented semantically.
- In the acoustic domain, the output of an algorithm for detecting the onset of notes may be probabilistic, and so may yield a probability distribution over a short time period, rather than an exact onset time.
- In the auditory domain, different listeners may infer different structures from the same acoustic stimulus.

Therefore, it is necessary to represent disjunction (either/or) in the representation (a feature which is very unusual in music representation systems, MEI[44] and TabXML[45] being two exceptions), and also to allow disjuncts to carry associated probabilities. It is necessary further, at least in principle, to admit continuous distributions (to address, for example, the need to express precisely a likelihood of an acoustic analysis, as above). This last is perhaps surprising, since such

---

Computable Numbers, with an Application to the Entscheidungsproblem', *Proceedings of the London Mathematical Society*, 2/42 (1936): 230–65): it is not possible in general to give a procedure to determine whether a program will or will not terminate in finite time, though to be precise this is semi-decidable: if the program does terminate in finite time, then we can in principle find this out, though it may take a while.

43 Extensional, here, is the opposite of 'intensional' (see n. 41).

44 Roland, 'Design Patterns in XML Music Representation'.

45 F. Wiering, T. Crawford and D. Lewis, 'Fretting with the Computer: Designing a Markup Strategy for Digital Critical Editions of Lute Tablatures', MedRen, Tours 2005 <http://people.cs.uu.nl/fransw/presentations/WieringMedRen2005.pdf>

an acoustic analysis will nearly always have been performed on quantized, sampled data. However, if a continuous distribution is known, storing it literally (and presumably parametrically), rather than storing its application to that data is preferable for the purposes of *post hoc* reasoning, because doing so gives an account of *why* the data is as it is.

4.10 Time and its representation

Marsden[46] and others have used temporal logic to represent order and overlap of musical events (mostly conceptualized as notes). It is not immediately clear that the case for doing so has been made, because the same inferences are derivable from the more obvious time-line representations espoused by, for example, Wiggins et al.,[47] in which time is explicitly represented at some appropriate level of abstraction, rather than being implied by notions such as simultaneity, precedence and so on. However, temporal reasoning may well be useful in less prosaic contexts, such as in representing musics that are not scored with respect to a particular time base. There is an unresolved philosophical issue here: is it actually meaningful to reason about a time-based art such as music at a level where the basis of time is abstracted away? In other words, even when a piece of music is specified at the *intensional* level without a time base, can we reason about it *qua music* without *extending* (or *extensionalizing?*) it onto a particular time base as we do so?

Perhaps a more generally important application of temporal logic in music representation is at the meta-level with respect to the musical surface: denoting information *about* the music, rather than denoting the music itself. In this context, for example, it may be useful to abstract information to the extent of saying that one event appears before another without saying exactly when or by how much; but, again, it is always possible to do this in terms of a time-line using existential quantification,[48] even if an exact date or time is unknown. The need for specialized temporal logic is therefore an open question in this context. It seems likely that explicit temporal logic and associated inference will be nothing more than syntactic sugar in most cases – but perhaps this will be a valuable level at which to work in practical terms.

4.11 Building representation systems

In this section, I have presented a sort of shopping list of desirable properties of generic music representation systems. The vast majority of music representation systems will not require all of these features, and I do not claim to have listed all the features they might require; however, I suggest that systems conforming

---

46 Marsden, *Representing Musical Time*.

47 Wiggins et al., 'Representing Music for Analysis and Composition'.

48 Existential quantifiers allow logics to express predications about objects that are known to exist, without saying exactly what they are.

to the specifications implicit in my shopping list have a better chance of being interoperable, and hence useful, than those which do not. I also suggest that applying the methodologies implicit in this section is likely to enlighten, or at least clarify, our thinking about the music we choose to represent.

5. XML

No discussion of music representation would be complete without mention of XML and the XML sub-languages devoted to music, most specifically MusicXML[49] and MEI.[50] Other extant systems are MPEG4 Structured Audio, which allows structured representation of audio signals,[51] and MPEG7 Notation.[52]

My position is that XML-based languages are inappropriate for the generalized markup of musical metadata, because XML imposes a single fixed hierarchy on the data it marks up. In music, however, it is very easy to construct examples in which one requires multiple hierarchies, as outlined in section 4.3. This problem is not restricted to music, but there is evidence that the XML research community treats it as a problematic property of data, known as 'overlapping', rather than as a shortcoming of the representation language. For example, DeRose writes:

> OSIS ..., a standard schema for biblical and related materials, has to deal with extreme amounts of overlap. The simplest case involves book/chapter/verse and book/story/paragraph hierarchies that pervasively diverge; but many types of overlap are more complicated than this.

> The basic options for dealing with overlap in the context of SGML or XML are described in the TEI guidelines. ... Thus, I present a variation on TEI milestone markup that has several advantages. This is now the normative way of encoding non-hierarchical structures in OSIS documents.[53]

The telling phrase, here, is at the end. In fact, the data described is not non-hierarchical, but *multiply* hierarchical (in other words, the structure is, formally, a graph, or maybe a semi-lattice, but not a tree). The use of the term 'nonhierarchical' here suggests that the author believes that only tree structures are actually hierarchical – an archetypal case of a hammer owner requiring everything to be a nail.

It is worth emphasizing that this does not mean that we *cannot* use XML-based representations for multiply hierarchical structures. We can easily do so

---

49 Recordare, 'MusicXML Definition, v. 2.0'.
50 Roland, 'Design Patterns in XML Music Representation'.
51 Lazzaro and Wawrzynek, *The MPEG-4 Structured Audio Book.*
52 Zoia et al., 'Proposal for Music Notation Modelling'.
53 D. DeRose, 'Markup Overview: A Review and a Horse', *interChange*, March (2005), p. 16.

by using the XML component simply as a syntax checker for whatever it is we are representing; in some contexts, this may even be useful. Further, there are certainly musical contexts where fully multiple-hierarchical representation is not necessary. The important distinction is between merely using the *syntax* of XML (or other representation, for that matter) and using its *inference capabilities*. If we merely use the syntax, we gain few, if any, of the advantages of the system, but nevertheless import all the extra work and complication it implies, which then raises the question of why we bother to use it at all.

The upshot of XML's restriction to trees is that the advantages of using the language can only be applied to a simplistic subset of musical markup, without adding non-uniform extra features (such as the 'milestone markup' mentioned above). This in turn draws the use of XML for music representation[54] into question, because it becomes necessary either creatively to abuse existing features of the language (as above), which is undesirable, or to implement the mechanism properly to represent one's data on top of XML, in which case one is needlessly (and therefore unacceptably) increasing the mechanistic overhead of one's representation. Either of these approaches might be described as bad engineering.

Furthermore, XML is not really intended to be a knowledge representation language, but rather a data interchange format. As such, we might question whether it *should* be used for knowledge representation of any kind, or whether it would be better viewed purely as a means for encapsulating data for efficient storage and transfer.

The minimal expressive power required to represent the multiple hierarchies of music is that of the directed graph; sometimes, acyclicity may be appropriate, but not in general. Trees, as represented by XML, are a relatively small subset of the set of directed graphs, and therefore unenhanced XML is inadequate, in general, for the fully detailed representation of properly structured musical knowledge. As such, I would advocate the use of XML for data interchange at the level of syntactic descriptions of graphs with whatever annotations are appropriate for music, and not for the representation of music directly.

6. Conclusion

In this chapter, I have presented ten general requirements for music representation, at various levels ranging from the level of effective engineering to the philosophy of knowledge representation. I argue that any general representation for music will require all of these features if it is truly to serve the needs of the computer-based musicologists and musicians of the future.

---

54 Or, indeed, for representation of anything multiply hierarchical.

Acknowledgements

I gratefully acknowledge the input, direct or indirect, of my valued colleagues Samer Abdallah, Michael Casey, Alastair Craft, Tim Crawford, Mitch Harris, Kjell Lemström, David Lewis, Alan Marsden, Dave Meredith, Eduardo Miranda, Alan Smaill and Frans Wiering, all of whom have influenced my thinking in this work very greatly. This work was funded by a Programme Officer's grant from the Andrew W. Mellon Foundation.

Chapter 3

Digital Critical Editions of Music:
A Multidimensional Model

Frans Wiering

1. Introduction

The aim of this chapter is to think through some implications that ICT may have for critical editing and scholarly editions of music. These implications are likely to go far beyond currently accepted practices such as the use of music notation software for the preparation of scores, the online distribution of music in PDF format or even the interchange of score data in some encoded format. Yet there is an almost complete silence as to the more radical possibilities for innovation. This is rather surprising, perhaps even worrying, since the 'critical edition in the digital age' has been an issue of debate for at least ten years in literary studies[1] and musicologists are generally well aware of developments in that area. So why this silence? Are musicologists disappointed by ICT after so many failed promises? Is current technology not mature enough for digital critical editions of music? Or is there no perceived use for these?

1.1 Outline

It is mainly the last question that will be addressed in this chapter. To prepare the ground, I will examine editorial methods in literary studies and musicology. Then I will present a generic, multidimensional model for digital critical editions of music, which is illustrated by means of four case studies. The chapter finishes with a critical evaluation of the model and a discussion of some obstacles that must be overcome before digital critical editions of music will be routinely created and used by musicologists.

1.2 What this chapter is not about

This chapter describes an abstract model for multidimensional editions of music as finished, relatively stable applications. Two issues are specifically not addressed: the implementation of such editions, and the process whereby editors might create

---

1 L. Breure, O. Boonstra and P.K. Doorn, *Past, Present and Future of Historical Information Science* (Amsterdam: NIWI-KNAW, 2004), pp. 39–45.

them. As part of the former, a solution for the encoding of text-critical features was proposed by Wiering et al.;[2] the latter was briefly discussed by Wiering et al.[3] It is also important to note that the case studies in this chapter are conceptual and do not describe current initiatives for creating digital critical editions, with the exception of the Electronic Corpus of Lute Music (ECOLM).

2. Literary studies

By tradition, the object of a scholarly edition is to establish a well-reasoned text of a document. Methods for doing so have been around for centuries. The most influential of these is the stemmatic method developed by Karl Lachmann in the early nineteenth century.[4] Its aim is to reconstruct, by comparing the surviving sources of a text and by evaluating their differences, the archetypal document from which these sources descend. Since Lachmann's days, many alternative approaches have been proposed; all of these combine one or more reconstructed texts with an account of the source network. An important part of the latter is the critical apparatus, a list of corrected errors and variant readings that have not made it to the final text.

Three technological developments – structured markup, hypertext and mass digitization – have fundamentally affected critical editing. Structured markup became virtually identical with SGML after 1986, when it was released as an ISO standard; it is now superseded by the closely related XML recommendation. Document encoding using structured markup has two important characteristics that distinguish it from desktop publishing formats (and flat text representation). First, it separates the logical structure of a document from its visual presentation. As a consequence, multiple 'views' can be generated from one encoded document. For example, one view of a book is its full-text content, another the table of contents. Second, it allows the document to be enriched with additional information. An example is the encoding of both source errors and their correction, so that an apparatus can be automatically created. Both features of structured markup are exploited in the TEI markup scheme, which is used successfully in many

---

2 F. Wiering, T. Crawford and D. Lewis, 'Creating an XML Vocabulary for Encoding Lute Music', in *Humanities, Computers and Cultural Heritage: Proceedings of the XVIth International Conference of the Association for History and Computing*, 14–17 September 2005 Amsterdam. (Amsterdam: Royal Netherlands Academy of Arts and Sciences, 2005), pp. 279–87.

3 F. Wiering, T. Crawford and D. Lewis, 'Fretting with the Computer: Designing a Markup Strategy for Digital Critical Editions of Lute Tablatures', presentation held at MedRen2005, Tours (2005). Available online from <http://people.cs.uu.nl/fransw/presentations/WieringMedRen2005.pdf>, accessed 21 April 2009.

4 J. Grier, 'Editing', in S. Sadie and J. Tyrrell (eds), *The New Grove Dictionary of Music and Musicians* (London: Macmillan, 2001), vol. 7, pp. 885–95.

digital editions projects that focus on the information contained in the edited documents.[5]

Hypertext, which first reached the general public through Apple's HyperCard (released in 1987) and later through the World Wide Web, allows documents to be structured in a non-linear way. A hypertext edition therefore may present more than one reading of a text, presenting alternative continuations of a text where the sources differ, or coordinate a number of completely encoded sources of a single document. McGann's notion of HyperEditing, briefly discussed below, provides a theoretical justification for such an approach.

Mass digitization arose in the 1990s, stimulated by the ever-decreasing prices of storage space and by the availability of standard technology for creating and processing digital audio, images and video. A large number of digital libraries, archives and museums have emerged over the last decade, giving scholars access to documents with unprecedented ease. Even though metadata are routinely attached to digitised sources, their content is still undigested: therefore they provide no alternative to critical editions. However, models for digital editions do often include digital facsimiles as a way of presenting the raw materials on which the edition is based.

2.1 HyperEditing

From the many scholars who have examined the consequences of these developments for critical editing, I have singled out Jerome McGann[6] for particular discussion because he draws the attention to the limitations of the book format itself: a book cannot contain and coordinate all source materials that an edition is based on. The analytical tools an edition in book format contains, notably the critical apparatus, are shaped by this fact: these abbreviate and restructure information from many different sources in such a way that it fits the book format (see Figure 3.1a). The price one pays for this in terms of usability is quite high. For example, it is hard to reconstruct a primary source from editorial text and the evidence in the apparatus, and virtually impossible to get a full picture of the source network. Another issue McGann raises is that the book format does not allow the inclusion of non-textual information such as performances of a play or song, or even the physical features of a source.

The solution McGann proposes is HyperEditing, the creation of critical, fully networked hypermedia archives. This concept is illustrated in Figure 3.1b. A critical archive consists of virtual copies of the sources, connections between

---

5 An example in musicology is *Thesaurus musicarum italicarum*, which contains nearly 30 Italian music treatises edited with TEI markup (<http://www.euromusicology. org>, accessed 21 April 2009).

6 J. McGann, 'The Rationale of HyperText' (1995). Available online from <http:// www.iath.virginia.edu/public/jjm2f/rationale.html>, accessed 21 April 2009.

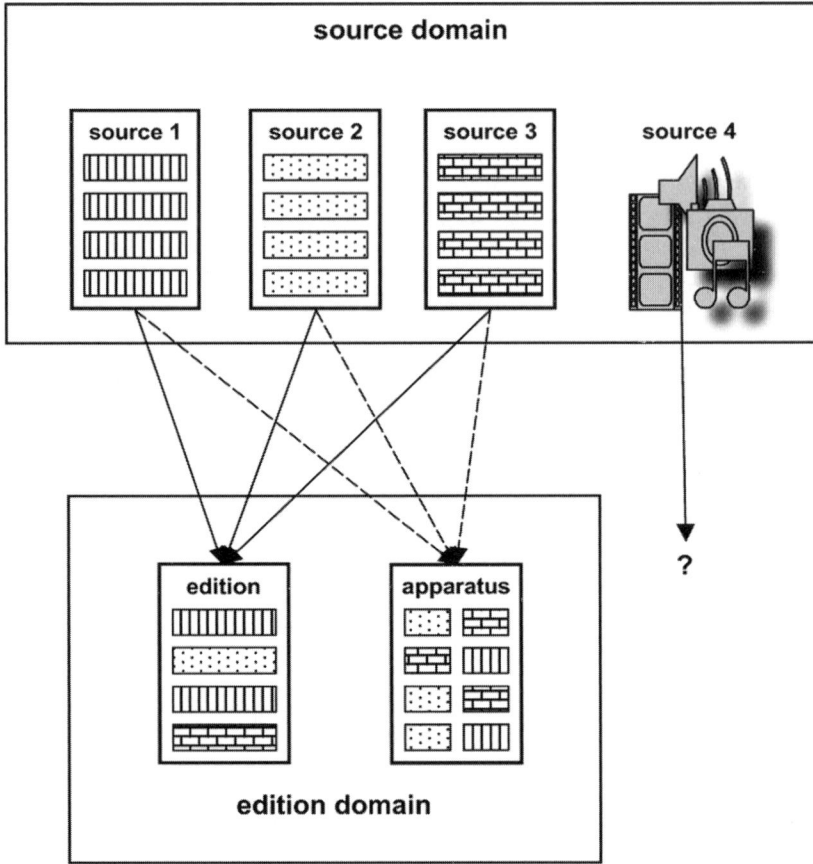

Figure 3.1a   Different models of editing: the book format

these, annotations with critical and contextual information, and analytical tools for searching and comparing the materials.

As a networked model, the critical archive documents the genesis, transmission and reception of a text through the material instances by which it survives. It is not a hierarchical model that aims at a reconstruction of the author's intention. Yet such a reconstruction can be incorporated into the model, for example by defining an edition as a 'reading path' through the critical archive. (A related notion of reading path can be found in Kress and in Darnton.[7])

---

7 G. Kress, 'Reading Images: Multimodality, Representation and New Media' (2004). Available online from <http://www.knowledgepresentation.org/BuildingTheFuture/Kress2/Kress2.html>, accessed 21 April 2009; R. Darnton, 'Old Books and E-Books. The Gutenberg Prize Acceptance Speech of 2004', *Gutenberg-Jahrbuch* (2005): 17–20.

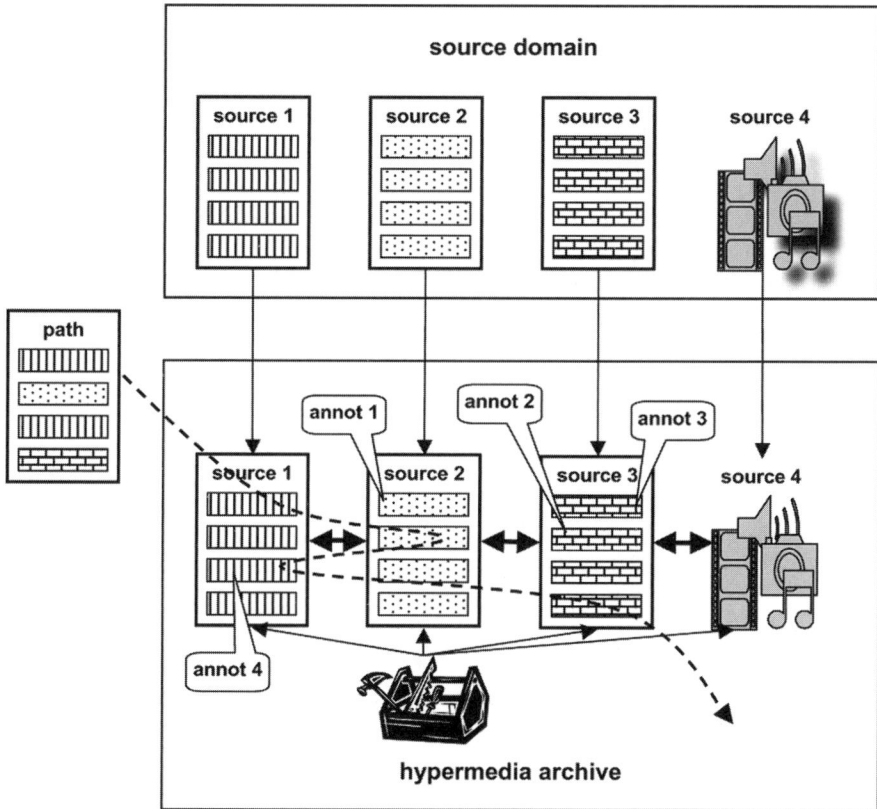

Figure 3.1b   Different models of editing: HyperEditing

HyperEditing deals with material instances of texts rather than with idealized works abstracted from those instances. This seems a promising perspective for musicological editing, especially if one considers written sources as instructions for – and often the only remaining traces – of past performances.

3. Critical editing in musicology

Critical editing in music has been shaped after traditional models of literary editing.[8] In music too, the task of the editor is to establish the text of a composition by some accepted method, whether this is by means of a stemmatic, best-text or copy-text approach. (From here on 'text' is short for the 'musical text' of a composition.) This text is then transcribed or adapted to modern notational conventions, so

8 Grier, 'Editing'.

that it is easily legible. Missing information is supplied (e.g. text underlay) and perceived ambiguities are resolved (e.g. *musica ficta*). All of this makes critical editions usable in performance. At the same time expert performers and scholars may feel that such adaptations add an unwanted layer of interpretation to the work. Transcription and the level of editorial intervention are therefore much more an issue of debate than how to establish the composition's text.

Philip Brett[9] observed that there are very few successful applications of the stemmatic method in music. The fundamental problem here is the meaning and weight one attaches to variants that occur between sources of the same work. Text-based editorial methods tend to treat variants as corruptions, whereas in fact they may often reflect adaptation to performance circumstances. To take Brett's argument one step further, to create an edition as a reconstruction of the 'work itself' and not to give full access to the 'instances' that together constitute this work is to misrepresent the inherent flexibility and adaptability of a very large repertoire of music.

Music publishing has been strongly affected by ICT, but mainly at a practical level. Scores prepared using music notation software are routinely distributed via the internet. A large number of choral works in decent, practical editions is available through the Choral Public Domain Library.[10] At the scholarly end of the digital publication spectrum stands a website containing diplomatic transcriptions of the works of the fifteenth-century composer Caron.[11] Other examples of the influence of mass digitization include a range of conventional digital library projects such as Variations 2[12] and more advanced ones such as the Digital Image Archive of Medieval Music,(DIAMM)[13] which features digital restoration of scanned images, and the Online Chopin Variorum Edition,[14] where sections from different sources can be aligned and compared.

Apart from the last example, hypertextual editions of music do not seem to exist yet, but structured markup has reached music in several ways. An important early example is Standard Music Description Language (SMDL).[15] SMDL distinguishes four domains in which a composition exists: visual (score), gestural (performance), analytical and logical. The last abstractly represents compositional intent, for which SMDL defines an SGML vocabulary. SMDL was never implemented

---

9 P. Brett, 'Text, Context, and the Early Music Editor', in N. Kenyon (ed.), *Authenticity and Early Music: A Symposium* (Oxford: Oxford University Press, 1988), pp. 83–114.

10 <http://www.cpdl.org>, accessed 21 April 2009.

11 <http://www.une.edu.au/music/Caron>, accessed 21 April 2009.

12 <http://variations2.indiana.edu>, accessed 21 April 2009.

13 <http://www.diamm.ac.uk>, accessed 21 April 2009.

14 J. Rink, 'Online Chopin Variorum Edition (OCVE), funded by the Andrew W. Mellon Foundation' (2006). Available online from <http://www.ocve.org.uk>, accessed 21 April 2009.

15 S.R. Newcomb, 'Standard Music Description Language Complies with Hypermedia Standard', *Computer*, 24/7 (1991): 76–9.

except in a few demos, but conceptually it influenced several XML-based music encoding systems. The best known of these is MusicXML.[16] Its purpose is to allow interchange of musical data, particularly between music printing applications, and it has many facilities for precisely recording layout. The Music Encoding Initiative (MEI) is less detailed about layout, but has some basic text-critical structures.[17]

Some attempts have been made to provide deeper access to the materials from which an edition is created. Thomas Hall[18] experimented with computer-based stemmatics for the New Josquin Edition, but there has been no follow-up to his experiments. Standard databases can be effectively configured for storing musical variants, as Yo Tomita did in his studies of J.S. Bach's WTC II.[19] A drawback to this approach is that the information is logically separated from the score. Experiments in integrating the two, using a TEI-based tagset, have been carried out as part of ECOLM.[20] The separation of logical structure and visual presentation is especially exploited in the *Corpus Mensurabilis Musicae Electronicum*.[21] Out of one encoded score, different transcription styles can be generated: one can for example choose between original and modern clefs, and different barline styles. CMME will also provide access to variants and manuscript context of works.

4. A multidimensional model

I perceive several open issues in current methods of critical editing of music:

- No clear distinction between establishing the text of a composition on the one hand, and transcription style and supplying performance information on the other.
- Loss of information about the notation in the sources.
- The weakly acknowledged role of variants to the understanding of a musical work.

---

16 M. Good, 'MusicXML for Notation and Analysis', *Computing in Musicology* 12 (2001): 113–24; <http://www.recordare.com>, accessed 1 September 2007.

17 P. Roland, 'The Music Encoding Initiative (MEI)' (2005). Available online from <http://www.lib.virginia.edu/digital/resndev/mei/>, accessed 1 September 2007.

18 T. Hall, 'Some Computer Aids for the Preparation of Critical Editions of Renaissance Music', *Tijdschrift van de Vereniging voor Nederlandse Muziekgeschiedenis* 25 (1975): 38–53.

19 Y. Tomita and T. Fujinami, 'Managing a Large Text-critical Database of J.S. Bach's *Well-tempered Clavier II* with XML and Relational Database', in I. Asselman and B. Bouckaert (eds), *International Musicological Society: 17th International Conference, 1–7 August 2002, Leuven* (Leuven: Alamire, 2002), pp. 256–7.

20 <http://www.ecolm.org>, accessed 21 April 2009.

21 T. Dumitrescu, 'Corpus Mensurabilis Musicae Electronicum: Toward a Flexible Electronic Representation of Music in Mensural Notation', *Computing in Musicology* 12 (2001): 3–18; <http://www.cmme.org>, accessed 21 April 2009).

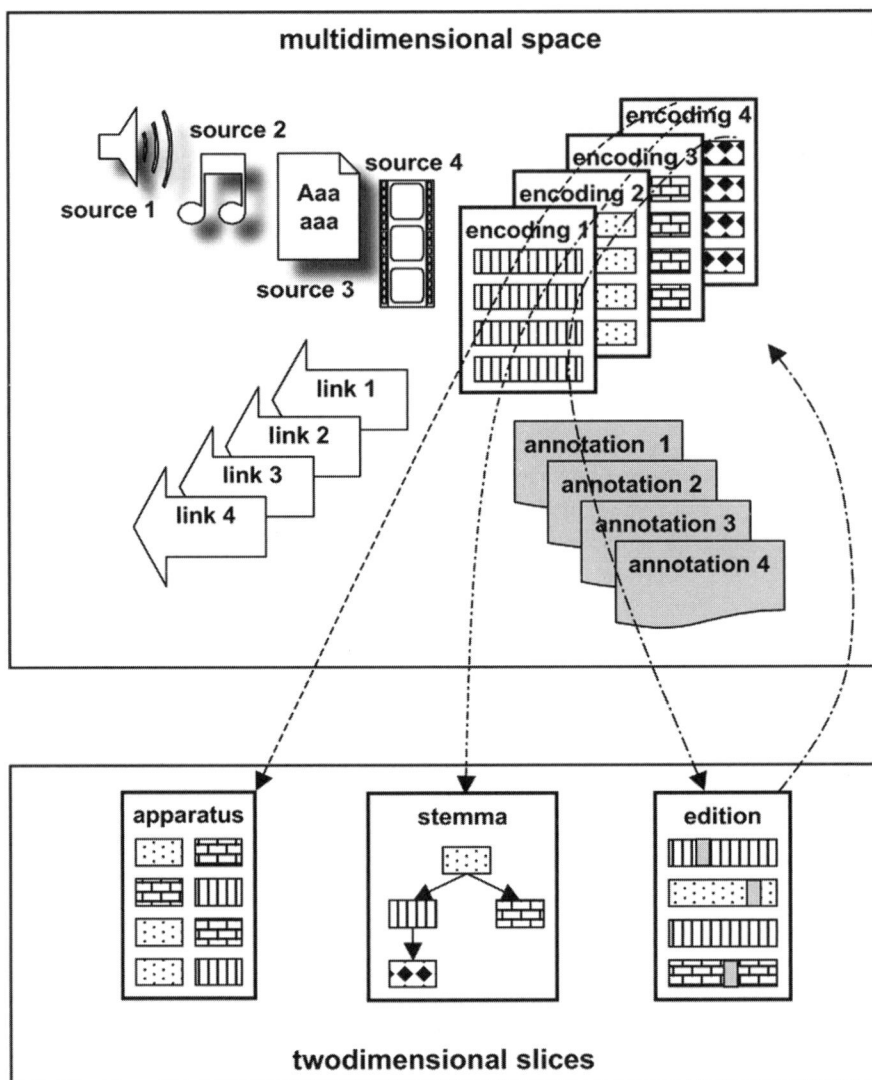

Figure 3.2   Multidimensional model for a digital critical edition of a composition

- The usability of text-critical data, particularly when the context from which it is abstracted matters.

All of these relate to the limitations of the book format as a visual, static, two-dimensional representation of a composition. As in literary studies, a HyperEditing approach might offer some solutions for music too. This is the purpose of the multidimensional model that is proposed in this chapter and illustrated in Figure 3.2.

A digital critical edition of music may ideally consist of the following, interconnected components:

- Digitized sources, from any relevant medium: usually these will be score facsimiles, but video and audio recordings are explicit options.
- Source encodings, making the information content of the sources suitable for computer processing.
- Annotations; categories include text-critical features, inferences (e.g. related to performance), musicological knowledge.
- Links to related works.

Such a collection of information can be imagined as a multidimensional space, in which different categories of information each occupy a different axis. For example, in addition to the two dimensions of the score, one can imagine versions, emendations, transcription styles and adaptations to performance as additional dimensions to the edition. These are not so much dimensions in a mathematical sense, but ways of accessing the edition, for example by projecting information onto a plane or by taking two-dimensional slices from it. Examples of such views are a diplomatic or emended transcription of a source, an apparatus, a stemma, or an edition conceived as a reading path through sources and annotations. At least as important is the possibility of switching views, for example from an apparatus view of a particular passage to the context in which it appears in a source, or – when multiple works are edited in this way – from a collection of similar features to the works in which they appear. Users can contribute to the edition by adding their own views and annotations.

Quite a sophisticated set of tools will be needed to realize these possibilities – but a discussion of these falls outside the scope of this chapter. The music representation these tools will work on has one important requirement that distinguishes it from the ones mentioned above. It is not a representation of the musical surface of a finished product (see Wiggins, this volume, Chapter 2, section 4.2), nor one of the musical logic that underlies it; instead it represents ideally all the information contained in the source that is necessary for deriving, whether by computer or human intelligence, meaningful views of the composition.

Two examples may illustrate this:

- Logically, CMN orders notes in bars of a predictable length, demarcated by barlines; so notes can be represented as the content of a bar, and barlines need not be explicitly indicated. When encoding a source, one can generally not assume that the length of the bar is predictable or correct, or even that a barline has the function it has nowadays. A non-hierarchical representation of the source text is therefore needed.
- Likewise, CMN has clear rules for accidentals, which makes it possible to

represent the accidental as part of the pitch of a note. In mensural notation, it is not always clear to which note(s) an accidental should be applied, so it should be represented separately.

The requirement is thus that the input to the edition, the notational, visual and possibly material aspects of the sources, is represented; editorial decisions about their meaning belong to a layer of inferences that comes on top of the source representation. Formats that encode the 'logical content' of a work are unhelpful for supporting the editorial process, which also follows from the fact that, if such a thing as the logical content of a composition exists at all, the task of the editor is to *establish* the logical content rather than to assume its existence.

It is important to note that the model, even though it is presented as an abstract and generic one, simplifies reality. This is especially important at the representation level. Minute details of ink and damage can sometimes lead to fundamental decisions about the editorial text of a composition, but this does not mean that such details must be routinely encoded. There will always be a negotiating process between simplicity and comprehensiveness, aimed at reaching an optimum effectiveness. Therefore each repertoire will require its own specific representation. At the same time, to allow interchange, it should conform to the requirements formulated in Wiggins (Chapter 2, this volume). The simplification inherent in modelling also explains why the model includes a digital facsimile: it puts a lower boundary on the level of detail of the encoding, and it allows an immediate check for problems and ambiguities in the source that may have been left unencoded.

The multidimensional model solves the issues mentioned at the beginning of this section by giving full access to as many source representations as one needs, by defining an edition as an adaptive layer on top of the sources, and by offering flexible generation and presentation of text-critical information. The model also raises a number of new questions. How can the model be realized in practice, which dimensions does it contain and how useful is it? The following four case studies will help in finding some answers.

5. Case studies

5.1 Ma bouche rit: anonymous mass and Ockeghem's chanson

An anonymous Missa 'Ma bouche rit' survives in the early sixteenth-century manuscript VienNB 11883 (fols 285v–294r). It is remarkable for its exceptional treatment of the model on which it is based: all three voices of Johannes Ockeghem's chanson are used as *cantus firmi* in at least one of its movements.[22] If these *cantus*

---

22 K. Olive, 'The Anonymous *Missa Ma bouche rit*, Vienna, Österreichische Nationalbibliothek, Ms. 11883: A Study and Modern Edition', undergraduate thesis, University of Manchester, 2003.

firmi are compared to Wexler's edition of the chanson,[23] there appear to be more than ten consistent differences that affect pitch and/or rhythm, one of which is shown in Example 3.1.

fort   qui___   m'ai -   -   - de

Example 3.1a   Ockeghem, 'Ma bouche rit', superius bars 40–42 after Ockeghem (1992)

Example 3.1b   Missa 'Ma bouche rit', superius bars 40–43. All note values quartered

Obviously, the mass is not based on this reading of *Ma bouche rit*, which is a 'best-text' edition derived from the manuscript PNiv.[24] As 17 sources of Ockeghem's chanson survive, one wonders if another one has a closer relation to the mass. The key to the answer is the edition's apparatus, a fragment of which is shown in Figure 3.3.

> 39/1-2 bl sbr, bl m (*MunSche*); 41/1-2 mi col (*BerGlo, Cop 1848, Dij, FBNC 176, FR 2356, MunSche, NHMel, PBN 4379, PCord, PPix, RCG XIII.27, WLab, Wol 287*); 41/2 c fu, b fu (*RISM 15389*); before 42/1 sharp (*NHMel*); 42/3-43/2 bl sbr,

Figure 3.3   Fragment of apparatus for Ockeghem, 'Ma bouche rit', after Ockeghem *Motets and chansons*, p. lxxx; line breaks as shown in original

---

23 J. Ockeghem, *Motets and chansons*, *Collected Works*, vol. 3, ed. Richard Wexler with Dragan Plamenac (Urbana, IL: American Musicological Society, 1992).

24 Ibid., p. lxxviii.

First, this fragment demonstrates three reasons why it is hard to use an apparatus: it presents source data outside the context of the score, it uses a specialized 'code' for these data and it breaks the connection between data from a single source. Second, it appears that the variant from Example 3.1 does not occur elsewhere. In total, the mass contains at least five variants that make musical sense but are not known from any of the chanson's sources.[25] It is unlikely that these are Ockeghem's, but they are surely relevant to a study of the transmission and reception of the chanson.

The principal contribution of a digital critical edition of Ockeghem's chanson would be to allow direct access to the sources through a third dimension of the edition, rather than indirect access only, through the apparatus. A second contribution would be to make it possible to upload a new source (or reconstruction of a source) to the existing edition. Finally, the mass (and other arrangements of 'Ma bouche rit') could be linked to the edition in such granularity that the user can see how they relate to the model.

5.2 J.S. Bach, Mass in B Minor

J.S. Bach's *Mass in B minor* (BWV 232) has a very complex source situation, the bare outlines of which are shown in Figure 3.4[26] and discussed below after Butt,[27] Wolff [28] and Rifkin.[29] Bach commenced work on the autograph score in 1733. The work at that stage consisted only of the 'Missa', i.e. *Kyrie* and *Gloria*. Most of its twelve movements are parodies from cantatas, but not all of the models survive. A set of mostly autograph parts from 1733 also survives, adding a level of performance detail that is missing from the score. These parts were never altered, unlike the score, which was subjected to a series of additions and revisions. The most important of these took place in 1748–50, when Bach expanded the Missa into a complete Mass. Again, most movements were based on earlier works: the *Sanctus* of 1724, a Credo intonation of c. 1740 and numerous cantata movements. The *Confiteor* and possibly the *Et incarnatus est* were newly composed. There are many signs of revision for all movements including the Missa. Owing to his failing eyesight Bach also introduced a number of errors, particularly in the *Sanctus*. After Bach's death the manuscript passed to his son Carl Philipp Emanuel, who added several layers of alterations. The first of these correct apparent errors and improve legibility; later ones are connected to a performance of the *Symbolum Nicenum* (the movements setting the *Credo* text) in 1786. Several sources that

---

25 A complete reconstruction of the model is available at <http://www.cs.uu.nl/people/fransw/>, accessed 21 April 2009.

26 An animated version of the overview is available at <http://www.cs.uu.nl/people/fransw/>, accessed 21 April 2009.

27 J. Butt, *Bach: Mass in B Minor* (Cambridge: Cambridge University Press, 1991).

28 J.S. Bach, *Messe in h-Moll*, ed. C. Wolff (Frankfurt: Peters, 1997).

29 J.S. Bach, *Messe in h-Moll*, ed. J. Rifkin (Wiesbaden: Breitkopf & Härtel, 2006).

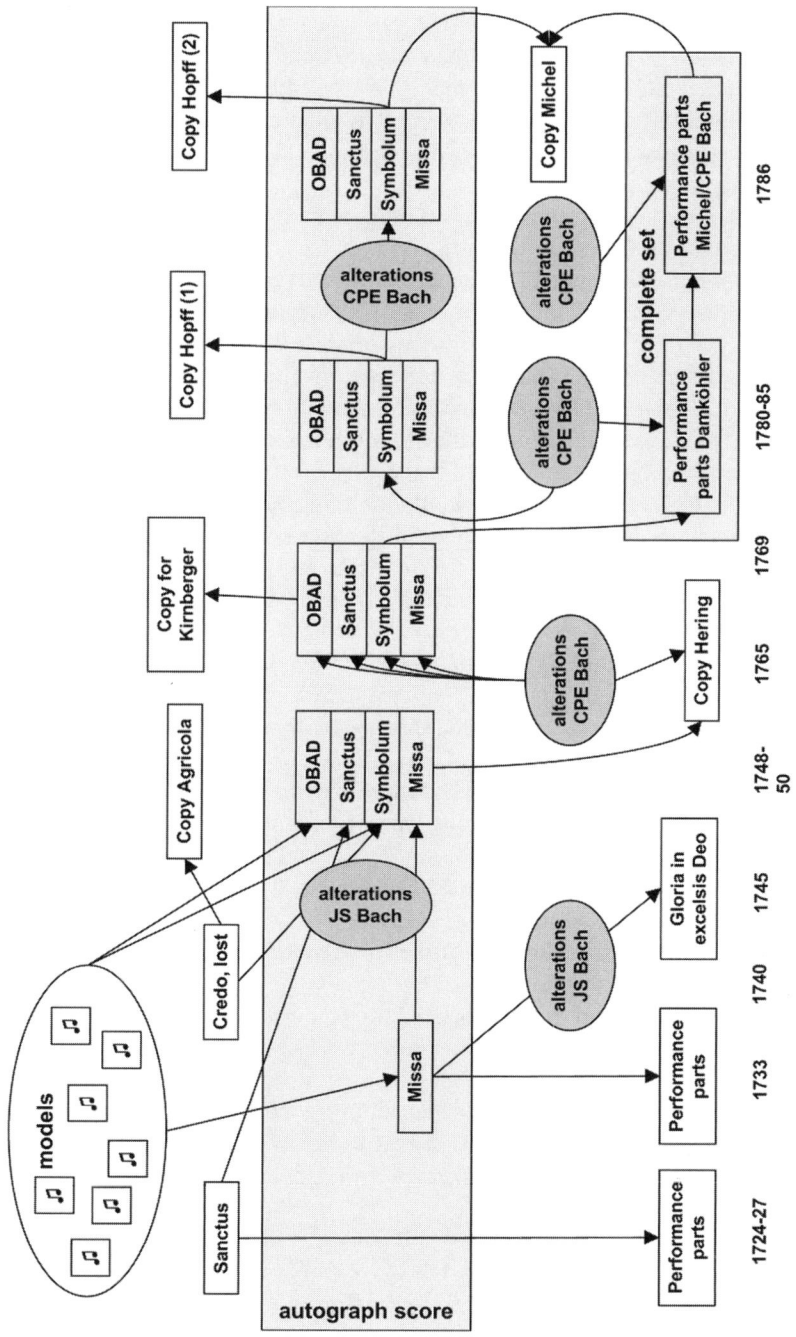

Figure 3.4   J.S. Bach, *Mass in B Minor* (BWV 232), relationships between sources, with approximate dates

derive from the main manuscript reflect earlier stages of the manuscript and may therefore be used to distinguish between layers of alteration. The most important of these are the cantata *Gloria in excelsis Deo* of 1745, a copy of the *Mass* in J.F. Hering's hand (c. 1765), one made for J.P. Kirnberger in 1769, and a set of parts (containing an earlier and a later layer) and several scores of the *Symbolum Nicenum* dating from the 1780s.

At least three possible strategies for editing the complete *Mass* emerge from this overview. One is to reconstruct the score as Bach left it at his death and emend it only where it is in error. Another is to construct an 'optimum text' by selecting the musically most satisfactory variants from the score, the 1733 parts and possibly also from the models of the movements. The third is to focus on performance and add to the score as it was in 1750 the kind of detail that the parts written in 1733 and 1786 offer. Every consecutive strategy involves a larger number of subjective decisions than the preceding one, but at the same time represents an equally legitimate view of the same underlying source materials. A multidimensional edition of the Mass would therefore represent the information content of the sources and allow a range of different views to be generated from these. Note that it is not the purpose of this model to enforce a particular editorial method: the only requirement is that an edition is a view on the source materials, no matter how and why it is created.

A well-known problem in the *Domine Deus* may illustrate this position.[30] Example 3.2 shows the beginning of the movement, in which the main instrumental motif is played first by the two flutes and then by the first violin. The 1733 parts however indicate performance by flute 1 only; moreover the first bar of the flute is notated with a different rhythm, which reappears in the second violin and viola, bar 27, but nowhere else. Three questions emerge from this situation:

- What does this variant indicate: (an approximation of) a rhythm, a reinforcement of the articulation, or both?
- How should other appearances of the same motif be treated, for example first violin, bar 2?
- What is its relevance to the scoring and performance of the final version of the work?

The answers to these questions influence an editor's rendition of the passage, but as important as the editorial decision is access to the evidence. One might even claim that the variants together convey a better understanding of this movement than a single editorial solution.

In addition to offering a range of possible views of the 'text' of the work, the added value of a digital critical edition is to give direct access to the underlying evidence. An exploration of the work could start from an overview such as that

---

30 For the details, see G. Herz, 'Der lombardische Rhythmus im "Domine Deus" der h-Moll-Messe J.S. Bachs', *Bach-Jahrbuch*, 60 (1975): 90–97.

Example 3.2a   J.S. Bach, 'Domine Deus', bars 1–3 from *Mass in B Minor* (BWV 232) after manuscript score

Example 3.2b   J.S. Bach, 'Domine Deus', bars 1–3 from *Mass in B Minor* (BWV 232) flute 1 after 1733 parts

in Figure 3.4, from which the user could zoom in to the required level of detail along different dimensions: sources, source layers, relations to models, editorial preferences and emendations, visual presentations and recordings. It is to be expected that in such an environment a user might like to contribute annotations or to create their own view of the work. Thus, the distinction between user and editor begins to fade, and a concept of editing as an on-going, collective process emerges (Robinson[31] makes the same observation for textual editions). In complex cases such as Bach's *Mass* in particular, this seems an attractive mode of operation, as there is so much evidence involved that it is an almost superhuman task for a single researcher to collect it from scratch and to digest it into a finished product.

5.3 V. Galilei, Fronimo

This case and the next are based upon practical experiments undertaken for the ECOLM project. The aim of ECOLM is to make sources of lute music accessible to scholars, lute players and others. Accessibility means more than just displaying the edited content of the sources. Since the sources employ a specialist form of notation – tablature – they are virtually inaccessible to non-players, including musicologists. Transcription to CMN or sound is not an added extra but an essential property of such an edition in order to give this relatively neglected repertoire its proper place in music research. However, such transcription involves both the addition and the loss of information.

Plate 3.1, taken from Vincenzo Galilei's lute treatise *Fronimo* (1568),[32] illustrates this. The principle of French and Italian lute tablatures is to indicate the moment on which certain frets must be stopped and certain courses (i.e. string or pair of strings) must be struck. Durations and voices are not indicated, and neither is pitch spelling. Therefore, a polyphonic transcription, such as the one shown in Example 3.3, requires a great deal of editorial inference, sometimes even involving durations that are physically absent but plausibly supplied in the listener's mind. At the same time, precise instructions about frets and courses, which influence timbre, are lost.

This particular composition from *Fronimo* also gives a dramatic example of a situation that is itself not uncommon, namely, that two or more different realizations can be derived from one score or set of parts. Adaptability to circumstances (liturgy, resources) seems to be the most common explanation. Here the reason is different: black symbols render straightforward transcriptions of the vocal models, whereas the black and red symbols together constitute ornamented intabulations.

The first task a digital critical edition of these works must be able to perform is to separate the two versions. It would also allow transcriptions to be shown. Chordal transcriptions require only a small amount of knowledge to be done automatically. Despite several decades of research, satisfactory algorithms for polyphonic transcriptions have not been found yet, although there is some hope

---

31 P. Robinson, 'Where We Are with Electronic Scholarly Editions, and Where We Want to Be', *Jahrbuch für Computerphilologie* (2002): 4. Available online from <http://www. computerphilologie.uni-muenchen.de/jg03/robinson.html>, accessed 21 April 2009.

32 V. Galilei, *Fronimo dialogo ... sopra l'arte del bene intavolare* (Venice: Scotto, 1568).

Example 3.3   V. Galilei, *Fronimo*, 'Lieti felici spiriti', transcription bars 1–4

that in the future techniques for phrase extraction developed in Music Information Retrieval may help. To generate passable MIDI or audio from tablature is not too hard, for two reasons: pitch-class information is exact and durations are not that critical because of the quick decay in amplitude of the lute's sound.

5.4 S.L. Weiss, Bourrée

Our final case study illustrates some possibilities in displaying text-critical information. As an example we use Silvius Leopold Weiss's *Bourrée* (from Sonata 44, composed c. 1710–14). It survives in seven sources; four of these were encoded as one document using TabXML.[33] From this encoding we generated a series of visual presentations by means of XSLT sheets and slight adaptations of the standard ECOLM software.

Example 3.4a   S.L. Weiss, *Bourrée*, bars 1–11

---

33 Wiering et al., 'Creating an XML Vocabulary for Encoding Lute Music'.

Example 3.4b   S.L. Weiss, *Bourrée*, bars 1–10, transcription of Paris source

VarNr	Paris	Brno	Dresden	Harrach
1	3E	S	E	S
2	(C)		(C)	
3			S	
4		u		
5		E		E
6	E	S	E	S
7	(C)		(C)	
8	S		S	
9		u		
10		E		E
11	,	,		
12	,			
13	,	,		
14	(C)	(C)	(C)	
15	(C)	(C)	(C)	
16	(C)	(C)		
17		,		
18	(C)			
19		u		
20	(C)	(C)	(C)	

Figure 3.5   S.L. Weiss, *Bourrée*, first items of critical apparatus

Note: Numbers correspond to the footnote numbers in Example 3.5

Example 3.5   S.L. Weiss, *Bourree*, bars 1–11 with variants in parallel

The simplest of these are diplomatic transcriptions of the sources, as in Example 3.4. From the same encoding, a critical apparatus can be generated (Figure 3.5). It is here shown as TabCode,[34] which is only slightly more cryptic than the apparatus shown in Figure 3.3 (section 5.1 above).

Example 3.5 gives a more intuitive view of the text-critical information, by showing one source and differences in other versions in parallel. It is easy to see now that the sources contain three interpretations of the rhythm of the first bar that differ from the Paris source (Example 3.6; cf. Example 3.4b). Taken together the variants suggest a performance style in which subdivisions of the beat were played

34 T. Crawford, 'Applications Involving Tablatures: *TabCode* for Lute Repertories', *Computing in Musicology* 7 (1991): 57–9.

Example 3.6 S.L. Weiss, *Bourrée*, rhythmic patterns for bar 1 in the Brno, Dresden and Harrach sources

inégale. This parallel view already allows zooming out from character level to the level of source relationships.

The third view (Plate 3.2) shows the number of diverging sources for each vertical sonority in the source: the darker the background colour is, the more variants there are. This view captures in one glance how unique a source is and how variants are distributed over the piece. In quite a different way from a printed apparatus we can put variants in context and create high-level views of them.

6. Dimensions and views

The model presented in this chapter is based on the central idea that all information relating to the edition of a composition is ordered in a multidimensional space, from which views of a lower dimensionality may be generated according to user preference.

Table 3.1   Dimensions of the model

Visual: written sources	Logical: edition
problems in source text	preference (Bach)
emendation	adaptation to CMN conventions
uncertainty	transcription (Ockeghem, Galilei, Weiss)
source layers	inference (Galilei, Weiss)
scribal correction (Bach)	**Gestural: performance**
improvement (Bach)	ensemble composition
performance alternative (Galilei)	interpretation
explication (Bach)	recording
different sources	**Analytical**
variants (Ockeghem, Weiss)	knowledge (Bach)
intertextuality (Ockeghem, Bach)	linking (Ockeghem, Bach)

Table 3.1 summarizes the dimensions we have found so far and several we assume exist in other repertoires. These are classified by SMDL domain (see section 3). Written sources are placed in the visual domain, performances in the gestural domain, and annotations and links in the analytical domain. The dimensions

related to classic editorial tasks are placed in the logical domain (see section 4). Table 3.2 provides a similar listing of views traced so far.

Table 3.2   Sample views that can be generated from the model

Linear renditions (notation or sound)
diplomatic transcription
layers in source
emended source
edition (reading path)
Composite views
aligned sources, editions
apparatus
stemma, source relationships
musical relationships

7. Evaluation

The multidimensional model has the following advantages:

- It represents a data-rich approach, allowing automatic extraction of information, for example by using information retrieval or statistical techniques.
- It can deal satisfactorily with different instances of a single work.
- It can incorporate performances.
- It prevents information loss caused by transcription.
- Source information can be directly accessed.
- Views can be adapted to specific requirements.
- A composition's musical context is made explicit by linking it to other compositions.
- Editing can be done incrementally and collectively, preventing duplication of work.
- An edition stores knowledge about the composition.
- Distribution is fast and cheap.

Most importantly, it aims at enhancing accepted musicological methods by overcoming certain shortcomings: for example, scarcity of data or difficulty in dealing with context. If a significant quantity of multidimensional editions becomes available, I expect the strong distinction that now exists between generic and specific approaches to music (e.g. between work analysis and the study of musical style) to blur or even to disappear.

I am aware that the model has a number of potential disadvantages, most of which are not specific to music but pertain to textual editions as well (where some of the solutions may also be found). These include:

- The complexity of the model itself, with its many dimensions and views.
- The required infrastructure, comprising data structures, software and services.
- The technical expertise editors will need to acquire.
- The instability of online resources: they move or disappear.
- Referring to editions that themselves are dynamic.
- The intellectual property of the contributing scholars and the rights of the owners of the sources.
- The status of digital publications, which are often considered less prestigious than paper publications with a renowned publisher.

Even though the model proposed here presents an abstract, extreme view and concrete implementations are likely to be much simpler, creating digital critical editions of music will be a complex task. It is likely to involve a team of specialists, each responsible for a certain aspect of the edition. This is a conspicuous difference from traditional editions, where an editor is typically in charge of almost the entire process. Generally, teamwork is not nearly as common in the humanities as in science, and editing music is very often part of PhD research, which is individual by nature and in practice leaves very little time for learning peripheral skills.

However, it appears that many scholars are willing to acquire complex technical skills, such as the use of music notation software. This type of software maintains the illusion that one is working in the same way as on paper, merely in a different, but neutral, medium. As said above, models simplify reality with a particular aim in view. With a few exceptions, the vast majority of those involved in music research are not used to this type of scientific approach to models. Their closest counterparts in music are theories such as Schenker's, which are more in the nature of belief systems that may be applied to a very wide range of tasks. As a result they are usually rich in escape mechanisms for solving unexpected problems. Formalized models do not allow for such mechanisms and may therefore seem too simplistic or rigid to the uninitiated. This may be the most serious obstacle to the acceptance of digital, multidimensional music editions. A significant effort to educate the profession seems to be needed to remedy this. However, this burden could be shared with those promoting other areas of computational or empirical musicology, in which the same problem exists.

Future work on the multidimensional model must also address its implementation. For a concrete repertoire only a restricted number of views and dimensions will be needed. This suggests a modular approach. Similarly, it must be possible to edit a work incrementally, by adding new layers of information to the existing ones. A great deal of this research will be done in projects that follow on from the ECOLM project. Other areas where pilot multidimensional editions might be relevant are liturgical music, which must often be adapted to the occasion; popular music, in which performance is more important than notation; and folksong, where oral transmission has caused much variation. Once a satisfactory incremental model for creating digital critical editions has been created, it makes sense to integrate those efforts with other attempts at digital corpus creation for music analysis, music information retrieval and performance research.

This chapter has sketched only the barest outlines of a model for digital critical editions of music. Before the model is ready to be used in actual implementations, many open issues need to be resolved that have been insufficiently debated within the broad community of historical musicology. I am therefore even more interested in critical reactions, counterproposals and so on to this chapter than in the actual dissemination of this model, and hope that a debate will emerge from it that is similar in passion and richness of ideas to that taking place in literary studies.

Acknowledgements

The research was supported by EPSRC grant no. GR/T19308/01. I would like to thank Kara Olive and Joshua Rifkin for giving us access to their unpublished work, Tim Crawford and David Lewis for numerous discussions about the ideas presented here and Peter Boot, Joshua Rifkin, Hans Voorbij and Anita de Waard for their comments on the draft of this chapter.

Chapter 4

Filling Gaps between Current Musicological Practice and Computer Technology at IRCAM

Michael Fingerhut and Nicolas Donin

Knowledge build-up is a process which involves complex interactions between intellectual pursuits and the tools used to examine reality. While the interdependence between research and its instruments is more readily apparent in such fields as (say) neurophysics or microbiology, it is usually obscured in musicology, where the nature of the knowledge that is produced is rarely explicitly correlated to the devices that allow for its emergence.

Computers provide new ways to interrelate, organize, process, ascribe meaning to and reuse a wide variety of musical information – whatever lends itself to digitization (from traces of the compositional process, such as sketches, notes and so on, to computer 'patches', musical scores, books and other forms of publication about the work, recordings of live events and information about them) – to unprecedented depth and breadth, and thus cannot but have a major impact on contemporary musicology. Their use addresses a multiplicity of related domains (including acoustical, perceptual, musical, technological, historical, social, legal …) and levels of interpretation (physical, symbolic, semantic, cognitive …).

Placed as it is at the crossroads of the musical creative process – production and performance on the one hand, and research and development in the related sciences and technologies, on the other – IRCAM is in a unique position to examine these interdependences in conjunction with the development of specific tools. Based on this reflection, in this chapter, we will attempt to present some examples of the musicologist's ideal instrumentation, as well as some of the concepts and tools which are already in use or in the course of realization.

* * *

Computers have been used in the classroom situation at least since the late 1950s with the innovative Plato project at the University of Illinois at Urbana-Champaign.[1]

---

1 PLATO, 'PLATO reports, PLATO documents, and CERL progress reports, 1958–1993' (1993). Computer-based Education Research Laboratory, University of Illinois at Urbana-Champaign. Available online from <http://www.cbi.umn.edu/collections/inv/cbi00133.html>, accessed 21 April 2009; M. Szabo, 'Enhancing the Interactive Classroom through Computer Based Instruction: Some Examples from Plato', *Computer-Mediated*

Since then, a plethora of educational CD-ROM and software packages have appeared, including a number to be used in music-teaching situations.[2] However, computers have barely been used for interaction with the material used in music theory or history classes except in very specific situations (such as in relation to a specified piece of music, say), nor have they so far provided a working environment for the musicologist.

In a 2000 paper,[3] Alain Bonardi listed the technical requirements for an environment that, in his view, would be of help to musicologists:

1. A rich view of the work including: score, sonogram, diagrams, and so on; sound recording(s); symbolic representations and so on.
2. Views of related works.
3. Annotation of a view.
4. Form recognition and identification.

At the centre of his analysis he identified the need to access (find and extract) and use information that is related to musical works (as embedded in the works themselves), to the processes in which they are involved (creation and performance) and to their context (historical, social, economic and so on). While this kind of information can usually be found in libraries on physical media, the development of digital technologies (computer speed, storage volume, networking – and their implications with regard to programming and systems), together with the phenomenal increase in the availability of content in digital form locally and remotely, has affected these practices. Plate 4.1 maps the principal types of information relating to this domain and their levels of abstraction.[4] Red arrows indicate known computable derivations.

These issues are the subject of intense research and development in the emerging multidisciplinary domain called *music information retrieval* (or MIR).[5]

Communications and the Online Classroom, vol. 1 (New Jersey: Hampton Press, 1994). Available online from <http://www.quasar.ualberta.ca/edmedia/readingsnc/cmc/cmc.html>, accessed 21 April 2009.

2 Including from IRCAM: see, for example, the Music Lab 1 software package (<http://www.ircam.fr/237.html?&L=1>, accessed 21 April 2009) and the MusicWeb consortial project (<http://musicweb.koncon.nl/>, accessed 21 April 2009).

3 A. Bonardi, 'Information Retrieval for Contemporary Music: What the Musicologist Needs', *Proceedings of the [First] International Symposium on Music Information Retrieval*, Plymouth, MA, October 2000. Available online from <http://mediatheque.ircam.fr/articles/textes/Bonardi00a/>, accessed 21 April 2009.

4 M. Fingerhut, 'Music Information Retrieval, or How to Search for (and Maybe Find) Music and Do Away with Incipits', IAML-IASA 2004 Congress, Oslo, 8–13 August 2004. Available online from <http://mediatheque.ircam.fr/articles/textes/Fingerhut04b>, accessed 21 April 2009.

5 A series of annual conferences in this domain, ISMIR, has been established in 2000. For its history, see D. Byrd and M. Fingerhut, 'The History of ISMIR – A Short Happy

The advances in science and technology that it has produced have helped reshape our imagination. As a result, our expectations of a better software environment for the musicologist and the music teacher are greater and more focused. The criteria include:

- The ability to interact with a work through annotation and manipulations of its score, by allowing one to focus, say on a section or a phrase, on the melody or on parts of the polyphony; to highlight it visually and aurally; to alter the piece at the overall structural level or in some of its constituents (including tempo, pitch relations, sound balance between instruments) and listen to the result so as to test the coherence of the original work; to find and select individual notes, pitch sets, harmonic patterns and so on, produce an analytical reduction of the work and listen[6] to the resulting remix.
- The ability to search for similar instances of an aspect under scrutiny (such as a harmonic progression) in the same and other works of the same or different style and period, by defining the desired kind and degree of similarity.
- The ability to compare students' analyses (calculations, analytical scores, rewritings and so on) of the same work; combine some of their proposals into a collective classroom reading of the piece; and show how it stands against other known work from the past in order to build an evolutive pedagogy.

Recent and on-going projects at IRCAM have addressed some of these points, which we will now discuss.

1. Production and annotation of rich views of musical works

Careful reading is an activity that, more often than not, involves annotation. Many tools exist to perform this action for text; IRCAM has been working on developing a toolbox for music annotation, to be used both for teaching and studying music (see Plate 4.2). It is part of the Music Lab 2 project on behalf of the French Ministries

---

Tale', D-Lib Magazine, 8/11 (2002). Available online from <http://www.ismir.net/texts/Byrd02.html>, accessed 21 April 2009. Full online cumulative proceedings of almost all the papers presented at the conference are available in ISMIR, Online Proceedings of the ISMIR Series of Conferences, 2000–2005 (2005). Available online from <http://www.ismir.net/all-papers.html>, accessed 21 April 2009. Information on past and future conferences is available at <http://www.ismir.net>, accessed 21 April 2009.

6 Following Agawu's interesting suggestion of playing Schenkerian graphs: K. Agawu, 'Schenkerian Notation in Theory and Practice', *Music Analysis*, 8/3 (1989): 275–301.

of Culture and Education, whose goal is the development of a suite of software applications for teaching music at high school and music conservatory levels.[7]

The aim of this component, called ML-Annotation, is to experiment with new, manual and computer-assisted syntactic and semantic annotation and visualization paradigms of complex multimedia objects (using automatic music summaries, libraries of music annotation symbols and so on). As IRCAM has been active in research in these domains (in particular, audio summarization[8] metadata modelling and automatic extraction, semantic tagging, synchronization), this development aims at integrating these advances into a usable application which provides multiple views of a single work: sketches, score, recordings, comments and so on. It is to be used in stand-alone systems as well as in distributed online digital libraries, thereby providing tools for the exploration of vast collections of such objects and their appropriation by individual users for personal, educational and professional uses.

The source material concerning a single work (in this case musical, but the model fits many other intellectual productions) comes in a multiplicity of forms and media. These may be static (text, hypertext, images – for example, of musical scores, but these could be any still pictures) or time-dependent (audio and video recordings – of performance, of master classes, or of any other relevant situation). In order to provide meaning to this variety of material, several classes of non-destructive operations are needed for the construction of time-dependent, multi-layered interactive presentations:

- Synchronization, comparison, summarization.
- Tagging and time-dependent annotation.
- Visualization.

Synchronization is the operation by which different documents are tagged so as to indicate the occurrence of corresponding temporal events, even when the document is static (a text, a sketch, a musical score, a still picture) and multi-page, or when there are several documents with a different notion of time (distinct performances, for example). It can then be used for the manual or computer-assisted comparison of documents of the same nature (audio recordings of different performances of the same type[9]), as well as for multimedia visualization (such as score-following of a recording).

---

7 See V. Puig et al., 'Musique Lab 2: A Three Level Approach for Music Education at School', *Conference Proceedings International Computer Music Conference* (ICMC), Barcelona, 4–10 September 2005, pp. 419–422.

8 See G. Peeters, A. La Burthe and X. Rodet, 'Toward Automatic Music Audio Summary Generation from Signal Analysis', *Proceedings of the Third International Conference on Music Information Retrieval* (ISMIR), Paris, 13–17 October 2002. Available online from <http://ismir2002.ismir.net/proceedings/02-FP03-3.pdf>, accessed 21 April 2009.

9 For example, G. Peeters, 'A Large Set of Audio Features for Sound Description (similarity and classification)', internal report (IRCAM, 2004).

Automatic summarization allows for the provision of bird's-eye views of complex documents (long audio recordings, in this case), so as to ease the task of navigating them, as well as of collections of documents. It consists in analysing the timbre features of the audio signal, and then in selecting one or several characteristic segments of varying duration according to various criteria.[10] While this works well for popular music, which usually has a simple timbral structure, it may also be adapted to some extent, by varying its parameters, to other genres of music. A separate application, developed in 2005 in the Multimedia Library, allows for the selection of 'profiles' (families of parameters) deemed to be appropriate to a specific recording or collection of recordings, and performs automatic summaries of all the selected items.

Annotations are visuals (shapes, text, hypertext, symbols of varying size and colour) meant to draw the attention to specific parts of documents as they unfold in time. They may be tagged, manually or with the help of computer pattern and characteristic extraction from any of the representations of the document (symbolic, spectrograms, sonograms, etc.), so as to attach semantics to documents. Both may be later used as indexes to searches on single documents as well as on a collection of documents. At any point, the resulting rich document can be viewed statically (as if leafing through the score) or played, giving the user the ability to select the kind of information displayed.

This application currently allows the user to synchronize a sound file (typically, a recording of a performance of a piece of music) with one or more images (typically, the score, but it could be any still or moving image), and then add annotations of various shapes (rectangles, ovals, lines, images and so on), colours and textual content, set to appear and disappear at specific points during the music or to appear throughout the piece.

Annotations can be grouped in layers, which may be shown selectively when the music plays. They may represent distinct aspects of a single analysis (e.g. voice leading, melody, tonality), or may be used to compare analyses made by different people, say students in a classroom. The score, actually a multi-page arbitrary image, is a layer in itself, and can be displayed or hidden when the music plays. When it is on screen, a cursor follows the sound as it is played, and repeats and page turns are performed as appropriate. Several different recordings (e.g. performances) can be synchronized with one single annotated score and thus compared.

This process is non-destructive, as it references only the sound and image files. The annotations are kept in a separate file (in XML). It can thus be safely added to an existing digital music library and make full use of the audio documents it contains.

---

10 Including legal ones: it transpires it is easier to obtain the rights to provide a one-segment summary, i.e. an excerpt, rather than a 'compilation' of excerpts.

A related development[11] has directly addressed the comparison of performances of a single specific work, the first prelude of J.S. Bach's *Well-tempered Clavier*, using a combination of manual annotation and digital signal processing algorithms. An audio alignment algorithm uses a MIDI file as a reference structure in order to get a precise onset estimation in the corresponding audio file. When several versions of the same classical work are to be compared, the MIDI file acts as the common 'score' for the distinct sound files; the algorithm then evidences even the tiniest time variations between the interpretations.

This tool allows the user to switch between different representations. The general view (see Plate 4.3a), in which all performances are aligned with respect to a common piano roll, provides automatically computed information on tempo variations. A windowing and zooming facility (see Plate 4.3b) allows one to concentrate on a few bars and see graphical indications of the duration and intensity of the individual notes. In this representation, textual annotations may be added anywhere, and saved together with the parameters of the view.

This experimentation will hopefully lead to the development of a generic performance comparison toolbox applicable to a wide range of pieces, which will provide built-in additional music-savvy computations. This will open a fascinating field of empirical research in the historical and analytical study of performance.

2. Navigation within individual sound documents

A music work has structure. Like a book subdivided in chapters, it can be composed of movements (acts and scenes in opera). At a deeper level, it may have a formal structure too (subject, countersubject and so on). Indeed, this is true of any audio document (e.g. spoken word). While it is easy to browse through a text document, as its structure may be apparent to the eye, and as hypertext may be used to highlight it, this is not the case for sound without visual cues. On compact discs, for instance, a table of contents on the cover allows for associating some structure with the audio contents (tracks), while current players show a one-dimensional view of the contents.

Since 1995, at IRCAM we have been faced with the need to provide our users with mechanisms of this type to access our online sound archives. While several emerging standards currently allow for describing the structure of multimedia documents (such as METS[12]) and for providing so-called hypermedia navigation

---

11 N. Donin, 'Problèmes d'analyse de l'interprétation. Un essai de comparaison assistée par ordinateur d'enregistrements du Premier prélude du *Clavier bien tempéré*', *Musurgia, Analyse et pratique musicales*, 12/4 (2005), pp. 19–43.

12 Metadata Encoding & Transmission Standard, used to encode metadata on objects in a digital library. See <http://www.loc.gov/standards/mets/>, accessed 21 April 2009, for details.

capabilities 'into' those objects, (such as SMIL[13]), this was not the case when we began. So we designed our own simple structured metadata schema representation of pieces and their movements, and developed a stand-alone player (see Plate 4.4) capable of displaying this structure and allowing the listener to move from piece to piece or movement to movement.

More recently, we have been working on the design and development of a network of servers hosting heritage sound collections (mostly spoken or sung) belonging to French institutions, which have been digitized under the aegis of the Ministry of Culture.[14] As some of the audio documents last well over an hour, it was necessary to provide tools to navigate within them. The holding institution, the French National Archives, uses EAD[15] to describe each individual document: topical segmentation with incipits, indexation (dates, places etc.), which we transform automatically into a modified SMIL object, including its own navigation capabilities, which can be viewed by an enhanced Flash[16] Player. These objects are integrated in the overall system and their 'internal' metadata (used to describe their structure and content) are indexed along with the external metadata (used to describe the collections and the files as single elements).

Needless to say, this can be used for any kind of sound recording, including classical and contemporary music. The annotation tool mentioned above could be used to provide this type of navigation metadata.

3. Sharing music information sources

In addition to its catalogue of books, scores and periodicals, the IRCAM Multimedia Library holds the digitized sound archives and concert notes of its public concerts, supplemented by a collection of compact discs of mostly contemporary music, both available online. A separate database, BRAHMS,[17] provides biographies of hundreds of living composers and detailed information about their works. Another database contains online versions of the publications of its researchers in all its domains of inquiry (science, technology, musicology and related fields). An online

---

13 Synchronized Multimedia Integration Language, an HTML-like language allowing for the authoring of interactive audiovisual presentations. See <http://www.w3.org/AudioVideo>, accessed 21 April 2009, for details.

14 It is available online at the following address: <http://www.archison-culture.fr.eu.org>, accessed 21 April 2009.

15 Encoded Archival Description, an XML schema used to encode archival finding aids. See <http://www.loc.gov/ead/>, accessed 3 September 2007, for details.

16 See <http://www.macromedia.com/software/flash/>, accessed 21 April 2009, for details.

17 Base Relationnelle d'Articles Hypertextes sur la Musique du 20ᵉ Siècle (relational database of hypertext articles about twentieth-century music), available here: <http://brahms.ircam.fr/>, accessed 21 April 2009.

calendar lists the events of its musical season, a year of concerts which culminate in its spring festival, Agora.

Faced with this multiplicity of sources of information about the work and its many contexts, the question arises as to how to provide an efficient way of accessing all these distinct sources and browsing rapidly in their contents. This is the gist of a project currently under way at IRCAM, whose goal is to devise a single access point for a federated search through these sources, using the OAI-PMH[18] protocol to collect the metadata records from each individual source, transforming them into a common model and allowing the user to search within this common pool through specific indexes as well as through full text – in the metadata records and, if available online, in the document itself[19] (see Plate 4.5). When the intellectual property issues are resolved, we plan to integrate automatic summaries of audio contents as browsing aids in the online sound collections.

While the common records are less detailed than those found in each individual database, they provide enough information to satisfy most queries, and include music-specific information, such as instrumentation of musical works. Thus, upon searching, say, for a specific work of music by composer and title, this system will return the location of the (physical) scores of this piece and of monographs about it, provide online access to available recordings from past concerts together with the digitized concert notes from those events as well as to online notes about the piece from the BRAHMS database, list dates of future concerts where this piece will be played and so on. This system also allows users to access the original records as found in the specific databases if they wish.

To implement this system, we have been using SDX,[20] which not only allows for the indexation and retrieval of XML documents (including the use of one or several thesauri), but also comprises an OAI module, which is used to query all the relevant databases. This usually requires minor adjustment[21] to enable it to respond to these queries, as the protocol is relatively simple to implement.

---

18 Open Archive Initiative Protocol for Metadata Harvesting, a protocol used to *harvest* (collect) metadata records (coded in XML) from possibly heterogeneous *repositories*, usually so as to provide a combined data store as a single search point for all harvested sources. This protocol is much 'lighter' to implement and use than Z39.50, but a comparison is beyond the scope of this paper. See <http://www.openarchives.org/> and <http://www.loc.gov/z3950/agency>, both accessed 21 April 2009, for details.

19 Full-text search in metadata, while very powerful, is not good enough to provide relevant replies to precise queries (such as, say, instrumentation). It is thus useful to combine it with searches within specific indexes.

20 System for Documentation in XML, an open source search engine and publishing framework for XML documents. See <http://adnx.org/sdx/>, accessed 21 April 2009, for details.

21 Provided the database software is extensible (i.e. its software can be extended). Where this is not the case (such as in our library system), alternative ways of exposing the metadata records can be developed.

As this system uses open standards, it can include external sources (which it clearly identifies as such), provided they respond to OAI queries. An interesting source to include would be the Grove Dictionary. We also envision the extension of this system to operate as a common portal to French contemporary music resources.[22]

4. Model validation and genetic approaches

Another application in the Music Lab 2 suite, ML-Maquette, is a tool which can be used to validate a model of a musical work resulting from its analysis. It is developed in the OpenMusic environment,[23] an object-oriented computer-assisted composition environment allowing for the manipulation of musical symbolic elements in order to produce music sequences.

It is based on the concept of the *maquette*, a 2-dimensional drawing-board, whose horizontal axis represents time, while the vertical one can represent any predetermined variable (e.g. pitch, volume). Temporal objects can be laid out and edited in this space: single notes, chords, rhythmic or harmonic sequences, envelopes and so on, but also audio files, to which tonal and non-tonal transformations can then be applied (e.g. transposition, arpeggiation, inversion).

While this environment may be used to compose, it can also be used to *re*compose a piece of music, starting from the constituents which a prior analysis has identified, such as its melodic elements and various transformations such as sequencing, inversion, transposition (see Plate 4.6). The resulting music sequence can then be compared with the original work. This has already been used for such works as the Busoni transcription of the *Chaconne* from J.S. Bach's *Partita* in D minor and Gérard Grisey's *Partiels*.

Once a model has been elaborated and validated, alternative parameters and combinations can then be tried interactively so as to examine different solutions to a given musical problem that the original work addresses. This is precisely the process to which Bonardi[24] alludes when he writes: 'The musicologist is at the same time a listener and a composer, since analyzing a piece a music leads to "rewriting" it.'

* * *

---

22 This portal opened up on the Web in December 2007. See <http:// www. musiquecontemporaine.fr> accessed 18 March 2009. It includes references from the Grove Dictionary.

23 J. Bresson, C. Agon and G. Assayag, 'OpenMusic 5: A Cross-platform Release of the Computer-Assisted Composition Environment', 10th Brazilian Symposium on Computer Music, Belo Horizonte, October 2005. Available online from <http://mediatheque.ircam. fr/articles/textes/Bresson05b/>, accessed 21 April 2009.

24 Bonardi, 'Information Retrieval for Contemporary Music'.

A multimedia project on a recent work by French composer Philippe Leroux (*Voi(rex)*, for voice and six instrumentalists, which premiered in 2002 at IRCAM) allowed one of the authors to experiment with new ways of explaining music and guiding the listener using a genetic musicology approach. It involved web technologies combined with IRCAM software.

The visualization interface aims to be a 'genetic navigation' tool: it follows the processes adopted by the composer and provides, in addition to the score and sound recordings, the same manipulations that were used in the composition process – such as simulation of an OpenMusic patch, demix of a movement that had been designed in part with ProTools – and includes scanned sketches from the composer's archive.[25]

Additional features allow the user to explore a database of documents – annotations and analytical texts – which help to make explicit the relation between the sketches and the score. These documents were produced in the course of an empirical musicological study that included interviews with the composer and whose goal was the reconstruction of the compositional process. Finally, the interface provides every user with means to add their own observations and hyperlinks to the database and to view them in conjunction with the score (see Plate 4.7).

A generic interface will be developed in order to facilitate critical editing of other contemporary music works using genetic research.

5. Conclusion

The potential contribution of computers for analysis can be summarily reduced to two major operating paradigms:

1. Abstraction (pattern extraction, recognition, comparison and so on).
2. Synthesis (generation of sequences from a model).

It is the second of these that has made the advances described in this chapter possible and that addresses many of the points in Bonardi's actualized wish list. The greatest challenge, form recognition and identification, belongs to the first category and is far from being resolved.[26] The higher up we are in the information space shown in Plate 4.1, the harder it is to make generalized determinations automatically (sometimes this is difficult even by hand).[27] Contemporary

---

25 See N. Donin, S. Goldszmidt and J. Theureau, 'De *Voi(rex)* à *Apocalypsis*, fragments d'une genèse. Exploration multimédia du travail de composition de Philippe Leroux' (DVD-ROM), in *L'Inouï. Revue de l'Ircam*, 2 (2006).

26 New algorithmic techniques such as unsupervised learning show promising results.

27 For very simple music, this may be computationally feasible: many of the test corpora described in the ISMIR papers (see ISMIR, passim) consist of 'songs'.

compositions, which usually avoid adherence to well-known musical models from the past – and sometimes from the present as well – are even harder to analyse.[28]

Yet the fact that a tool like ML-Maquette is built on an environment that is also used for composition, and can communicate and exchange analysis data with ML-Annotation,[29] may herald the emergence of new tools for musicologists and thus help reshape their conceptual tools.

With the advent of an increasingly huge amount of digitized sound, we are seeing the emergence of a computer-assisted musicology of performance through quantitative analysis, making increasing use of measuring, averaging, comparison, navigation at the micro- and macro-levels of the work and the corpus, and of wider classification paradigms (e.g. not just traditional thesauri but also folksonomies). Historical musicology will probably be affected, too, as it is now increasingly possible to build a historically valid model of recording and listening, as well as to perform more effective stylistic comparisons of past performances. But insights could also be gained from the capacity, anticipated in the near future, to analyse and manipulate the constituents of the recorded sound of public performances (e.g. the spatial positions of the instruments, hall response, the mixing process).

As these tools develop, they will no doubt allow musicologists to address unforeseen questions that will in turn affect the whole field of musicology. It is all the more necessary then that they be involved in their development.[30]

---

28 See Bonardi, 'Information Retrieval for Contemporary Music'.

29 As well as with a third program, ML-Audio, part of the same suite. See Puig et al. (2005).

30 This is precisely what the IRCAM Analysis of Musical Practices group, headed by Nicolas Donin, is currently researching. For online examples of results, see <http://apm.ircam.fr>, accessed 23 March 2009.

Chapter 5

The Computer and the Singing Voice

David M. Howard

1. Introduction

The application of sound spectrography to human speech production, begun over half a century ago following the ground-breaking work by Potter et al.,[1] has facilitated and continues to add to our understanding of the acoustics of human voice production. Coupled with the pioneering work of Fant[2] on the acoustic theory of speech production, the foundations were laid for the now rapidly growing field of speech science. The ubiquity of home and office multimedia computers has fuelled this growth in recent years, because today's computers are more than capable of carrying out acoustic analyses of singing, which were only previously possible in specialist engineering and speech sciences laboratories.

There are many research areas that share the major goal of working to understand better exactly which acoustic features of particular sounds are most crucial to human production and perception, including: speech and singing analysis, speech and singing synthesis, room acoustics, forensic phonetics, linguistics, forensic analysis of music, music technology, audiology, communication systems design, sound recording and reproduction equipment design, psychoacoustics and psychology. The home or office computer provides a means of exploring such features. Many professional singing teachers and students are showing increasing interest in the possibility of using computers in lessons and practice. Real-time visual displays can be used to support professional voice skill development, for example for: actors in training;[3] adult singers;[4] children;[5] and girl and boy cathedral

---

1 R. Potter, G. Kopp and H. Green, *Visible Speech* (New York: Van Nostrand Company, 1947).

2 G. Fant, *Acoustic Theory of Speech Production* (The Hague: Mouton, 1960).

3 D.P. Rossiter, D.M. Howard and R. Comins, 'Objective Measurement of Voice Source and Acoustic Output Change with a Short Period of Vocal Tuition', *Voice* 4/1 (1995): 16–31.

4 D. Rossiter and D.M. Howard, 'ALBERT: A Real-time Visual Feedback Computer Tool for Professional Vocal Development', *Journal of Voice*, 10/4 (1996): 321–36; D.M. Howard, 'Variation of Electrolaryngographically Derived Closed Quotient for Trained and Untrained Adult Singers', *Journal of Voice*, 9/2 (1995): 163–72.

5 D.M. Howard and J.A.S. Angus, 'A Comparison between Singing Pitching Strategies of 8 to 11 Year Olds and Trained Adult Singers', *Logopedics Phoniatrics Vocology*, 22/4 (1997): 169–76.

choristers.[6] Real-time visual feedback has been previously used successfully with primary school children[7] and adult singers.[8] Our own experience with such displays has suggested that they are of greatest benefit when they are easy to use by non-specialists, providing information that is readily understood, meaningful, valid and useful. This chapter considers the use of computers with the human singing voice both for analysis and real-time visual displays for singing training.

2. Computer analysis of singing

The source-filter model of human voice production[9] underpins all computer analysis of singing, and here the source and filter will be referred to as the *sound source* and the *sound modifier*, respectively.[10] There are two *sound sources* available during singing (or speech) production, *voiced* sounds, such as the vowels in 'soon' or 'bin', and *voiceless* sounds, such as the initial consonants in 'shop' or 'flight'. Both sound sources can occur simultaneously during sounds with *mixed* excitation, such as the initial consonants in 'zoo' or 'victor'. The filter in the model describes the acoustic effect of the shape of the vocal tract on the source as the acoustic pressure wave passes from its source to the local environment via the lips and/or nostrils of the speaker, known as the *sound modifier*. The vocal tract shape varies as different sounds are articulated – this is the sound modifier, and each shape has different acoustic properties that manifest themselves acoustically as a number of resonance, or *formant*, peaks in the vocal tract acoustic frequency response. As the vocal tract shape is varied, the centre frequencies of the formants change, and the filtering effect on the source also varies, thereby characterizing acoustically one sound from another.

A common task in computer analysis of singing is to quantify acoustic aspects of the source and/or the filter. In the case of the source this might be to measure the fundamental frequency and/or other parameters relating to vocal fold vibration

---

6 G.F. Welch and D.M. Howard, 'Gendered Voice in the Cathedral Choir', *Psychology of Music*, 30/1 (2002): 102–20.

7 G.F. Welch, D.M. Howard and C. Rush, 'Real-time Visual Feedback in the Development of Vocal Pitch Accuracy in Singing', *Psychology of Music*, 17 (1989): 146-57.

8 C.W. Thorpe, J. Callaghan and J. van Doorn, 'Visual Feedback of Acoustic Voice Features for the Teaching of Singing', *Australian Voice*, 5 (1999): 32–39; G. Nair, *Voice: Tradition and Technology* (San Diego: Singular Publishing Company, 1999); D.M. Howard, G.F. Welch, J. Brereton, E. Himonides, M. DeCosta, J. Williams and A.W. Howard, 'WinSingad: A Real-time Display for the Singing Studio', *Logopedics Phoniatrics Vocology*, 29/3 (2004): 135–44.

9 Fant, *Acoustic Theory of Speech Production*.

10 D.M. Howard and J.A.S. Angus, *Acoustics and Psychoacoustics*, 3rd edn (Oxford: Focal Press, 2006).

during voiced speech,[11] while for the filter, the task might be to measure the formant frequencies during different sounds or to characterize the effect of vocal projection or the acoustic space in which any accompaniment is operating.[12] Standard home or office multimedia computers are able to do this in real-time, which is why such analyses are now potentially available on a widespread basis to singers and their teachers.

2.1 Sound source analysis: fundamental frequency

The perceived pitch of the singing voice indicates which note is being sung, how in-tune it is, and the nature of any variation, such as vibrato or flutter, that is being applied by the singer. The prime acoustic change that cues pitch variation is fundamental frequency ($f0$). However, it is important to note that $f0$ is not solely responsible for pitch changes, particularly when considering fine degrees of intonation or subtle tuning differences, because timbre and loudness can also have an effect, albeit small.[13] At present, it is not possible to quantify the secondary small effects on pitch relating to timbre and loudness; these require the active judgement of a human listener. Pitch is therefore a *subjective* judgement made by a human listener, and $f0$ measurement is an *objective* measurement that can be made algorithmically by a computer. The term *pitch extraction* is commonly used in the literature, and *pitch detection algorithm* is used throughout the highly comprehensive work on the subject by Hess,[14] when what is actually meant is $f0$ estimation.

The measurement of $f0$ relies on the fact that the waveform of a sung note exhibits repetition, or *periodicity*; the section that repeats being known as a *cycle*. A periodic signal has a harmonic spectrum, where harmonics are integer multiples of $f0$ ($1{\times}f0$, $2{\times}f0$, $3{\times}f0$, $4{\times}f0$ ...). Computer systems that measure $f0$ are either detecting features which occur once per cycle during sung notes, such as the major positive or negative peaks or positive-going or negative-going zero crossings, or they are measuring $f0$ by locating one or more of the harmonics themselves. All methods are prone to some errors, and the choice of an $f0$ estimation technique for a given application is based on the selection of one that has the least intrusive errors in the context of that application. For a fuller account of $f0$ estimation, see Hess.[15]

11 E.g. Howard, 'Variation of Electrolaryngographically Derived Closed Quotient for Trained and Untrained Adult Singers'.

12 E.g. J. Sundberg, *The Science of the Singing Voice* (Dekalb, IL: Northern Illinois University Press, 1987).

13 Howard and Angus, *Acoustics and Psychoacoustics*.

14 W. Hess, *Pitch Determination of Speech Signals* (Berlin: Springer Verlag, 1983).

15 Ibid.

An alternative and generally more accurate method of *f0* estimation is electrolaryngography[16] or electroglottography.[17] These rely on the same basic technique, which involves the measurement of the electrical impedance between two neck electrodes placed externally on the neck at larynx level secured with an elastic neckband. Electrolaryngography or electroglottography are widely used as reference *f0* estimation systems in the speech science laboratory[18] due to their immunity to acoustic noise such as banging doors, equipment noise and other people talking in the vicinity, as well as to the acoustic properties of the local environmental including reverberation.

Figure 5.1 shows a display of *f0* for a quartet singing the first few lines of 'The First Noel' to the tune of that name harmonized by Sir John Stainer. Each singer wore an electrolaryngograph during this recording, allowing the four singers to sing together without their acoustic outputs interfering with each another. The analysis of *f0* is carried out on a standard PC using the SPEAD software from Laryngograph Ltd.[19] The individual notes can be followed in the figure, and varying degrees of vibrato are evident in the output from each singer. A measurement of *f0* is made for each cycle of vocal fold vibration, so the output trace from an electrolaryngograph analysis can be viewed on a cycle-by-cycle basis at a resolution such as that in the figure to enable complete lines to be seen. A number of statistical analyses of the measured *f0* values for a recording, including the mean, mode median, standard deviation, and 80 per cent and 90 per cent ranges are available as shown in Figure 5.2 for the soprano line of 'The First Noel' shown in Figure 5.1. The total number of vocal fold closures for these few lines is over 17,000 (the 'samples' value). The distribution has a number of peaks because the sung input consisted of discrete notes. The output for a speech sample would usually consist of a single wide peak because spoken *f0* variation is continuous rather than centred around discrete *f0* values.

The use of a computer to measure *f0* in this way has enabled fine-tuning between members of a quartet to be investigated, to establish whether or not they sing in just intonation with the consequence that they must go out of tune. Initial results[20] suggest that singers will allow overall tuning to be compromised in order to keep individual chords consonant, beat free or close to just tuning. A keyboard cannot be tuned throughout in just tuning in all keys if the octaves are to be kept in tune

---

16 E.g. E.R.M. Abberton, D.M. Howard and A.J. Fourcin, 'Laryngographic Assessment of Normal Voice: A Tutorial', *Clinical Linguistics and Phonetics*, 3 (1989): 281–96.

17 E.g. R.J. Baken, *Clinical Measurement of Speech and Voice* (Boston, MA: Little Brown, 1987).

18 W. Hess and H. Indefrey, 'Accurate Pitch Determination of Speech Signals by Means of a Laryngograph', *Proceedings of the IEEE International Conference on Acoustics Speech and Signal Processing* (1984): 1-4; D.M. Howard, 'Practical Voice Measurement', in T. Harris, S. Harris, J.S. Rubin and D.M. Howard (eds), *The Voice Clinic Handbook* (Whurr Publishers, 1998).

19 <http://www.laryngograph.com>, accessed 21 April 2009.

20 D.M. Howard, 'A Capella SATB Quartet In-tune Singing: Evidence of Intonation Shift', *Proceedings of the Stockholm Music Acoustics Conference*, 2 (2003): 462–6; 2006.

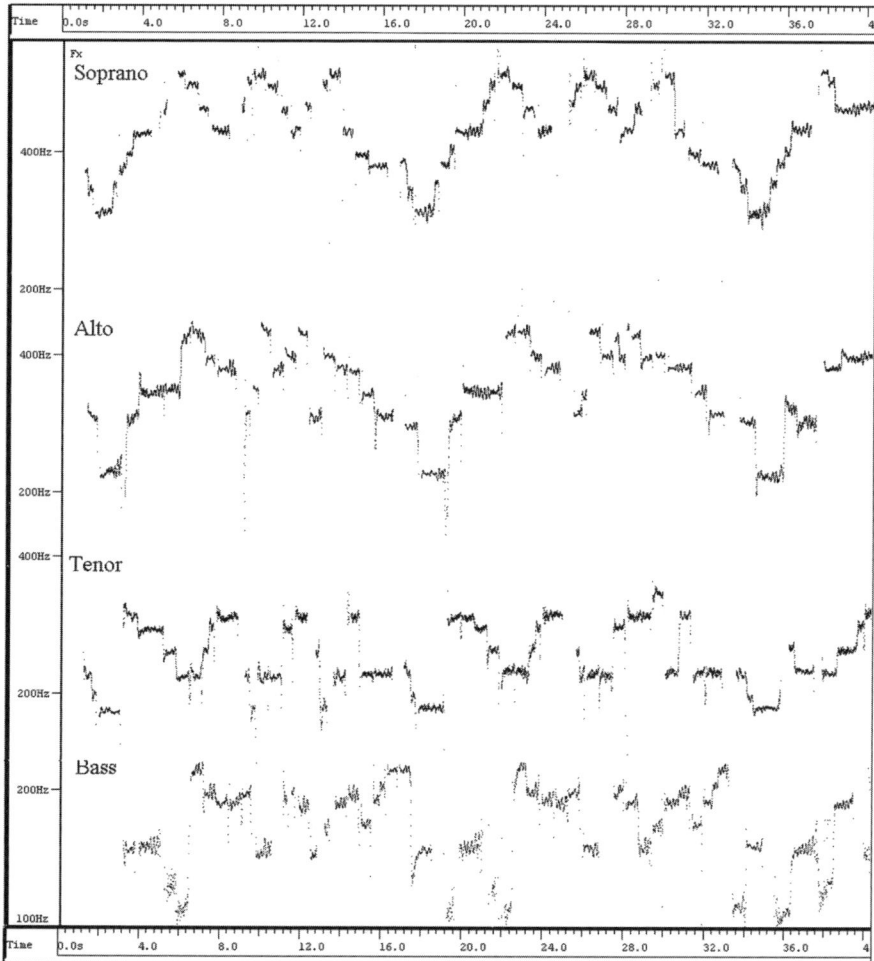

Figure 5.1 *f0* **traces derived from four electrolaryngographs, one per singer, for an SATB (soprano, alto, tenor, bass) quartet singing the first few lines of 'The First Noel' to the tune of that name harmonized by Sir John Stainer**

Note: The traces are combined from analyses made using SPEAD software from Laryngograph Ltd.

(something that is sacrosanct in Western music), and this led to a plethora of tuning systems in the Baroque era, and ultimately to the universal equal-tempered tuning we have today. The fact that singers will allow overall pitch to change in order to maintain just intonation within the harmony, despite their own backgrounds of listening and probably rehearsing (with a piano or organ) in equal temperament themselves is rather remarkable.

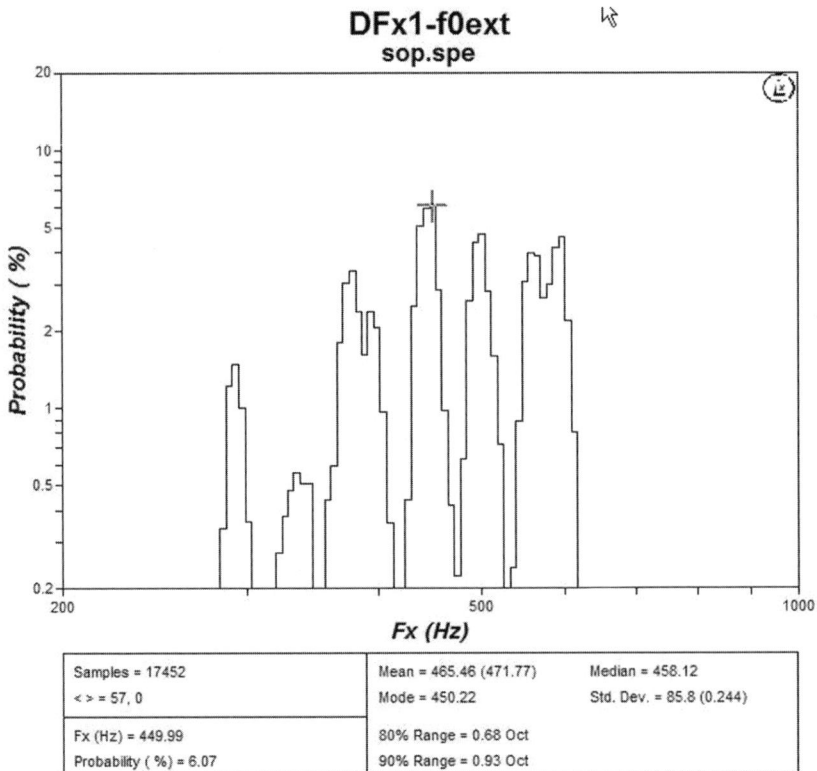

DFx1-f0ext
sop.spe

Samples = 17452	Mean = 465.46 (471.77)	Median = 458.12
< > = 57, 0	Mode = 450.22	Std. Dev. = 85.8 (0.244)
Fx (Hz) = 449.99	80% Range = 0.68 Oct	
Probability (%) = 6.07	90% Range = 0.93 Oct	

Figure 5.2 *f0* **distribution measured from the electrolaryngograph output for the soprano singing the first few lines of 'The First Noel'**

Note: Summary statistics are given for all the f0 values, of which there are 17,452. The *Fx* (equivalent to *f0*) and probability values shown at the bottom left are those at the mode of the distribution marked by a plus sign on the display. The plot was made using QAnalysis software from Laryngograph Ltd.

2.2 Sound source analysis: larynx closed quotient

When the vocal folds vibrate, they come together and move apart once every cycle. The electrolaryngograph enables the degree of contact between the vocal folds to be monitored as the *larynx closed quotient* (CQ), which is defined as the percentage of each cycle for which the vocal folds remain in contact.[21] Details of the algorithm employed are available in. CQ has been found to vary with singing

---

21 Details of the algorithm employed are available in Abberton et al. 'Laryngographic Assessment of Normal Voice'.

experience and/or training for adult males,[22] for adult females[23] and for children.[24] CQ also varies when a singer sings in different styles[25] and when sopranos sing in operatic and Broadway Belt styles.[26] These findings suggest that a raised CQ (the vocal folds spend longer in contact in each cycle) is beneficial to singing, and that this is achieved through training and/or experience, albeit in different ways for different singers. CQ is also higher when singing in a Broadway Belt style compared to an operatic Bel Canto style. Howard et al.[27] offer three suggestions as to why a raised CQ might benefit the acoustic efficiency of the professional singer:

1. Less stored air is vented in each cycle (the vocal folds are closed for longer in each cycle), which enables more notes to be sung on one breath or notes to be sustained longer, thereby improving the efficiency of the usage of the power source.
2. The time for which there is an acoustic path to the lungs via an open glottis is reduced, which results in a reduction in the total acoustic energy transmitted to the essentially anechoic environment on the lungs (an effect known as *sub-glottal damping*) and therefore loss to the listener.
3. The perceived voice quality is less breathy.

The studies on CQ for adults and children reveal the trends illustrated in Figure 5.3, where each dashed plot represents the area in which the individual points (*log f0*, CQ) typically occur when an individual subject sings. The more trained/experienced adult male singers exhibit CQ values that increase with increasing *f0*.

22 D.M. Howard and G.A. Lindsey, 'New Laryngograms of the Singing Voice', *Proceedings of the 11th International Congress of Phonetic Sciences*, 5 (1987): 166-9; D.M. Howard, G.A. Lindsey and B. Allen, 'Towards the Quantification of Vocal Efficiency', *Journal of Voice*, 4/3 (1990): 205-12 (See also Errata, *Journal of Voice*, 5/1 (1991): 93-5.)

23 Howard, 'Variation of Electrolaryngographically Derived Closed Quotient for Trained and Untrained Adult Singers'.

24 D.M. Howard, C. Barlow, J.E. Szymanski and G.F. Welch, 'Vocal Production and Listener Perception of Trained English Cathedral Girl and Boy Choristers', *Bulletin of the Council for Research in Music Education*, 147 (2000): 81–6; C.A. Barlow and D.M. Howard, 'Voice Source Changes of Child and Adolescent Subjects Undergoing Singing Training', *Logopedics Phoniatrics Vocology*, 27 (2002): 66–73; C. Barlow and D.M. Howard, 'Electrolaryngographically Derived Voice Source Changes of Child and Adolescent Singers', *Logopedics Phoniatrics Vocology*, 30, 3/4 (2005), 147–57; Williams et al., 2005

25 D.M. Howard, 'Quantifiable Aspects of Different Singing Styles: A Case Study', *Voice*, 1/1 (1992): 47-62.

26 M. Evans, M. and D.M. Howard, 'Larynx Closed Quotient in Female Belt and Opera Qualities: A Case Study', *Voice*, 2/1 (1993): 7-14.

27 Howard et al., 'Vocal Production and Listener Perception of Trained English Cathedral Girl and Boy Choristers'.

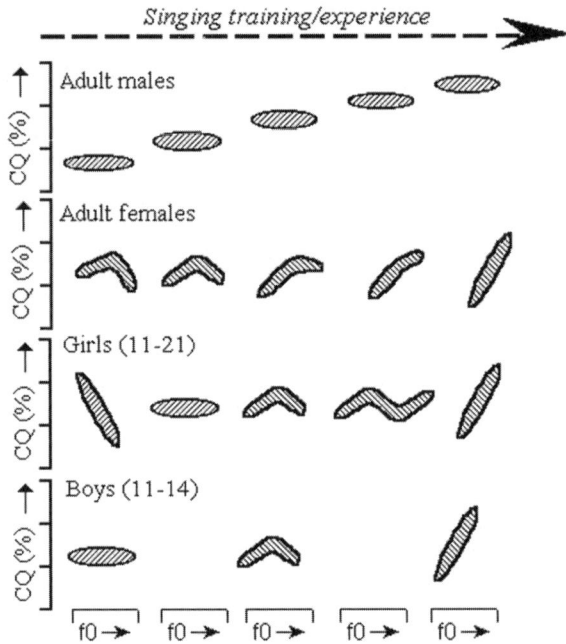

Figure 5.3   Variation in CQ with *f0* patterns for adult males, adult females and children as a function of singing/training experience.

Note: Each dashed plot represents the area in which the individual points (log f0, CQ) typically appear when an individual subject sings.

For adult females, CQ varies with *f0* so that for the highly trained/experienced, CQ rises linearly as *log f0* rises, whilst for the less trained/experienced, CQ tends to rise, fall or stay constant with *f0* in different parts of the range to differing extents. For children, the CQ/*f0* variation appears very similar to that obtained for adult females.

2.3 Sound modifier analysis: spectral measurements

Each sung sound is uniquely perceived by the listener based on its unique acoustic components, or *acoustic cues*. These acoustic cues are related primarily to the acoustic properties of the sound modifiers, and they vary as different sounds are articulated. The action of the sound modifiers is usually quantified in terms of the frequency components that exist in the acoustic output. Whilst it should be remembered when considering the results from such an analysis that they represent the combination of the acoustic spectrum of the sound source *and* the sound modifiers at that instant of time, this is not usually an issue in practice since

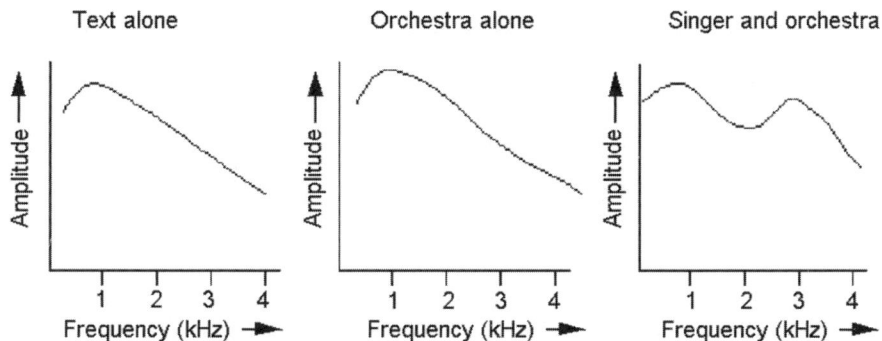

Figure 5.4 Long-term average spectral distribution of acoustic energy with frequency for a singer speaking the text of an opera aria (left), the orchestra playing the accompaniment (centre), and the aria being sung with orchestral accompaniment (right)

it can generally be assumed that the acoustic spectrum of the sound source itself remains essentially constant.

One essential achievement of the Bel Canto school of Western operatic singing is that it enables singers to be heard over vast orchestral forces in large spaces without amplification. Figure 5.4 illustrates the acoustic principles behind this. The overall spectrum of the sound modifiers can be best viewed as an average spectrum, usually taken over a long time (in comparison with the length of a syllable for example). This is referred to as a *long-term average spectrum*, or LTAS. When a singer speaks the words of an aria for example, the resulting LTAS will have the shape shown in the left-hand section of Figure 5.4, consisting of a low-frequency peak and a gentle fall-off in amplitude with frequency. When the orchestra plays the accompaniment to the aria, its LTAS (centre of the figure) exhibits essentially the same shape, albeit with a higher overall amplitude (the amplitudes in the figure have been normalized for convenience). When a professional opera singer sings the aria with orchestral accompaniment (right-hand side of the figure), the LTAS has an additional peak between approximately 2.5 kHz and 4 kHz, known as the *singer's formant*.[28] This peak provides a spectral region in which the singer can focus sound without acoustic competition from the orchestra, and its presence is often perceived as a form of resonance and referred to as voice projection.

Changes that occur on a note-by-note level over time happen over a short term, and the main tool for observing these is the *spectrogram*, which is usually described in terms of a fixed bandwidth filter bank analysis which is either *wide* or *narrow*. If a good time response is required, a wide-band filter is employed, and for a good frequency response a narrow-band filter is employed. In this context, the terms 'wide' and 'narrow' refer to the filter's bandwidth being greater or less

---

28 Sundberg, 'The Science of the Singing Voice'.

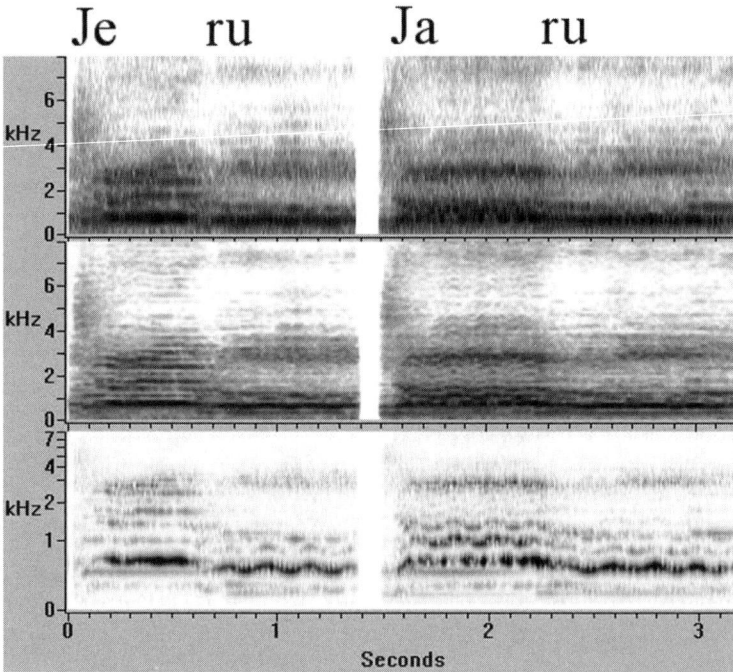

Figure 5.5 Top: wide-band (300 Hz); centre: narrow-band (45 Hz); and bottom: Gamma Tone spectrograms for the first two syllables of 'Jerusalem' from bar 17 of recitative 'Comfort ye' from Handel's *Messiah* sung twice with different vowels by an adult male amateur singer

than the $f0$ of the sound being analysed respectively. When analysing singing, the choice of a wide- or a narrow-band spectrogram should be made according to the acoustic features of interest. The spectrogram provides the eye with a picture that to a first approximation relates to that provided to the brain by each ear. Nowadays, more is known about the peripheral human hearing system[29] and this knowledge can be used in spectrographic analysis. The bandwidth of the ear varies with centre frequency; essentially the ear has narrow-band filters for low frequencies and wide-band filters for high frequencies.

Figure 5.5 shows wide, narrow and human hearing modelling spectrograms for the first two syllables of 'Jerusalem' from bar 17 of recitative 'Comfort ye' from Handel's *Messiah* sung twice with different first vowels by an adult male amateur singer. The use of two different vowels relates to a specific discussion during a singing lesson, when the teacher was expressing concern over the lack of perceived

---

29 E.g. Howard and Angus, *Acoustics and Psychoacoustics*.

resonance in the first sung syllable.[30] The teacher's suggestion was that the student should make more use of a more open vowel during the first syllable, which he described vocally as being more like 'jar' than 'jer'. The main acoustic difference here is in the region between the first and second formants (in the vicinity of 1 kHz). Differences are apparent in all three spectrograms, but overall, the Gamma Tone spectrogram provides the most useful discriminator in this example due to its quasi-logarithmic frequency scale and the fact that the harmonics are clearly separated in this region. In addition, only the Gamma Tone spectrogram gives a clear indication of the nature of the vibrato being employed by this singer as well as the relative importance of acoustic energy at the frequency extremes of the spectrogram, which is most likely to be background noise.

3. Real-time visual displays for singing training

Our experience in the provision of real-time visual displays started with a system for the development and assessment of pitching skills in primary school children, known as SINGAD (SINGing Assessment and Development). It was first implemented in the mid-1980s on the Acorn BBC range of microcomputers which were then commonly available.[31] Pitching was assessed by measuring the $f0$ of notes sung in response to three- or five-note patterns played by the computer. For pitching development, a real-time display of $f0$ against time is provided on the screen to enable pitch changes to be observed. Memory limitations of the BBC microcomputer meant that only the $f0$ values could be stored and the sung sounds themselves could not be retrieved, and this led to SINGAD being ported to the Atari ST range of computers.[32] The usefulness of SINGAD in the classroom for pitching skill development was confirmed by Welch et al.[33] Howard and Angus[34] used the SINGAD system to investigate how pitching accuracy varies with school year, and they identified the following trends across primary years:

• Pitching accuracy improves with age.
• Girls develop pitching accuracy earlier than boys.
• The first note of a trial is least pitch accurate.

30 Howard et al., 'WinSingad'; Howard and Angus, *Acoustics and Psychoacoustics*.

31 Howard and Lindsay, 'New Laryngograms of the Singing Voice'.

32 D.M. Howard and G.F. Welch, 'Microcomputer-based Singing Ability Assessment and Development', *Applied Acoustics*, 27/2 (1989): 89–102.

33 Welch et al., 'Real-time Visual Feedback in the Development of Vocal Pitch Accuracy in Singing'; G.F. Welch, C. Rush and D.M. Howard, 'A Developmental Continuum of Singing Ability: Evidence from a Study of Five-year-old Developing Singers', *Early Child Development and Care*, 69 (1991): 107–19.

34 Howard and Angus, 'A Comparison between Singing Pitching Strategies of 8 to 11 Year Olds and Trained Adult Singers'.

- Wide musical intervals are pitched less accurately than narrow intervals.
- All ascending intervals are pitched flat.
- All descending intervals are pitched sharp.

The SINGAD system has been ported to Windows as WinSingad,[35] taking advantage of processor speed, memory and disk space offered in modern PCs to enable a number of other displays to be included. WinSingad provides its displays on panels within the main program window, and which outputs are visible on the screen is left to the choice of the user. Each panel has the same screen width and they share an equal proportion of the height available. One panel can be made higher than all of the others if desired, in order to home in on a particular feature. Audio input is via the soundcard, and recorded audio data can be saved and replayed. The WinSingad displays currently available are:

- input waveform
- fundamental frequency against time
- short-term spectrum
- narrow band spectrogram
- spectral ratio against time
- oral tract area
- mean/min vocal tract area against time.

In addition, it has been found useful to add a webcam placed to one side of the singer, with its output over part of the WinSingad display, to allow posture to be viewed via what is in effect a 90-degree mirror.

Plate 5.1 shows a screen of a real-time $f0$ and spectrogram display from WinSingad for a C major arpeggio on the vowel in 'bee' sung in a trained (left) and untrained (right) style by an adult male singer. The presence of energy in the singer's formant region is very clear in the trained example, and the user is guided to this region by horizontal lines across the spectrogram at 2000 Hz and 4000 Hz. This representation has been found to be very useful in singing lessons.[36]

WinSingad also offers a display of the oral tract area, which models the vocal tract in terms of either the areas, diameters or radii of a set of tubes of equal length between the larynx and the lips. The lower plot in Plate 5.2 shows an example oral tract area display for the vowel in the second syllable of the word 'comfort' from bar 8 of 'Comfort ye' from Handel's *Messiah*, which is sung unaccompanied by a tenor on B3 (247 Hz). The glottis and lips are at the left and right edges of the plot respectively. The shape of the oral tract is displayed to enable observation of the nature of the shape of the oral tract during the production of sustained sounds such as vowels. WinSingad also enables summary plots of the average, minimum or maximum vocal tract area against time, and the mean oral tract area is shown

---

35 Howard et al., 'WingSingad'.
36 Howard and Angus, *Acoustics and Psychoacoustics*.

in the upper plot of Plate 5.2 for the phrase 'comfort ye'. The purpose of this display is to enable some indication of oral tract constriction and openness to be observed.

There are two other real-time systems that are aimed at the singing studio: Voce Vista[37] and SingandSee.[38] Voce Vista allows a detailed examination to be carried out of the acoustic waveform, spectrum and spectrogram as well as the output from the electrolaryngograph or electroglottograph. Of particular interest for users of Voce Vista is the ability to observe the interrelationship between the excitation and the acoustic output within each cycle of vocal fold vibration. Voce Vista allows around 8 seconds of data to be recorded at once. SingandSee has a fixed group of displays associated with the acoustic pressure waveform, a spectrum and spectrogram, waveform energy and a number of pitch displays including a score, note-name and piano-roll display. Experience with all three suggests that they are useful in singing lessons to reinforce learning but that their use needs to be supervised to ensure that a correct method is being employed by the singer to achieve the desired output; often there is more than one way of achieving the goal on the display, and sometimes the alternatives are not vocally healthy.

4. Conclusions

Computers are now widely used both for singing analysis and in support of singing teaching. The widespread availability of home and office multimedia computers that are more than capable of analysing singing in real time is fuelling interest amongst singing professionals in using computers in their work. Real-time visual feedback has been shown to be useful in singing training. It should be noted, however, that there are caveats to be borne in mind when analysing singing with a computer, and these relate to the way in which the algorithms themselves are set up and adjusted by the user. Many users are totally unaware that there are controls available which enable the algorithms to be fine-tuned, and that the display may or may not be a true record of the singing material under examination.[39] In some cases, there are no controls available: the programmer has made a 'best guess' at appropriate default values.

There is clearly value in using computers for the analysis and training of the singing voice in terms of the enhanced learning gained by singers and the potential for tracking progress for the teacher. However, no computer system will ever replace a singing teacher for developing the musical skills that are essential to effective performance including:

---

37 Nair, *Voice* and <http://www.vocevista.com>, accessed 21 April 2009.

38 Thorpe et al., 'Visual Feedback of Acoustic Voice Features for the Teaching of Singing' and <http://www.singandsee.com>, accessed 21 April 2009.

39 For more details, see Howard, D.M., 'The Real and Non-real in Speech Measurements', *Medical Engineering and Physics*, 24 (2002): 493–500.

- Working with a conductor
- Stagecraft
- Interpreting a score
- Understanding the composer's intentions
- Working with a director
- Singing with others
- Working with an accompanist or orchestra
- Holding the audience.

The application of technology in the singing studio has the potential to free time for the development of such skills, something it is hoped teachers will want to embrace.

Chapter 6

Mapping the Use of ICT in Creative Music Practice

Celia Duffy

1. Introduction

Creative music practice, encompassing the world of performance and composition, has not, until recently, been closely associated with the scholarly concerns of musicology. However, the trend over the past twenty years has been one of convergence: researchers in university music departments now take performance as seriously as they have always taken composition and their colleagues in conservatoires (now often with institutional degree awarding powers) undertake research. Music is perhaps the broadest of disciplines and the old boundaries are fast dissolving. With such a diversity of teaching, learning and research as a backdrop, this chapter focuses on the wide scope of ICT application in creative musical practice. In the particular context of the AHRC and the UK research establishment, there is a case for paying special attention to creative practice as a still-emerging research area and one that provides examples of some of the most exciting ICT developments. The multidisciplinary nature of ICT and music research and the interests of audio engineering and computing science in the topic also push and cross more familiar musicological boundaries. But quite apart from the academic establishment, there is a side of ICT and creative musical practice that is opening up a world of creative opportunity to a very much wider population and so this chapter also covers non-professional and informal creative ICT uses and users.

This chapter attempts neither prospect nor proposal, but rather identifies on-the-ground realities across the territory of creative musical practice. This territory embraces ICT-assisted tools for performance training and analysis, and distribution and dissemination of audio materials. The world of ICT-assisted composition and creative music making across various genres is well documented, investigated and theorized[1] and although directly relevant, its very breadth sets it outside our scope here. However, there are some highlights that should be mentioned: for

---

1 For example, see the excellent and exhaustive annotated bibliography at the De Montfort University Music, Technology and Innovation Research Centre: EARS: ElectroAcoustic Resource Site <http://www.ears.dmu.ac.uk>, accessed 21 April 2009. Other key sources from the UK are S. Emmerson (ed.), *Music, Electronic Media and Culture* (Aldershot: Ashgate, 2000) and T. Wishart, *On Sonic Art*, rev. edn (Routledge, 1996).

example, the free availability of compositional tools over the internet or packaged with a Macintosh that, even ten years ago, would have been the result of at least six months' hard labour at IRCAM, or the possibilities for collaborative creative work offered by the web offering radically new ways of creating, distributing and playing music.[2]

2. A music map

The rationale behind the mapping activity is simple: in the same way that Willard McCarty and Harold Short's landmark *Intellectual Map for Humanities Computing* in 2002[3] signalled a recognition of the maturity of humanities computing, the time is now ripe for a similar exercise in music. It is worth mapping both the discipline as a whole and its interactions with ICT. In recently published work Richard Parncutt[4] proposes that a broad and inclusive view of the wide field of musicology and its interrelations with other disciplines is beneficial. A consideration of various types of ICT tools, applications and approaches, what they are used for and why, what could be further developed and how, how best to support those developments, and what the relationships are between the various constituent parts both within the broad field of music and related disciplines complements that inclusive agenda.

---

2 The collaborative possibilities offered by Internet music are discussed in section 6. Although my contention is that free or open source software has become available to a wider community of users in the past ten years, there are some honourable and long-running precedents. CSound, the classic computer music program, has its origins in the 1980s, and another classic free program, Soundhack (<http://www.soundhack.com>, accessed 21 April 2009), has been well used for over 15 years.

Coming up to date, Audacity and Ardour are popular, free, cross-platform, stereo and multitrack recording and editing programs: Ardour is similar to Pro Tools, the ubiquitous recording environment. For live electronics and video there are MaxMSP, Jitter and Pure Data, a free equivalent. Many artists are making objects for MaxMSP/Jitter and Pure Data, as well as plug-ins for the recording environments which explore, often unusual, creative ideas; many are free.

GarageBand is a good example of the kind of program which is intended as a creative music tool for everyone; it's not technically free as it comes bundled with new Macs.

I am grateful to my RSAMD colleague Dr Alistair MacDonald for his help in selecting these examples of compositional software.

3 W. McCarty and H. Short, 'A Rough Intellectual Map for Humanities Computing', in *Mapping the Field* (Pisa: Association for Literary and Linguistic Computing, 2002). Available online at <http://www.allc.org/reports/map/mapping.html>, accessed 21 April 2009, to which I will return below.

4 R. Parncutt, 'Systematic Musicology and the History and Future of Western Musical Scholarship', *Journal of Interdisciplinary Music Studies,* 1 (2007): 1–32. Available online at <http://www-gewi.uni-graz.at/staff/parncutt/SMW.HTM>, accessed 21 April 2009.

A way of starting to draw a map for music is to mark a boundary between the use of ICT in assisting the study of musical *texts* (which until recently with the interest in performance studies[5] and with other honourable exceptions, for example the sub-discipline of ethnomusicology, has been musicology's main concern) and the study and production of musical *sounds* (the performer's main concern). A separate stake can be claimed for the use of ICT in composition. Leigh Landy's work in providing useful working classifications of the various genres of electroacoustic music[6] indicates that this is complex terrain, particularly bearing in mind that electroacoustic music is only one, relatively specialized, art-music genre.

The mapping project stems from an urge to try to create or impose some order on what seems to be an ill-defined situation as to how ICT is being used across this musical domain. ICT is now often a standard, or at least a widely used creative, analytical or distribution tool across this sector, and in some areas has been so accepted into the mainstream that it is rarely viewed as a specialized discipline in itself. In that regard it has much in common with the debates that surrounded humanities computing not long ago. So-called humanities computing[7] presents a picture of another, related, chaotic, organically developing discipline, as drawn in Willard McCarty and Harold Short's map. This map is now out of date – and we can be sure its authors knew it would be – but at the time it seemed to herald the arrival of humanities computing as a discipline in itself. So, like all new disciplines, it is fuzzy. It is rough, it is chaotic, provisional, organic with fluffy clouds rather than hard-edged boxes. But it's fascinating: it juxtaposes graphically some areas that are not usually conceptually related. It poses questions about methods (here computing methods), suggests links and relationships; it stimulates thinking, particularly about interdisciplinary matters and the place of humanities computing in them. It is also teasingly difficult to achieve.

McCarty and Short remarked of their map that 'the mapping activity instantiated here is the point rather than the map itself'. The same goes for this attempt: the results are tentative, but the activity may have some use to start movement along less-travelled lines.

Figure 6.1 presents a provisional map for music and ICT. Following the model of McCarty and Short, it presents four fuzzily defined areas of music, each with a particular focus, and four complementary or supporting areas of ICT. These are lined up vertically according to the strength of their connection (e.g. music education is strongly connected with educational technology), but there are a great

---

5 As exemplified by the activities of the AHRC Research Centre for the History and Analysis of Recorded Music <http://www.charm.rhul.ac.uk/index.html>, accessed 21 April 2009.

6 EARS, <http://www.ears.dmu.ac.uk>.

7 Although, following the welcome landmark decision this year by the UK's leading conference in humanities computing, DRH (Digital Resources in the Humanities) to restyle itself DRHA (+ Arts) perhaps even the label 'humanities computing' is now obsolete.

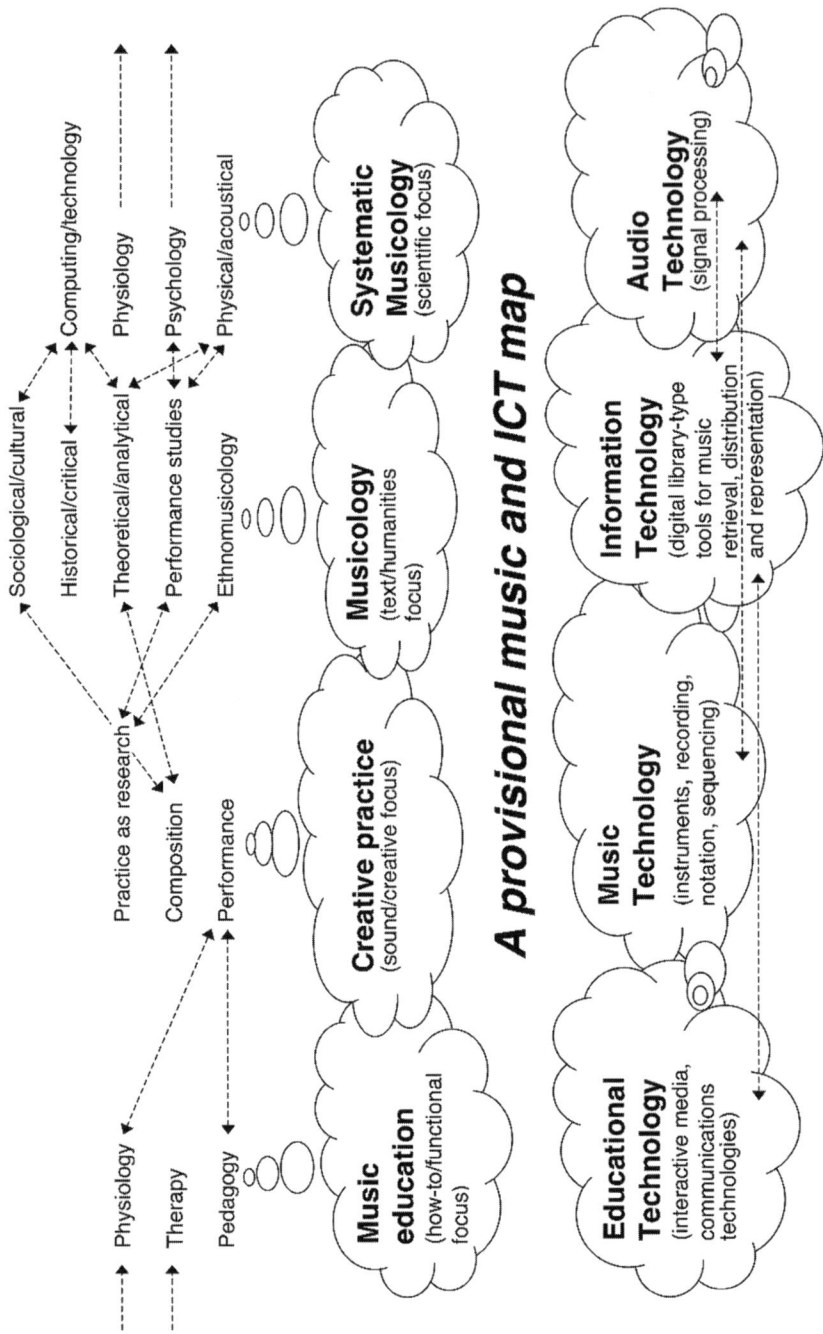

A provisional music and ICT map

Sociological/cultural
Historical/critical
Theoretical/analytical
Performance studies
Ethnomusicology
Computing/technology
Physiology
Psychology
Physical/acoustical

Practice as research
Composition
Performance

Physiology
Therapy
Pedagogy

Systematic Musicology (scientific focus)

Musicology (text/humanities focus)

Creative practice (sound/creative focus)

Music education (how-to/functional focus)

Audio Technology (signal processing)

Information Technology (digital library-type tools for music retrieval, distribution and representation)

Music Technology (instruments, recording, notation, sequencing)

Educational Technology (interactive media, communications technologies)

Figure 6.1   A provisional map for music and ICT

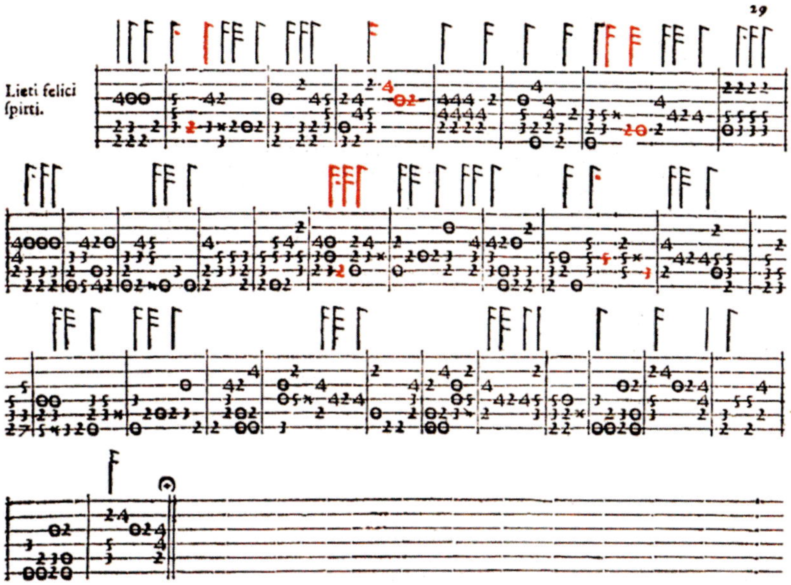

Plate 3.1   V. Galilei, *Fronimo*, 'Lieti felici spiriti', facsimile (digitally enhanced)

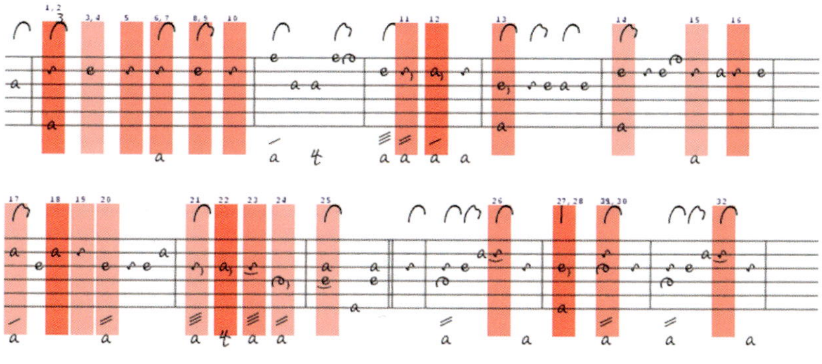

Plate 3.2   S.L. Weiss, *Bourrée*, bars 1-11, showing variant density

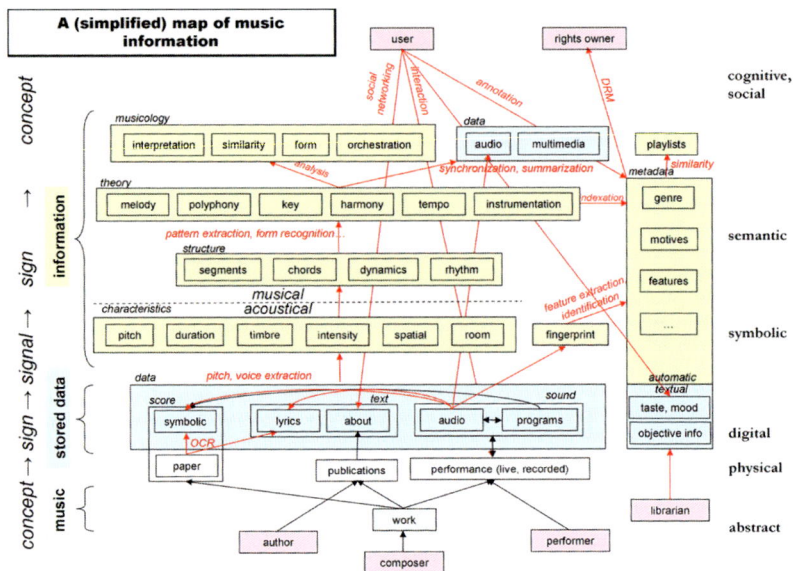

Plate 4.1   What music information retrieval is all about

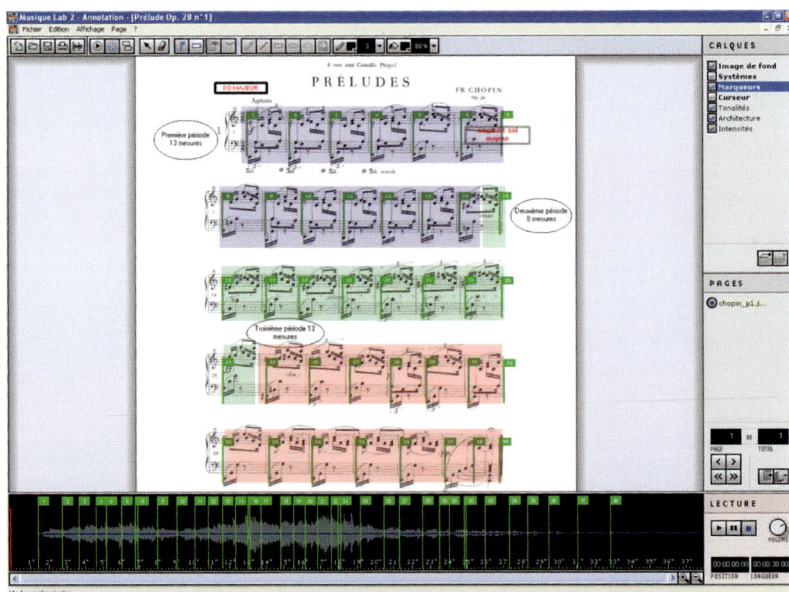

Plate 4.2   Annotation of F. Chopin *Prelude* Op. 28 No. 1

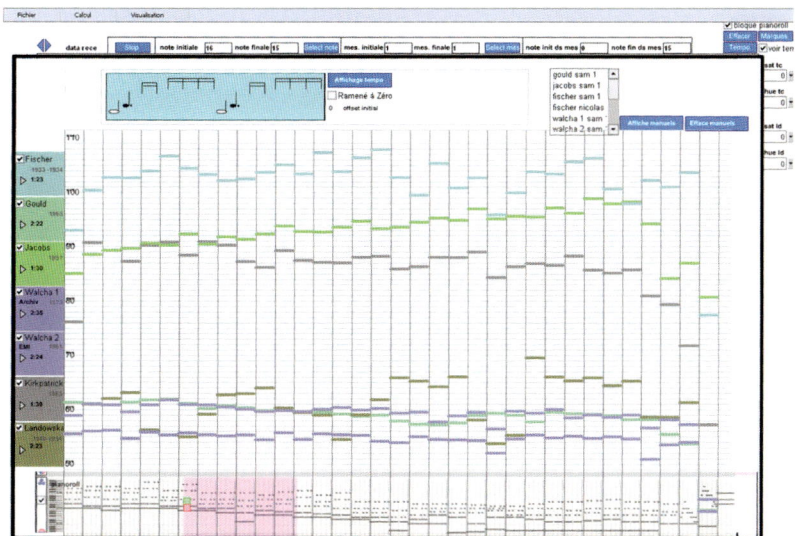

Plate 4.3a **Performance comparison of J.S. Bach's first 'Prelude'
(average tempo in seven performances)**

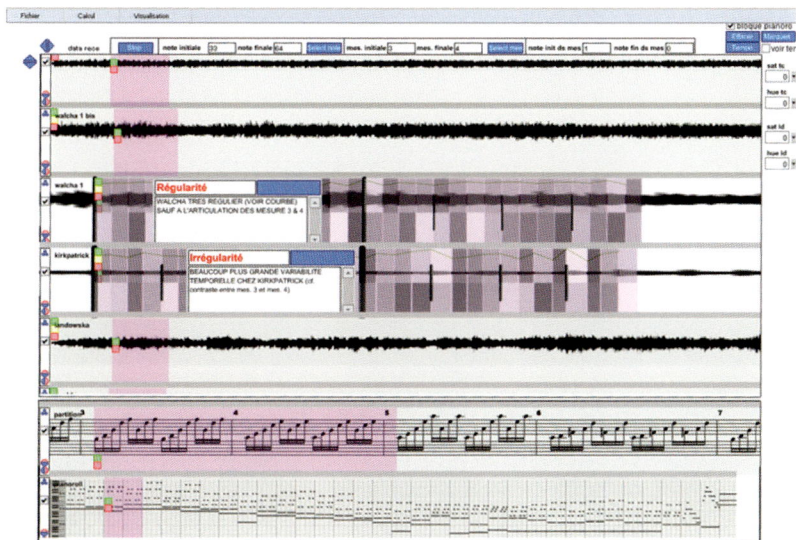

Plate 4.3b **Performance comparison of J.S. Bach's first 'Prelude'
(zooming in: Walcha vs. Kirkpatrick, bars 3–4**

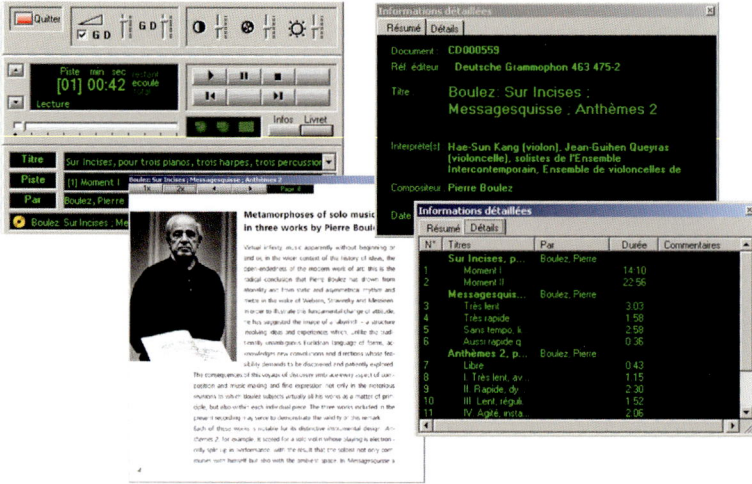

Plate 4.4   Audio player showing the musical structure and the program notes

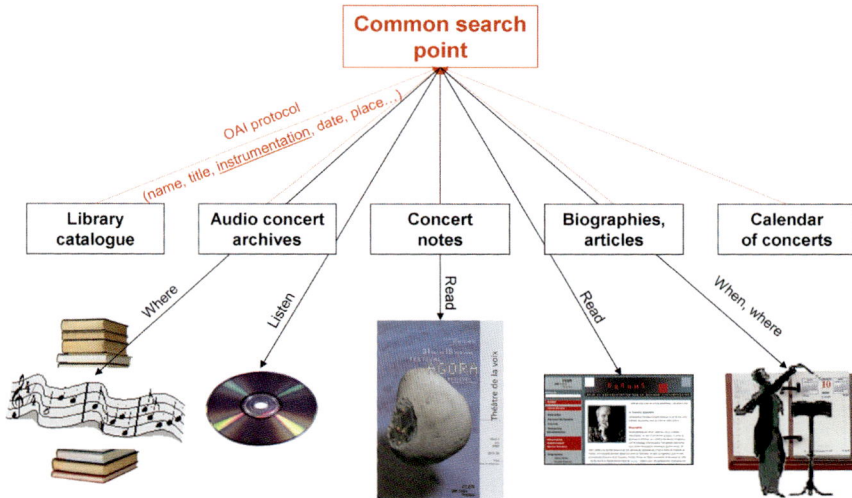

Plate 4.5   Sharing information sources with OAI

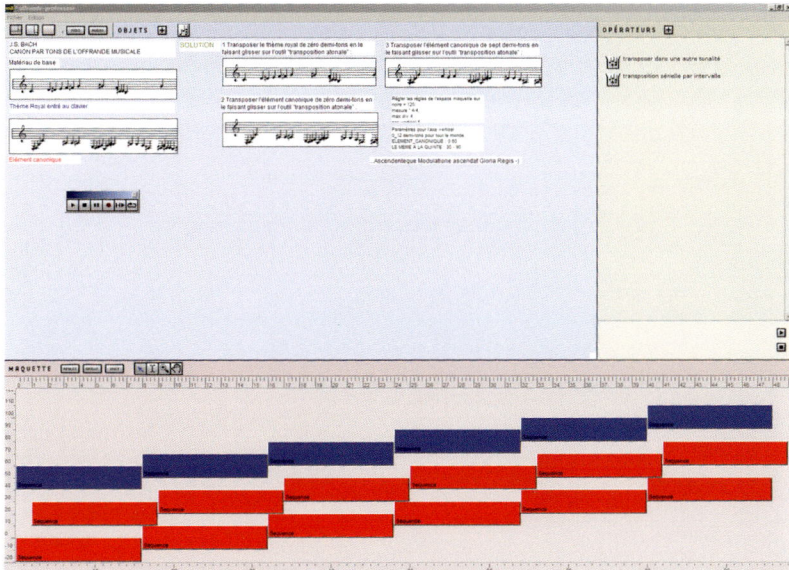

Plate 4.6   **Maquette of J.S. Bach's 'Canon 5 a 2 (per tonus)' from the**
Musical Offering

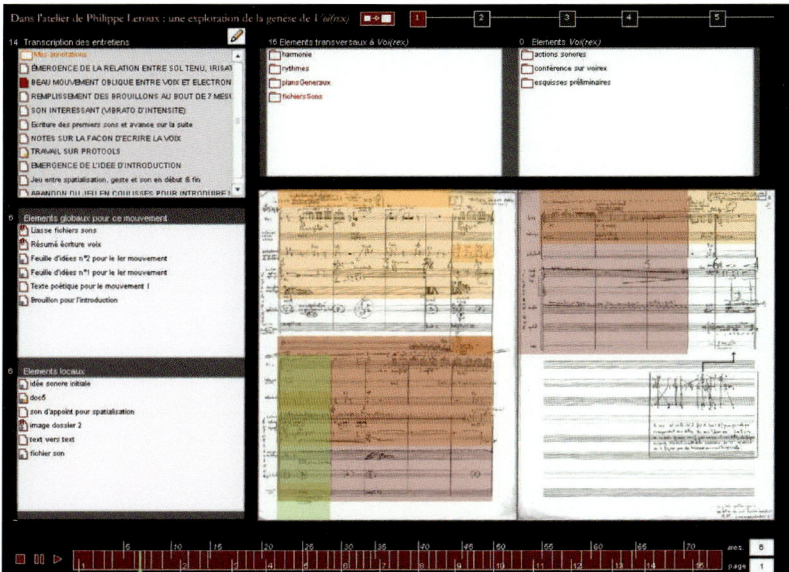

Plate 4.7   **'Genetic navigation' in P. Leroux's** ***Voi(rex)***

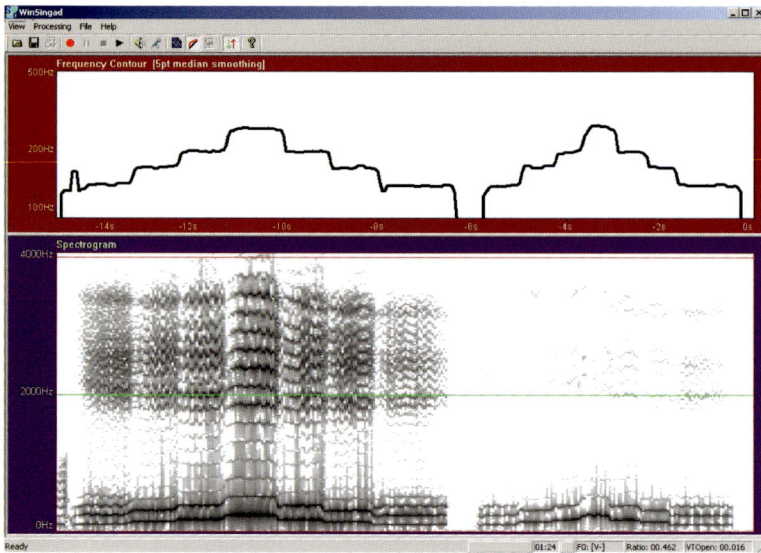

Plate 5.1   Real-time *f0* contour (top) and narrow-band spectrogram (bottom) for a C major arpeggio on the vowel in 'bee' sung in a trained (left) and untrained (right) style by an adult male singer

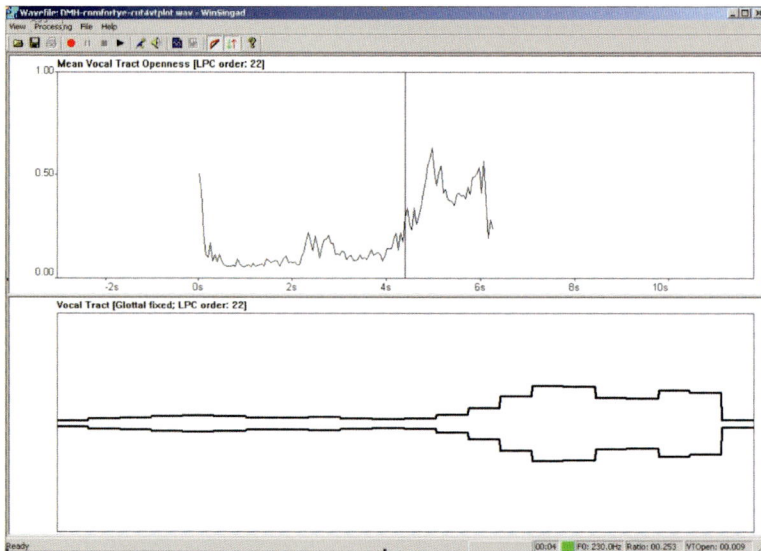

Plate 5.2   Display of the mean vocal tract area for the vowel in the second syllable of the word 'comfort' in 'comfort ye' in bar 8 of the tenor recitative of that name from Handel's *Messiah*

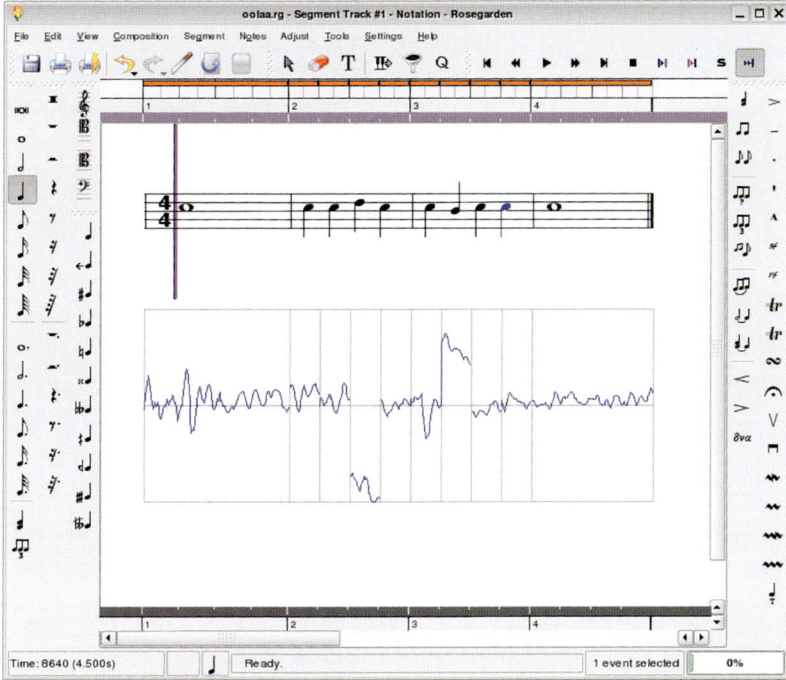

Plate 6.1   Screen shot from the Rosegarden Codicil microtonal pitch tracker

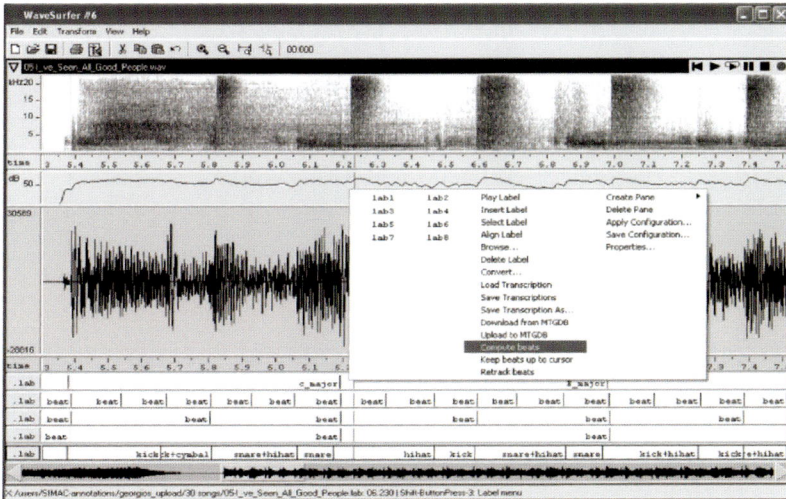

Plate 8.1   A screenshot of MUCOSA, with chord and beat annotations

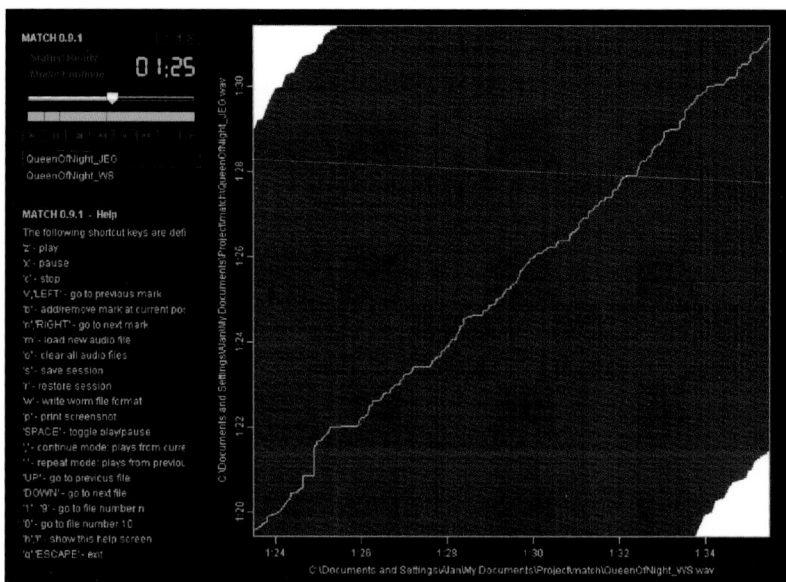

Plate 8.2   A screenshot of the MATCH toolchest comparing two renditions of Mozart's 'Queen of the Night' aria

many more overlaps and other interconnections between them. The four music areas are again divided into some sub-disciplinary offshoots, listed above. These also overlap, and strong connections are shown with dotted lines. Indeed all are interconnected in some way but even so there are likely to be more overlaps and connections than are shown here and some may be contentious; the nature of some of these connections is fuzzy. There are also very strong connections between the separate areas of ICT (e.g. audio technology as the foundation of music technology).

As far as definitions are concerned, this mapping adopts a term more commonly used in central Europe, that of *systematic musicology*, referring to primarily empirical and data orientated study.[8] Although the classifications differ in details, Parncutt's call for balance and positive and constructive interactions between musicological sub-disciplines is at the heart of the thinking here. The very term ICT (Information and Communications Technology/ies) itself is not without ambiguity; although more commonly used in the UK as a catch-all for a range of technologies for gathering, storing, retrieving, processing, analysing and transmitting data which also includes computing, networking and communications devices, hardware and software (which is the sense in which it is used here), as a term it sometimes retains an educational focus.[9]

Support for the use of ICT in the UK is almost as complex. Until very recently the UK research community was very well served in terms of central support for the use of ICT in arts and humanities research – indeed, so well supported that the AHRC ICT Programme found it necessary to produce another map which provided 'a brief description of the main providers, with links to further information on each one […] a simplified representation of their functions and the way they relate to each other'.[10] Since this map was produced, funding for the AHDS from the AHRC has ceased; its other major funder the JISC has also been forced to withdraw funding. The future of centrally funded, focused ICT support for the arts and humanities in the UK seems uncertain.

I have for several years been involved with support systems for learning, teaching and research in the arts and humanities with experience as a long-standing member of various JISC committees (in particular its Moving Image and Sound Working Group), through involvement with the (then-named) AHDS Performing Arts Data Service at its inception, and the AHRC and its ICT programme committee structure. My interest is in using technology to assist learning and teaching in music, and a particular niche interest is in tools to make sound archives as usable as possible.

---

8 Parncutt, 'Systematic Musicology and the History and Future of Western Musical Scholarship'.

9 Kent County Council, National Grid for Learning, <http://www.kented.org.uk/ngfl/ict/definition.htm>, accessed 21 April 2009.

10 AHRC ICT Programme, <http://www.ahrcict.rdg.ac.uk/ictmap/>, accessed 21 April 2009.

This is reflected in the HOTBED[11] project and currently in EASAIER,[12] an EU-funded project on access to sound archives. I chair the user panel of the JISC-funded British Library Archival Sound Recordings project which is providing several thousand hours of sound material to UK further and higher education online. The recent AHDS funding decision adds anxiety about how best to support the needs of learners, teachers and researchers on the ground.

The following sections follow and elaborate on the connections and intersections proposed in the map in Figure 6.1 and hover around several of its fuzzy boundaries. Concentrating on how ICT is used principally in, and in support of, musical performance, another taxonomy results which will form the structure of this chapter:

- Performance training
- Performance analysis
- Distribution and dissemination of performances
- Music making.

This cut starts from ICT used in support of performance training (from beginners to professionals), moves towards tools for analysis and dissemination (perhaps of equal interest to creative practitioners and researchers) and comes back to the perspective of the creative practitioner in the final section. Each section starts by characterizing the overall nature and function of the ICT type or tool, which constituency of users it is aimed at, and how it might intersect with other (sub)disciplines. These tools cover a very broad range: from advanced digital signal processing applications that accurately measure and analyse sound sources to Internet technologies that facilitate building linked communities of performers; from 'wired' conventional instruments to digital sound archives making available a hundred years of recorded music. The field is vast and varied and it is difficult to generalize or find common themes. Perhaps the most useful broad categories to consider are ICT tools that *assist* and *support* performance and creative endeavour (e.g. by analysis or interactive feedback or example) and those that help *create* performance (e.g. new instruments or technological extensions, creative compositional tools).

3. Performance training

The use of ICT in performance training is perhaps the area that has fewest intersections with conventionally defined musicological research. It tends to be

---

11 HOTBED (Handing On Tradition By Electronic Dissemination) <http://www.hotbed.ac.uk/>, accessed 21 April 2009.

12 EASAIER (Enabling Access to Sound Archives through Integration, Enrichment and Retrieval) <http://www.elec.qmul.ac.uk/easaier/>, accessed 21 April 2009.

supported more by educational and psychological research sources,[13] and it also has a significant commercial profile.[14]

The function of ICT tools in performance training includes analysing a user's performance (from either a digital or acoustic source), and giving feedback (visual/audio) or tutorial assistance, and adding 'peripherals', such as notation, transpositions, 'intelligent' accompaniments, backing or arrangements. There is a significant market for and widespread use of these tools for elementary performers and learners in the 'teach yourself' market, but specialized applications may also be used for advanced- and professional-level musical training. Playback/feedback functionality means that such tools are useful for research into pedagogy and have been used to collect data for music psychology research.

Starting with some examples from the bottom end of the market, there are a number of commercial 'teach yourself' or 'help yourself' applications, which are aimed at the elementary learner. Among these are applications like the Yamaha Digital Music Notebook[15] or SmartMusic,[16] a very fully functioned software package endorsed by the Associated Board of the Royal Schools of Music (ABRSM). The ABRSM is particularly interested in Smart Music's 'intelligent' accompaniment functions that follow the user's performance, unlike the old vanilla performances and set-in-concrete tempi of Music Minus One. SmartMusic has a large database of titles and can 'simulate a rehearsal environment and encourages students to listen to fellow musicians. Students play their individual part while listening to the piece as a whole in a rich musical environment that makes practicing fun and engaging.'[17] Both SmartMusic and the Yamaha application allow users to record their performance in either audio or MIDI, play it back, switch between and compare prerecorded demo data and their own recorded performance. The idea is to make it easy for users to focus on a difficult passage, slow it down, and try it over and over again.

SmartMusic has very specific visual feedback for users. Users play or sing their part with accompaniment and receive, in real time on the computer, detailed feedback on their performance. As the web blurb has it:

---

13 *The British Journal of Music Education* (BMJE), as the leading UK journal in this field, regularly covers use of ICT in music education. See <http://www.cambridge.org/journals/journal_catalogue.asp?mnemonic=BME>, accessed 21 April 2009.

14 Some of the many and varied commercial sites include AlphaTutors (<http://www.alphatutors.co.uk/virtual_learning_category_level.php?cPath=469>), Expert Village (<http://www.expertvillage.com/category/music.htm>) or IBegin (<http://www.original-works.co.uk/ibegin/index.html700>), all accessed 21 April 2009.

15 Yamaha Digital Notebook, <http://www.digitalmusicnotebook.com/>, accessed 21 April 2009.

16 SmartMusic, <http://www.smartmusic.com/>; 'SmartMusic and your students' <http://www.smartmusic.com/teachers/default.aspx?page=page1_1_1>, both accessed 21 April 2009.

17 From 'SmartMusic and your students'.

Instant feedback and assessment tools help students master material faster. As students play or sing, SmartMusic shows students how well they've performed. Correct notes appear on the screen in green. Wrong notes and rhythms display in red, and indicate if the note was played early or late. Fingering charts for every note appear on demand with a mouse-click.

With Smart Music's built-in assessment tools, students see their mistakes and how to correct them. As they practice, students see their SmartMusic grade climb higher and higher as red notes disappear and the screen fills with correct green notes. SmartMusic eliminates the danger that students will unknowingly repeat a mistake over and over again until their next lesson with an instructor. SmartMusic helps students improve each time they play.[18]

This approach seems of dubious pedagogical merit, a concern shared by a new European-funded music teaching and ICT project called I-Maestro.[19] In contrast to the SmartMusic blurb, I-Maestro's initial publicity declares: 'Music performance is not simply "to play the right note at the right time".'[20] Led by the University of Leeds Interdisciplinary Centre for Scientific Research in Music, I-Maestro lists a number of collaborators including IRCAM and City University, and the project is exploring innovative pedagogical paradigms including gesture interfaces and augmented instruments (using visual as well as audio rendering).

There are also interesting examples of educational studies using interactive musical applications. One such study[21] aims to understand how the use of interactive musical systems (such as the ones described above) can affect the learning and musical creativity of children (particularly younger children). This study uses a music system conceived at Sony CSL in Paris that is able to produce music in the same style as the person playing the keyboard (thus taking the SmartMusic intelligent accompaniments one stage further) and it looks at how children relate to this particular interactive system, what kinds of musical behaviours develop and how the system might be used in the educational field.

Moving on to more specialist applications, there has recently been a great deal of activity and research in pitch tracking for singers,[22] but even within this specialist

---

18 From 'SmartMusic and your students'.

19 I-Maestro, Interactive multimedia environment for technology enhanced music education and creative collaborative composition and performance <http://www.i-maestro. net/>; I-Maestro overview <http://www.i-maestro.org/contenuti/contenuto.php?contenuto_ id=39>, both accessed 21 April 2009.

20 From I-Maestro overview, <http://www.i-maestro.org/contenuti/contenuto. php?contenuto_id=39>.

21 F. Pachet and A.R. Addessi, 'When Children Reflect on their Own Playing Style: Experiments with Continuator and Children', *Computers in Education*, 2/1 (2004): 14.

22 D. Howard and G. Welch, VoxEd <http://www.voxed.org/>, accessed 21 April 2009.

area there are niche applications. One such is the charmingly named Rosegarden Codicil.[23] Named after the open-source Rosegarden sequencer from which it was developed, the codicil adds specialist functionality to deal with microtonal music, and is designed to help performers 'think' microtonally (in 19 tones to the octave). It gives performers practice routines, guide notes and visual feedback when going 'out of tune' (see Plate 6.1).

Finally, here are some examples from the professional end of performance training applications. There is the well-known crème de la crème of 'wired' acoustic instruments designed to give feedback on performance – the highly sophisticated Bosendorfer 290SE concert grand piano. Another such example is the cello 'hyperbow' developed by the MIT Media Lab in collaboration with the Royal Academy of Music.[24] The Bosendorfer instrument is fully geared up for both recording and playback of a pianist's actions and the keyboard data can be used to replay faithfully a pianist's performance. The Yamaha Disklavier is similar. These sorts of instruments have both pedagogical and research functions: they can be used by performers and their teachers for very detailed analysis, and by researchers into performance. Although useful for technical practice and detailed review, it is an open question as to how useful pianist-researchers concerned with aesthetic and creative experimentation find the accurate playback data that such instruments produce (and with possibly less-than-ideal keyboard action).[25]

A question for these applications is how effective they are in helping performers (of whatever level) improve, or better understand, their practice. Anecdotal evidence from a specialist singing teacher colleague at the RSAMD and corroborated by singing teachers at the Universität der Künste Berlin as demonstrated at a recent ELIA conference[26] suggests that visual feedback for singers can be useful.[27] This informal evidence is confirmed by studies into the application of technology in

---

23 The Rosegarden Codicil: A Microtonal Rehearsal Tool, University of Glasgow Centre for Music Technology <http://markov.music.gla.ac.uk/CMT/cmt.py/Projects/rgtracker.html>; Rosegarden pitch tracker <http://www.n-ism.org/Projects/microtonalism.php>, both accessed 21 April 2009.

24 D. Meredith, 'The Future of ICT in Music Research and Practice', workshop report, AHRC ICT Methods network <http://www.methodsnetwork.ac.uk/activities/act7report.html>, accessed 21 April 2009.

25 Although there is an extensive literature on the technical aspects of hyper instruments, there seems to be little research on or evaluation of their longer-term effectiveness for the performer.

26 'Research in and through the Arts', European League of Institutes of the Arts (ELIA), 2005 <http://www.elia-artschools.org/-downloads/publications/research_conference.pdf>, accessed 21 April 2009.

27 This is also endorsed by the account of electromyography (EMG) biofeedback for musicians reported in Meredith, 'The Future of ICT in Music Research and Practice', see n. 20. EMG feedback enables players to hear their performance at the same time as viewing their muscle activity graphically.

the singing studio by David Howard and Graham Welch.[28] The RSAMD singing teacher's comment was that it was most useful for certain types of student – and sometimes as a last resort if none of the specialist singing teacher's considerable and imaginative repertoire of methods seems to be getting through. Of course one person's research area is just another's ordinary professional routine: the RSAMD teacher has been using visual feedback software for several years as a matter of course and not regarding it as anything particularly out of the ordinary – another indication that ICT use in music has been absorbed into the mainstream.

4. Performance analysis

This section looks at how ICT tools can facilitate analysis of a pre-existing, recorded performance by presenting it in different, usually visual, formats, offering tools for segmentation, markup, annotation and manipulation, as well as tools for precise, recordable measurements. Much of this functionality overlaps with the previous section on Performance Training, but here the focus is on analysis not of the user's own performance (so there will be no specific 'tutorial' feedback intention), but of other pre-existing performances from which the user can learn, whether to inform their own performance or address wider analytical or stylistic questions. Such tools may be of use to performers, practice-based researchers, musicologists, particularly in performance studies, and ethnomusicologists.

As an example I will draw on the work of HOTBED (Handing on Tradition by Electronic Dissemination),[29] a JISC-funded project to evaluate the best ways of using networked sound material with undergraduate performance students. The materials in question included a collection of archival sound recordings from the School of Scottish Studies sound archive at the University of Edinburgh (otherwise very difficult to access), but also staff and students' own performances, fieldwork recordings, and videoed masterclasses. It was a rich mix from which we learned something about the sorts of tools that might benefit users. Thinking from HOTBED has informed the EU project, EASAIER (Enabling Access to Sound Archives through Integration, Enrichment and Retrieval).[30]

HOTBED, aimed at performance students in Scottish music, began with the question of how it is possible, through making available a collection of otherwise difficult-to-access performances, to adapt, incorporate and build on the tradition in students' own performances. The ethnomusicologist Peter Cooke helped shape thinking during HOTBED about what kind of tools might be useful to our practice-based consistency:

---

28 Howard and Welch, VoxEd. (See also David Howard's chapter in this book.)
29 HOTBED, <http://www.hotbed.ac.uk/>.
30 EASAIER, <http://www.elec.qmul.ac.uk/easaier/>.

In the Scottish-music context it is difficult to draw any line between practice-based research that has creative performance as the end aim, and research into performance for a better understanding of the techniques and style of a particular exponent. Both types call for focused, often repeated, listening that sometimes means researchers making their own detailed transcriptions of the music they listen to (whether it be to serve as a prescription or mnemonic aid for their own performance, or to help them to understand more clearly and precisely the instrumental or vocal techniques employed).

Researchers of both are as interested in such techniques and in the details that might have made a performance artistically successful, as they are in what is performed. Hence any serious study requires more than repeated listening to recorded performances delivered in real-time. Ethnomusicologists have for long taken for granted that their prime focus of study must be musical practice (or recordings of such) and that where they use notations they are usually their own, created as part of the work of analysis.[31]

On the topic of measurements and their purposes, Nicholas Cook,[32] in an address to the ISMIR conference in 2005, contrasted the CHARM Mazurkas project (correlating timing and dynamic information from recorded performances with the score) with Gerhard Widmer's OFAI project on very close analysis of pianists' styles (beat-level tempo, beat-level loudness analysis), a 'bottom-up [approach] giving rise to [...] extremely high-level characterisations of different great pianists' styles. Literate musical cultures, however, like that of Western "art" music, involve a constant tension between what is heard on the one hand and what is constructed or manipulated through notation on the other [...]'. There may also be a tension between perceptions of 'good' intonation in performance and the data from ICT-facilitated measurements that needs to be handled with sensitivity.[33] All this forms a nice contrast to the Scottish music examples, working with an aurally/orally transmitted musical culture that celebrates diversity in performance, in a format (networked provision) that facilitates aural analysis. Indeed it was decided after much debate, not to include any notation at all in HOTBED.

HOTBED came up with the following wish list for analytical tools to be used in conjunction with its networked collection of Scottish music, in this case often

31 Cooke, P., *On the Feasibility of a Scottish Music Performance Resource Centre as a Research Facility Principally Aimed at Performers and Composers*, RSAMD, 2003, unpublished report.

32 N. Cook, *Towards the Compleat Musicologist?*, invited talk at ISMIR 2005. Available online at <http://ismir2005.ismir.net/documents/Cook-CompleatMusicologist.pdf>, accessed 21 April 2009.

33 P. Johnson, '"Expressive Intonation" in String Performance: Problems of Analysis and Interpretation', in J. Davison, *The Music Practitioner: Research for the Music Performer, Teacher and Listener* (Aldershot UK and Burlington, VT: Ashgate, 2004), 79–90.

recorded in the field. Although this list arose from the Scottish traditional music domain, it has wide applicability to other musical genres and is corroborated by other user-needs studies in the area of networked audio resources.[34]

The project identified the need for:

- Fast playback for rapid scanning and comparison of musical structures.
- Slow tempo playback (half-speed, quarter-speed, or slower, but retaining pitch) to aid understanding or transcription of rhythmically dense or heavily ornamented music performances. Often performers can only really satisfy themselves that they have accurately 'heard' a performance, by checking at slower playback speeds. For example, fiddlers need slow playback in order to be able to note bow changes (especially if visual evidence is not available) and pipers find it difficult to perceive what precise cuttings and other ornaments have been used in bagpiping at normal playback speeds.[35]
- Changes in equalization so that audibility is preserved and/or to filter out unwanted pitch bands and artefacts (e.g. noise such as hiss and hum). Boosting specific pitch bands can help detect bow changes in fiddle performances or consonants in speech and song recordings.
- Loops (repeating passages of music) need to be readily created at will. If, for instance, a musical item is streamed, users need to specify exact points for the beginning and end of loops and to annotate them. This is one of the facilities already available in HOTBED.
- Markup and segmentation tools are also useful in repertories that use notation. Indiana University's Variations 2 project[36] has a suite of tools that allow users to create and save both visual (score-based) and audio annotations.
- Pitch adjustments are often necessary if performers wish to 'play along' with the performance they are studying (bagpipes often vary in pitch, and traditional fiddlers often tune their instruments to pitches other than the current standard).
- Adding of time clicks or drones on a parallel channel to the musical signal

---

34 S. Dempster, 'Report on the British Library and Joint Information Systems Committee Usability Evaluation Workshop, 20 October 2004', JISC Moving Pictures and Sound Working Group, London, 20 October 2004. HOTBED, <http://www.hotbed. ac.uk/>; 'Final Report of the American Memory User Evaluation, 1991–1993', American Memory Evaluation Team, Library of Congress, Washington, DC, 1993 <http://memory. loc.gov/ammem/usereval.html>, accessed 21 April 2009; EASAIER D7.1 Initial User Requirements and Evaluation procedures, January 2007, unpublished.

35 M.Gainza and E. Coyle, Automating Ornamentation Transcription, <http://www. elec.qmul.ac.uk/easaier/papers/automating%20ornamentation%20transcription%20-%20mikel%20gainza.pdf>, accessed 21 April 2009. Researchers on the EASIAER project are working on an ornamentation detector and transcriber.

36 Variations 2, Indiana University Digital Music Library Project <http://variations2. indiana.edu/research/>, accessed 21 April 2009.

is useful to explore questions of timing and rhythm (rubato) or pitch and intonation respectively.

- Visual aids and graphical display such as displaying and measuring the spectral content of notes and phrases. Of particular value to singers who may wish to test their own perceptions of pitch slides, vibrato etc. which the performers they are studying may have produced.
- Conversion to MIDI files, and via these, conversion to printed graphical musical notations via software such as Sibelius.
- Ease of juxtaposition of several different performances of an item (by the same or different musicians) to compare versions and styles.
- Source separation, for example separating a solo instrument from an ensemble, may be useful for close analysis of that solo.

Most of these tools are available, and useful for many different genres of music – the trick is to get them all in one box, easy to use and implement for the non-specialist. This is one of the aims of the EASAIER project. Analytical tools for manipulating audio source materials are valuable for performers themselves (particularly for traditional repertoires where a range of recordings may not be so readily available), as well as for the (ethno)musicological study of performance styles.

5. Distribution and dissemination

ICT enables digitized recorded music to be made available widely (e.g. providing access to archives, or shared collections) and, depending on access rights and software tools, makes available downloads and streams not just for listening, but for sampling and manipulating. It also enables recordings to be more easily discovered and retrieved.

ICT-based distribution and dissemination serve a very large constituency of music learners, teachers and researchers, an even larger one of general music lovers and a generation of 'born digital' creative music-makers. The effect of ICT-enabled distribution and dissemination on the creative constituency is double-edged: more opportunities than ever to put work in the public domain lead to greater likelihood of rights infringements. There are, of course, workarounds and many artists, having embraced internet distribution, have managed to find a business model that works (see section 6). As well as distribution of their own performance or compositional work, performers can benefit from the easy accessibility of recorded music archives. For example, the British Library Archival Sound Recordings project described below has a comprehensive collection, online, of Beethoven String Quartet recordings from the last hundred years – a performance practice treasure-trove.

The British Library Archival Sound Recordings project,[37] funded by the JISC, is providing nearly 4,000 hours of audio content (including music, actuality and sound effects and spoken word) in its first phase and has recently won additional funding for a second phase. Music content ranges from non-Western recordings such as Klaus Wachsmann's Uganda recordings (as curator of the Uganda Museum in Kampala, Wachsmann made invaluable recordings of Ugandan music and cultural activities, many of which are unpublished) and David Rycroft's South Africa recordings, to the Beethoven String Quartet performances noted above. The story of jazz in the UK, its varied styles, venues and characters as told by musicians, promoters and the label owners, is one of the oral history packages.

The user panel[38] has been engaged in very positive discussions with the British Library about what else we need to make these collections of recorded music most useful: for example, enhanced data such as record sleeves and labels; for Western classical performances, scores are an obvious extra; and in the case of vocal music, texts and translations. The question of the value of enriching users' experience with 'peripherals' in sound archives is also being addressed in EASAIER which is also set to work with large collections such as that of the British Library to add value with the sort of tools described in the previous section.

There is a need for rich documentation of the performance (and recording) context in helping the listener better to understand the performance under consideration. Again, in Scottish music, we need to know as much as possible about performers' interactions with listeners and with each other (whether it be in concerts, at dances and ceilidhs, festivals and competitions, in one-to-one interviews in their homes, or in recording studios) as it can directly affect the nature of the performances. It may seem obvious, but complete performances are important. However interesting 'sound-bites' might be for browsers, they are of little use for the serious study of musical performance. In the Scottish music content, researchers may need to discover, for instance, how a singer develops a song and handles or develops a strophic melody from verse to verse (often it takes a couple of verses for a traditional singer to arrive at their 'normal' version of a melody – if there is such a thing as a normal version).

A web repository of such documentation of the performance process is the aim of a recently funded project, called PRIMO (Practice-as-Research in Music Online),[39] that aims to support and document practice-based research. Launched in October 2007, it offers 'performers, composers and other researchers whose findings are best expressed through real-time and sonic events a new platform for the dissemination of their work, whilst scholars will find a wide range of practice-based outputs that have not heretofore been available to the research community'.

---

37 British Library Archival Sound Recordings Project <http://sounds.bl.uk/>, accessed 21 April 2009.

38 The author chairs the Archival Sound Recordings project user panel.

39 PRIMO <http://music.sas.ac.uk/research-projects/practice-as-research-online.html>, accessed 21 April 2009.

PRIMO is a very welcome development for the creative research community in music as in the specific area of performance documentation for research purposes, music lags behind associated disciplines such as drama.[40]

The foregoing has been quite specifically an education-orientated discussion of digitally enabled dissemination of recorded music (although experience with HOTBED indicated a strong feeling from the wider Scottish music community that it was its right and entitlement to be able to access its own musical heritage by digital means). The other side is the commercial (right side of the law?) and informal (wrong side?) networked distribution of music. The effect of networked distribution on the music industry and on music consumers, and the phenomenon of easily available and easy-to-use software for creative manipulation of networked music is touched on in the next section.

6. Making music

The use of ICT is so ubiquitous, standard, vital and important to so many creative musical constituencies that it is beyond the scope of this chapter to try to catch them all. ICT has a range of functions in this category. They include ICT acting both as a musical instrument and as a tool for playing/interacting with/composing for it; adding onto acoustic instruments, extending their ranges and capabilities (such as Jonathan Impett's 'Metatrumpet'[41]) or working in conjunction with other sources/signals (such as movement/gesture tracking via RFID tagging); and providing a vehicle for dissemination facilitating particular types of interaction (e.g. internet music).

Professional commercial and art performers and composers, research-led, practice-based performers and composers through to amateurs and 'bedroom' performers and composers – all interact with ICT in their creative activities. As mentioned above, not just new music, but also quite different types of musical behaviour arise from the opportunities that ICT provides for creative music-makers: for example, communities of musicians of every sort can be created, promoted and enabled through the web.

An example is internet music, defined by the De Montfort University EARS (ElectroAcoustic Resource Site) website as:

> Music in which the internet is integral either to its composition, or dissemination, or both. Currently, the main distinctive characteristics of internet music are:
> * Asynchronicity
> * Interactivity

---

40 Perhaps this is because in music, performance studies as an *academically-focused* discipline is so strong.

41 J. Impett, Metatrumpet <http://www.sara.uea.ac.uk/?artist&id=54>, accessed 21 April 2009.

- Multi-user
- Co-operation
- Emergence

Whilst the last two may also be said to be characteristics of conventional music making, the medium of the internet requires a special notion of social intercourse and co-operation which is peculiar.[42]

This notion of social intercourse, community building, and collaborative composition or performance bringing together geographically separated practitioners is a quite distinctive contribution of internet music. The word 'currently' in Landy's definition is also important: since this was written there has been an explosion in the phenomenon of sharing and social networking sites like FaceBook,[43] self-generating content and video sharing sites like YouTube[44] and online fantasy sites like Second Life.[45] Important social phenomenon, democratizing force[46] or sad reflections of ordinary real life, narcissism (YouTube's tag line is 'Broadcast yourself'), pornography and silliness, at the very least these sites provide performance and compositional outlets for creative practitioners.

Music software is now freely or easily available (especially to Mac users). One such software product, GarageBand, packaged with Macs and intended as a creative music tool for everyone, has been used by the band Nine Inch Nails in an interesting way. Trent Reznor comments on the band's website:

> well, the experiment of releasing the hand that feeds in garageband format was a resounding success. for those of you unaware, i essentially gave away the master multitrack sessions for that song for you to remix/reinterpret/ruin. last I checked, there were hundreds of remixes […] posted here alone.
>
> i've enjoyed and cringed at what you've done with my song. thank you (i think).
>
> again, there is no agenda here other than for you to explore, experiment, and have fun with it. depending on how this goes we may construct a more formal community for remix postings and/or possibly some sort of 'official' endorsement by means of an EP or something.[47]

---

42 EARS, <http://www.ears.dmu.ac.uk>.

43 <http://www.facebook.com>, accessed 21 April 2009.

44 <http://www.youtube.com>, accessed 21 April 2009.

45 <http://www.secondlife.com>, accessed 21 April 2009.

46 Although now already out of date in this fast-moving field, the democratizing possibilities of music technology for all are discussed by Timothy Taylor in *Strange Sounds. Music, Technology and Culture* (New York and London: Routledge, 2001).

47 T. Reznor, Nine Inch Nails Only Remix Downloads <http://www.nin.com/access/only/>, accessed 13 July 2007.

This says a great deal about a world in which communities of creative music-makers are, in this instance, being aided, abetted and encouraged by the copyright holder to manipulate the music. In the UK academic community there is now access to another collection via the JISC which is similarly completely rights-free and can be sampled, manipulated, pushed, pulled and used in whatever way users wish. This is the so-called Culverhouse collection of mostly mainstream Western classical repertoire.[48]

Sophisticated manipulation of an 'insider' community of users on the web has been used recently in a clever promotion of the currently much-hyped band, the Arctic Monkeys. One site puts it like this:

> The Arctic Monkeys are what we call a phenomenon. Built on a mass hype of no hype, word of mouth, downloads and official bootlegging has seen them championed as outsiders whilst manipulating the media. It's a clever move since the Arctics are no more than a very good next step in the contemporary zeitgeist of pop music. You know – smart-arse lyrics, Northern sensibility, drilled and frantic guitar riffs recognisable to followers of fashion.[49]

The effects of collaboration and cooperation, and construction of virtual, insider communities for music-making and music consumption, and of technology on musicians more generally, are far-reaching.[50] They present some radical paradigm shifts in creative musical behaviour.

7. Conclusions

The foregoing discussion has covered a wide scope of creative ICT users – from the bedroom composer to the professional pianist – and uses – from a play-along tutorial to sophisticated manipulation of digital sound archive material. A recurring theme has been how ICT opens up access to previously specialized activities and tools, and makes them available to a wider group of users. This democratization can be detected in 'new' musical practices: the effects of the web on participatory musical culture; the ease of access to and use of compositional software tools; the possibilities for close analysis of musical repertory. ICT also enhances and facilitates some 'old' practices: performance tutorials or access to exemplar performances.

---

48 Film and Sound Online Culverhouse Classical Music Collection, <http://www.emol.ac.uk/collections/culverhouse.shtml>, accessed 21 April 2009.

49 R.McGibbon, Artic Monkeys @ Blank Canvas, Leeds, 2005, Vanguard Online Gig Reviews <http://www.vanguard-online.co.uk/archive/music/0511LAM.htm>, accessed 21 April 2009.

50 Taylor, *Strange Sounds*.

Another outcome is the web of connections ICT promotes between the various branches of musical study and research, and with interdisciplinary thinking. ICT opens up possibilities for working with other disciplines such as audio engineering, computing and information science, psychology, education and pedagogy. For example, a new research group in Glasgow, n-ISM,[51] aims to produce significant and novel results in all its participating disciplines. The maxim in its first *microtonal-ism* project is that:

- Only a composer could have done the composition.
- Only a performer could have performed the piece.
- Only a software engineer could have implemented the software.
- Only a signal processing engineer could have made the measurements.

This acknowledgement of the vital and independent contribution of every discipline involved, but threaded through with and facilitated by ICT, is salutary. In the last decade there has been much debate about whether humanities computing should be acknowledged as a discipline in itself, and whether it enables new types of research that would otherwise be impossible to achieve, or rather whether it simply (and more humbly) functions as just another tool in the researcher's repertoire. In music, ICT often has a useful linking role among competing sub-disciplines and fast-emerging interdisciplinary constellations. It is best regarded in creative music practice as a ubiquitous and facilitating tool, and we might now be confident in striving for music and disciplinary 'pull', rather than (as has been the case for so long) technology 'push'.

However, it is an open question as to whether the creative music community as a whole is quite ready wholeheartedly to embrace these possibilities. A recent report indicates that there are still doubts about how the speed of change in new technologies leaves inadequate time for reflection and evaluation:[52] 'For a new technological "toy" to become a "tool" of creativity requires time for dialogue, both within the creative studio and without.' This is, perhaps, overcautious; musicians have always adapted technical resources for creative ends. For example in the electroacoustic music community, general purpose tools for audio (tape recorders, microphones, loudspeakers, test equipment) as well as software have been imaginatively put to use for unexpected creative means – and often adopted/adapted very quickly. Mainstream activities as well as enhanced, innovative practices can result from imaginative use of one of the myriad forms of ICT; creative musicians have always been among the early adopters of technology and continue in the vanguard.

---

51 n-ISM, the Network for Interdisciplinary Studies in Science, Technology, and Music, <http://www.n-ism.org/>, accessed 21 April 2009.

52 Meredith, 'The Future of ICT in Music Research and Practice'.

Acknowledgments

I am very grateful to two RSAMD colleagues, Dr Alistair MacDonald and J. Simon van der Walt for their good and timely advice on navigating the complex terrain of compositional software and the many forms of computer music.

Chapter 7

On the Use of Computational Methods for Expressive Music Performance

Werner Goebl and Gerhard Widmer

1. Introduction

The general availability of more and more powerful computers over the past two decades and the advent of a standardized symbolic communication protocol between music instruments (MIDI) have led to a downright boom in quantitative research on expressive music performance.[1] The number of papers exploring the various aspects of (predominantly piano) performance even increased towards the millennium.[2] This trend towards the constitution of an entire new field is also reflected in comprehensive compilations of pertinent studies.[3] In order to bridge the gap between theoretical and practical approaches and to connect knowledge from science and music practice, Parncutt and McPherson[4] collected a wide range of contributions on various aspects of music teaching, learning and performance, each written jointly by a researcher and an active musician. Similarly, the contributions collected by Williamon,[5] which deal with the various aspects of achieving excellence in music performance through refined techniques of practice, strongly refer to the current scientific literature.

---

1 R. Kopiez, 'Interpretationsforschung mit Hilfe des Computerflügels. Eine Studie zur Wahrnehmung von Interpretationsmerkmalen [Interpretation Research with the Help of Computer Pianos: An Analysis of the Perception of Features of Music Interpretation]', in K.E. Behne, G. Kleinen and H. d. la MotteHaber (eds), *Musikpsychologie. Empirische Forschungen, ästhetische Experimente*, vol. 10, *Jahrbuch der Deutschen Gesellschaft für Musikpsychologie* (Wilhelmshaven: Noetzel, 1994), pp. 7–23; C. Palmer, 'Music Performance', *Annual Review of Psychology*, 48 (1997): 115–38; A. Gabrielsson, 'Music Performance in D. Deutsch (ed.), *Psychology of Music* 2nd Edn (San Diego: Academic Press, 1999), pp. 501–502.

2 A. Gabrielsson, 'Music Performance Research at the Millennium', *Psychology of Music*, 31/3 (2003): 221–72.

3 J. Rink (ed.), *The Practice of Performance: Studies in Musical Interpretation* (Cambridge: Cambridge University Press, 1995); J. Rink (ed.), *Musical Performance. A Guide to Understanding* (Cambridge: Cambridge University Press, 2002).

4 R. Parncutt and G. McPherson (eds), *The Science and Psychology of Music Performance. Creating Strategies for Teaching and Learning* (New York: Oxford University Press, 2002).

5 A. Williamon (ed.), *Musical Excellence: Strategies and Techniques to Enhance Performance* (Oxford: Oxford University Press, 2004).

Parallel to these advances in more 'conventional' music research, extensive work on computational modelling of expressive music performance has been carried out, with partly astonishing results – for example, the automatic discovery of fundamental performance principles and rules, computer recognition of individual performers, and even artificial performances rendered by computer.[6] Another recent development in the scientific landscape that may help the study of music performance in the future, is the advent of the research field of 'music information retrieval', which has a strong focus on new methods for intelligent music and audio analysis.

As measured data on music performance quickly reaches enormous dimensions (just a single Mozart sonata contains around 8,000 notes, each associated with performance properties such as onset, offset and loudness, to name only the most obvious), the use of computers for data processing is virtually inevitable. Measuring, managing and making sense of these data requires several processing steps (e.g. onset detection, score-performance alignment, error correction). For each of these steps various computational solutions have been proposed in the literature; for some of them even freely available software has been provided on the internet. In the following, we report on the state of the art of such computational methods in order to provide an overview for both the musicologist with a strong technical interest, and the technical developer with an interest in helping the former. Naturally, a certain emphasis will be given to work that has been performed in recent years by our music groups in Vienna and Linz.[7]

For the purpose of this chapter, we define the term 'computational method' to include computational approaches to retrieving data from recorded performances as well as tools for the abstract display, visualization and automatic analysis of such data. However, we exclude studies from our survey that, for example, simply use a waveform display to manually read off onset times of certain tones, not because such studies might not be highly valuable for research, but because our focus here is on more advanced and autonomous computational methods.

Despite some excellent attempts to provide introductory texts for empirical research in classical musicology[8] and to bridge the gap between computational research and music education,[9] it is still not common to apply advanced tools from information technology in everyday musicological research or music education. We want this chapter to be helpful in this respect by describing current technologies

---

6 For exhaustive overviews, see G. Widmer and W. Goebl, 'Computational Models of Expressive Music Performance: The State of the Art', *Journal of New Music Research*, 33/3 (2004): 203–16; G. De Poli, 'Methodologies for Expressiveness Modelling of and for Music Performance', *Journal of New Music Research*, 33/3 (2004): 189–202.

7 The first author was formerly affiliated with the Austrian Research Institute for Artificial Intelligence in Vienna.

8 E.F. Clarke and N. Cook, *Empirical Musicology: Aims, Methods, and Prospects* (Oxford: Oxford University Press, 2004).

9 Parncutt and McPherson (eds), *The Science and Psychology of Music Performance*.

and proposing ways of using them in real musical applications. We will set out to describe computational means for establishing access to music performance data mainly through audio recordings (section 2). In order to understand (and eventually to interact with) performance data, it is indispensable to think about ways to display and visualize data that are intuitive and informative at the same time (section 3). Finally, section 4 will report on recent developments in the computational modelling of music performance.

2. Access to music performance

Expressive music performance is the process of singing or playing a musical instrument in order to create musical output. This process can be captured in multiple ways: the most common is to record its acoustic outcome with microphones; the recordings can be stored on different media such as tapes or computer hard disk. The digitized audio data are a good representation of the acoustical signal, but in order to understand the properties of the performance such as tempo variations, dynamics or articulation, these data have to be processed. A common first step is to distinguish entities such as notes or chords from the audio stream, determine the times of their onsets and offsets, and estimate their loudness values. Several computer programs have been developed to support such operations. We will discuss some of them in section 2.1 below.

Another common way of capturing the process of music performance is to record the movement of the parts of the musical instrument that are involved in tone production. A good example here is the action of a piano as a mechanical interface between the musician and tone production. Computer-monitored pianos that measure the speed and the timing of the piano hammers and output this information in a symbolic format (usually MIDI) have been developed exclusively for research purposes, such as the 'Iowa Piano Camera'[10] or Henry Shaffer's Photocell Bechstein.[11] Today, instruments such as the Disklavier by Yamaha or the computer-controlled pianos by Bösendorfer[12] are commercially available, not to mention the many digital pianos and synthesizer keyboards that are frequently used as well.

---

10 C.E. Seashore (ed.), *Objective Analysis of Musical Performance*, *University of Iowa Studies in the Psychology of Music*, vol. 4 (Iowa City: Iowa University Press, 1936).

11 See L.H. Shaffer, 'Analysing Piano Performance', in G.E. Stelmach and J. Requin (eds), *Tutorials in Motor Behavior* (Amsterdam: North Holland, 1980); L.H. Shaffer, 'Performances of Chopin, Bach and Bartòk: Studies in Motor Programming', *Cognitive Psychology*, 13/3 (1981): 326–76.

12 W. Goebl and R. Bresin, 'Measurement and Reproduction Accuracy of Computer Controlled Grand Pianos', *Journal of the Acoustical Society of America*, 114/4 (2003): 2273–83.

We called expressive music performance a 'process of singing or playing a musical instrument', a definition that logically entails the involvement of a human individual who produces all sorts of movements during performance that can be the subject of research.[13] These movements may contain large amounts of expressivity that can even override the acoustic information.[14] Thus, they should be regarded as an integral part of a music performance. In order to capture performers' movements, other monitoring techniques are required. They range from conventional video cameras or webcams[15] to complex three-dimensional motion capture systems.[16] While movement analysis will more and more become an integral part of music performance research, the present chapter will focus on performance analysis at a symbolic and acoustic level.

In the following, we describe ways of automatically or at least semi-automatically retrieving performance data from audio recordings (annotation), and ways of relating one performance to a score or multiple performances to each other (alignment). At this point we want to refer the reader to an outstanding introductory chapter on empirical methods for studying music performance[17] that discusses basic principles of data measurement and display as well as problems and shortcomings of quantitative as compared to qualitative methods.

2.1 Annotation

By music annotation, we understand the process of retrieving performance data from audio recordings or labelling audio files with content-based metadata. In the domain of music information retrieval, annotation refers not only to expressive performance data such as tone onsets, offsets or loudness, but also to more general aspects of transcription such as harmony or instrumentation.

---

13 J.W. Davidson and J.S. Correia, 'Body Movement', in R. Parncutt and G. McPherson (eds), *The Science and Psychology of Music Performance: Creating Strategies for Teaching and Learning* (Oxford: Oxford University Press, 2002), pp. 237–50.

14 K.E. Behne, '"Blicken Sie auf die Pianisten?!" Zur bildbeeinflußten Beurteilung von Klaviermusik im Fernsehen', *Medienpsychologie*, 2/2 (1990): 115–31; J.W. Davidson, 'What Type of Information is Conveyed in the Body Movements of Solo Musician Performers?', *Journal of Human Movement Studies*, 26/6 (1994): 279–301.

15 A. Camurri, G. Volpe G. De Poli and M. Leman, 'Communicating Expressiveness and Affect in Multimodal Interactive Systems', *IEEE Multimedia*, 12/1 (2005): 43–53.

16 See, for example, M.M. Wanderley, B. Vines, N. Middleton, C. McKay and W. Hatch, 'The Musical Significance of Clarinetists' Ancillary Gestures: An Exploration of the Field', *Journal of New Music Research*, 34/1 (2005): 97–11; W. Goebl and C. Palmer, 'Anticipatory Motion in Piano Performance', *Journal of the Acoustical Society of America*, 120/5 (2006): 3002.

17 E.F. Clarke, 'Empirical Methods in the Study of Performance', in E.F. Clarke and N. Cook (eds), *Empirical Musicology: Aims, Methods, and Prospects* (Oxford: Oxford University Press, 2004), pp. 77–102.

Any automated system for music transcription or beat-tracking will produce errors, even if only a small number. However, to use performance data for analysis, one requires data that is completely correct. A common solution is to provide a (graphical) user interface that allows the user to go through the audio recordings and check for possible errors. Recently, a number of systems have been proposed that support the semi-automatic gathering of performance data from musical audio signals.

A first system that provided a graphical front-end to check and manipulate the output of a sophisticated beat-tracking algorithm was BeatRoot.[18] It allows the user to derive the onset times of 'beats' relatively quickly from any type of musical audio file.[19] BeatRoot gives the user graphical and aural feedback concerning the placement of each beat (markers in the waveform on the screen, and click sounds in parallel with audio playback). When detecting errors, the user can correct them and re-run the beat-tracking algorithm from that point. The system then updates its beat hypothesis, taking into account the corrected information. By repeating these steps iteratively, the user can go through an audio file quite quickly. The determined beat times can be exported for further analysis in a text-based MIDI file format that can easily be imported into other software packages. The beat level at which a given piece is tracked can be chosen by the user. With this procedure, it is possible to obtain timing data from very regularly timed music (e.g. pop or jazz) virtually automatically, and from classical music in a fairly short time. It has already proved useful in several studies of music performance.[20] Gouyon et al.[21] implemented

---

18 S. Dixon, 'An Interactive Beat Tracking and Visualisation System', in A. Schloss, R. Dannenberg and P. Driessen (eds), *Proceedings of the 2001 International Computer Music Conference* (San Francisco: International Computer Music Association, 2001a), 215–18; S. Dixon, 'Automatic Extraction of Tempo and Beat from Expressive Performances', *Journal of New Music Research* 30/1 (2001b): 39–58.

19 A comprehensive description of this system can be found in G. Widmer, S. Dixon, W. Goebl, E. Pampalk, and A. Tobudic, 'In Search of the Horowitz Factor', *AI Magazine*, 24/3 (2003): 111–30.

20 S. Dixon, W. Goebl and G. Widmer, 'Real Time Tracking and Visualisation of Musical Expression', in C. Anagnostopoulou, M. Ferrand, and A. Smaill (eds), *Proceedings of the Second International Conference on Music and Artificial Intelligence* (Berlin: Springer, 2002), Lecture Notes in Artificial Intelligence 2445, 58–68; W. Goebl, E. Pampalk and G. Widmer, 'Exploring Expressive Performance Trajectories: Six Famous Pianists Play Six Chopin Pieces', in S.D. Lipscomp, R. Ashley, R.O. Gjerdingen and P. Webster (eds), *Proceedings of the 8th International Conference on Music Perception and Cognition*, CD-ROM (Adelaide: Causal Productions, 2004): 505–509; E. Stamatatos and G. Widmer, 'Automatic Identification of Music Performers with Learning Ensembles', *Artificial Intelligence*, 165/1 (2005): 37–56.

21 F. Gouyon, N. Wack and S. Dixon, 'An Open Source Tool for Semiautomatic Rhythmic Annotation', in *Proceedings of the 7th International Conference on Digital Audio Effects* (Naples, 2004), pp. 193–6.

a subset of BeatRoot as a plugin into the free audio editor WaveSurfer,[22] which was originally designed for speech signals. BeatRoot is available in the JAVA 1.5 programming language, which runs on multiple platforms;[23] it comes with an improved onset detection algorithm[24] and can be freely downloaded.[25] BeatRoot won the annual MIREX 2006 contest on audio beat-tracking.[26]

A software framework for annotation of musical audio signals is CLAM (C++ Library for Audio and Music), which contains an annotator tool that allows the user to modify any pre-processed low-level frame descriptor.[27] Low-level descriptors provided in the sample files are signal energy, centroid, flatness and the like, as well as higher-level descriptors referring to harmony (chord, note) and structure (chorus, verse, etc.). CLAM reads and writes its descriptors in standard XML text files so that a simple import of an audio file beat-tracked by BeatRoot would be easy to accomplish. At the time of writing this chapter (January 2007, CLAM 0.97), there was no tool for beat-tracking or transcription provided in the CLAM framework. However, due to its modular concept and its input and output in standard XML, any custom-made descriptor could be loaded and manipulated in this annotator tool. CLAM is available for multiple platforms at <http://clam. iua.upf.edu/> (accessed 5 September 2007).

Another advanced and flexible tool for annotating musical signals is the Sonic Visualiser[28] developed at the Centre for Digital Music at Queen Mary, University of London. It employs a multi-layer architecture that is designed to stack multiple analyses of the audio signal on top of each other (just as Adobe's Photoshop does for image processing) so that multiple views that are synchronized in time produce a comprehensive image of the audio signal for analysis and understanding. The graphical user interface provides rich facilities for visual data display (waveform and spectral representations), annotation (e.g. a time instants layer), as well as aural display of selected features. All displayed annotation layers can be manipulated, saved to and loaded from standard XML.

---

22 K. Sjölander and J. Beskow, 'WaveSurfer – An Open Source Speech Tool', in B. Yuan, T. Huang, and X. Tang (eds), *Proceedings of the International Conference on Spoken Language Processing* (Bejing, 2000), pp. 464–7.

23 Dixon, S., 'MIREX 2006 Audio Beat Tracking Evaluation: BeatRoot' (2006). Available online at <http://www. music–ir.org/mirex2006>, accessed 21 April 2009.

24 S. Dixon, 'Onset Detection Revisited', in *Proceedings of the 9th International Conference on Digital Audio Effects* (Montreal, 2006), pp. 133–7.

25 <http://www.elec.qmul.ac.uk/people/simond/beatroot/>, accessed 21 April 2009.

26 <http://www.music-ir.org/mirex2006/index.php/Main_Page>, accessed 21 April 2009.

27 X. Amatriain, J. Massaguer, D. Garcia and I. Mosquera, 'The CLAM Annotator: A Crossplatform Audio Descriptors Editing Tool', in *Proceedings of the 6th International Conference on Music Information Retrieval* (London, UK, 2005), pp. 426–9.

28 C. Cannam, C. Landone, M. Sandler and J.P. Bello, 'The Sonic Visualiser: A Visualisation Platform for Semantic Descriptors of Musical Signals', in *Proceedings of the 7th International Conference on Music Information Retrieval* (Victoria, 2006).

In order to expand the features of the Sonic Visualiser, custom-made plugins can be loaded and programmed (Vamp Plugins). At the time of writing, the authors found plugins for beat-tracking,[29] onset detection, and various spectral processors (from the Mazurka Project web page[30]). The beat-tracker did not perform well on the tested slow-paced classical pieces (like most other beat-trackers); however, since there is no re-track function built in, as in BeatRoot, getting a piece beat-tracked takes basically as long as a purely manual annotation. The onset detection plugin from the Mazurka Project produced very satisfying results although it missed some of the onsets, but not necessarily soft ones in general. Like the other packages described, Sonic Visualiser runs on multiple computer platforms and is freely available online.[31]

2.2 Alignment

Unlike a human music listener, none of the computational tools described above has any deeper knowledge of the music that it processes. A way to enhance the performance of beat-trackers and other feature extractors would be to give them access to, for example, symbolic score information. Such an approach would involve some sort of score-to-performance alignment procedure that – if working in real time – could be used for automatic accompaniment.

An alternative approach would be to use existing knowledge (e.g. previously annotated audio files) and to transfer these metadata to other performances of the same piece. A system that matches two audio files on to each other is MATCH (Music Alignment Tool CHest[32]). It finds the optimal alignment between pairs of recordings of the same piece of music and provides a time-warping function that has a pointer usually every 20 milliseconds. MATCH compares the recordings frame by frame, based on a spectral similarity measure, and computes the warping function with a dynamic programming algorithm that operates in linear time (as opposed to other algorithms whose processing time grows quadratically with the length of the files to be processed[33]).

An example of four automatically aligned performances can be seen in Figure 7.1. The multiple lines between the individual performances indicate the time-

29 M. Davies and M. Plumbley, 'Beat Tracking with a Two State Model', in *Proceedings of the IEEE International Conference on Acoustics, Speech, and Signal Processing* (Philadelphia, 2005), vol. 3, 241–4.

30 <http://www.mazurka.org.uk/>, accessed 21 April 2009.

31 <http://www.sonicvisualiser.org/>, accessed 21 April 2009.

32 S. Dixon and G. Widmer, 'MATCH: A Music Alignment Tool Chest', in *Proceedings of the 6th International Conference on Music Information Retrieval* (London, 2005), pp. 492–7.

33 See S. Dixon, 'An Online Time Warping Algorithm for Tracking Musical Performances', in *Proceedings of the International Joint Conference on Artificial Intelligence* (Edinburgh, 2005a), pp. 1727–8.

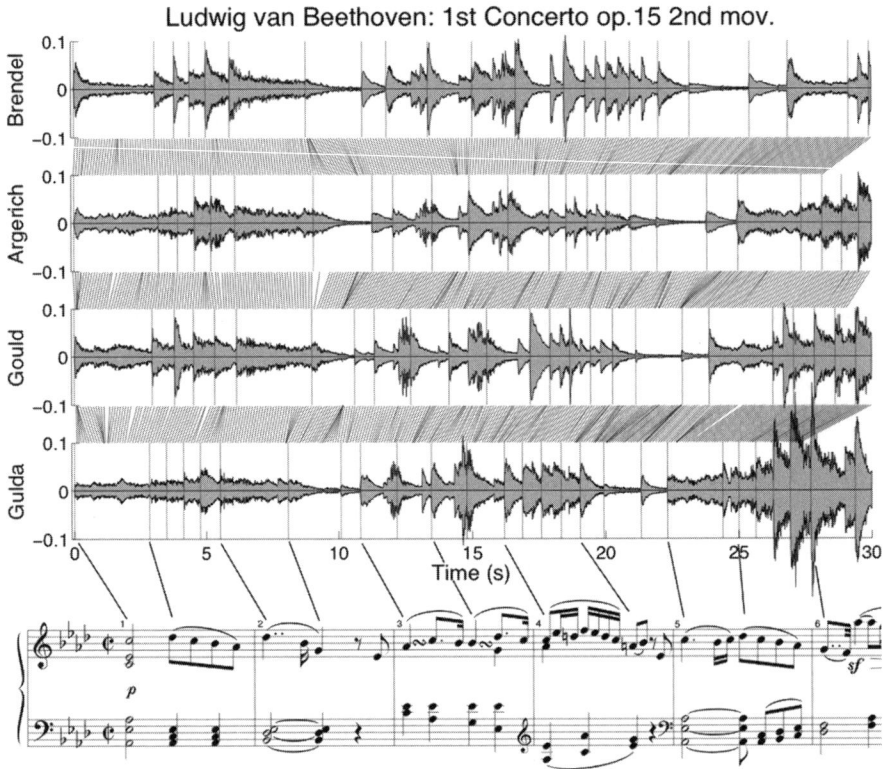

Figure 7.1   The waveforms show the first 30 seconds of four performances of four performances of Beethoven's first piano concerto, Op. 15

Note: The lines superimposed on the waveforms indicate manually annotated onsets at the eighth note level as a 'ground truth'. The solid lines between the panels show the time-warping functions between two neighbouring performances as automatically tracked by MATCH. In this figure, only warping lines every 100 ms are plotted, although the default window size of MATCH is 20ms. Compare the manually annotated onsets with the output of the algorithm that does not know anything about music. As we plot the same amount of time for each performance, a different excerpt relative to the score is shown because of the different performance tempi. We indicate the link between Gulda's performance and the music score shown by a line every half bar.

warping relations as output by MATCH (for the sake of clarity, a line is plotted only every 100 milliseconds). We invite the reader to compare this automatically produced output with the manually annotated 'ground truth' as marked by the solid lines superimposed on the waveforms. Although it gives slightly incorrect estimates at some points, it performs astonishingly well given the fact that neither onset detection nor any other higher-level processing or knowledge is involved.

Given this, a procedure that might be more efficient than direct beat-tracking or annotation might be to analyse one recording with the tools described above and then use MATCH to project these annotations automatically on to an arbitrary number of other recordings of the same piece. The output can then be reviewed and – if necessary – corrected with the software tools mentioned above. Another application that can be realized with MATCH is score-performance alignment in real time. The user would have to synthesize a score into an audio file which would then be aligned with the (live) input of a microphone listening to a performance of that score.[34] That could be used for real-time accompaniment and similar applications. MATCH runs on multiple platforms and can be freely downloaded on the internet.[35]

In some ways technically similar to the online version of MATCH, several automatic accompaniment systems have been proposed[36] that work on symbolic (MIDI) data as well as directly on audio.[37] They have been either commercialized or are not available from the researchers' homepages, so their application for performance research could not be directly assessed by the authors.

Other common demands from music researchers involve matching recorded expressive data to a score at a symbolic (usually MIDI) level. This problem has been addressed several times;[38] however, to date no conveniently working software has been provided that would offer symbolic score-performance matching interactively combined with a user interface for error correction.[39]

---

34 S. Dixon, 'Live Tracking of Musical Performances Using Online Time Warping', in *Proceedings of the 8th International Conference on Digital Audio Effects* (Madrid, 2005b), pp. 92–7.

35 <http://www.elec.qmul.ac.uk/people/simond/match/index.html>, (accessed 21 April 2009).

36 R. Dannenberg, 'An Online Algorithm for Real-time Accompaniment', in *Proceedings of the 1984 International Computer Music Conference* (San Francisco: International Computer Music Association, 1984), pp. 193–8; N. Orio and F. Déchelle, 'Score Following Using Spectral Analysis and Hidden Markov Models', in *Proceedings of the 2001 International Computer Music Conference* (Havana: International Computer Music Association, 2001), pp. 151–4; C. Raphael, 'A Hybrid Graphical Model for Aligning Polyphonic Audio with Musical Scores', in *Proceedings of the 5th International Conference on Music Information Retrieval* (Barcelona, 2004), pp. 387–94.

37 C. Raphael, 'Aligning Music Audio with Symbolic Scores Using a Hybrid Graphical Model', *Machine Learning*, 65/2–3 (2006): 389–409.

38 H. Heijink, L. Windsor, and P. Desain, 'Data Processing in Music Performance Research: Using Structural Information to Improve Score-performance Matching', *Behavior Research Methods, Instruments and Computers*, 32/4 (2000): 546–54; E.W. Large, 'Dynamic Programming for the Analysis of Serial Behaviors', *Behavior Research Methods, Instruments and Computers*, 25/2 (1993): 238–41; for an overview see H. Heijink, P. Desain, H. Honing and L. Windsor, 'Make Me a Match: An Evaluation of Different Approaches to Score-performance Matching', *Computer Music Journal*, 24/1 (2000): 43–56.

39 Ed Large and colleagues have developed an interactive user interface to the system described in Large, 'Dynamic Programming for the Analysis of Serial Behaviors', but

2. Performance visualization and interaction

After having retrieved and successfully post-processed (corrected) the performance data, one would want to see, explore and finally make sense of the collected information. In the following, we will present some ideas and techniques for visualizing music performance data with the help of computers. A crucial property of music performance is that it evolves over time. Therefore, one requirement of a visualization is that it should reflect or recreate this temporal process.

One such technique, developed and presented by Langner and Goebl,[40] combines the two most important performance parameters into one animated display. Instant tempo and loudness are displayed in a two-dimensional space in which a little disc indicates the current state of a performance at a particular moment in time. With time, the disc moves inside this space according to tempo and loudness measurements of a performance, leaving behind a trace that fades with time. The trace can be viewed as a performance trajectory that is specific for a particular performance. For obvious reasons, this display has elsewhere also been called the 'Performance Worm'.[41] This display technique has proven to be an excellent tool for performance comparisons to lay-audiences and musicians alike. The two-dimensional trajectory representation has also been used for computational analysis of larger corpora of performance data,[42] as well as to characterize the individual style of performers.[43]

To illustrate, we plot the performance trajectories of the first four bars of Alfred Brendel's and Glenn Gould's performances of the second movement of Beethoven's first piano concerto, Op. 15 (Figure 7.2; for the score, see Figure 7.1). Both trajectories are stopped at the beginning of bar 5 (cf. the number inside the circle) for comparison purposes. The two black discs within the tail indicate the phrase boundaries at bars 5 and 3. While Brendel shapes the first phrase (the first two bars) in a typical way by speeding up and slowing down in combination with a crescendo–decrescendo pattern, Gould does just the opposite: he slows down in the initial eighth notes and shortens the break before the second phrase. In the second part of this excerpt, our two pianists agree more in their interpretations:

---

it is at present being beta tested and not yet available online. Also, the Department of Computational Perception at the University of Linz is currently developing such a tool, which should be made available online some time in 2007.

40 J. Langner and W. Goebl, 'Visualizing Expressive Performance in Tempo–Loudness Space', *Computer Music Journal*, 27/4 (2003): 69–83.

41 S. Dixon, W. Goebl and G. Widmer, 'The Performance Worm: Real Time Visualisation Based on Langner's Representation', in M. Nordahl (ed.), *Proceedings of the 2002 International Computer Music Conference* (San Francisco: International Computer Music Association, 2002), pp. 361–4; Widmer et al., 'In Search of the Horowitz Factor'.

42 Goebl et al., 'Exploring Expressive Performance Trajectories'.

43 Widmer et al., 'In Search of the Horowitz Factor'.

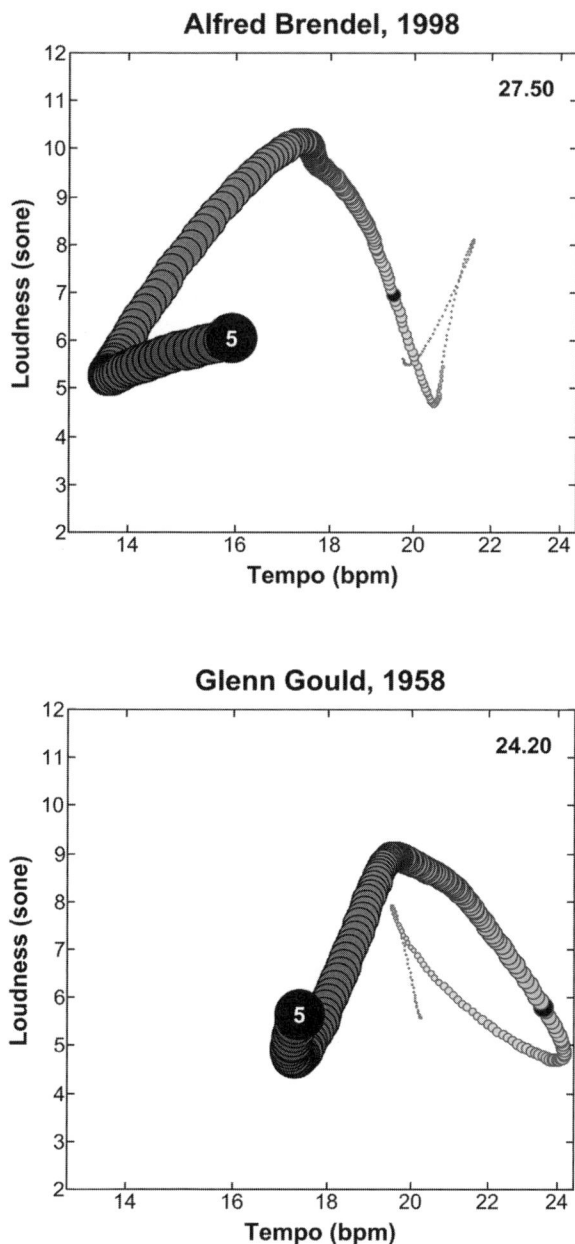

Figure 7.2 Tempo–loudness trajectories of the first four bars of the second movement of Beethoven's Op. 15 as played by (a) Alfred Brendel and (b) Glenn Gould

Note: The black discs indicate the beginning of bar 3 (smaller) and bar 5

they both employ an up-down pattern in their dynamics, while monotonically slowing down – probably in order to shape the turns more carefully.

Of course, the advantage that we claimed for the described display – its account of the temporal nature of performance via animation – is not visible in the static screen shots. Animated movies of this display can be downloaded from the internet.[44] Limitations of this way of showing performance are the loss of detail due to data smoothing and the absence of performance measures other than expressive tempo and (overall) loudness.

This tempo–loudness space has also been used to control expressive performance – a 'reversed worm', as it were. The user manipulates the current position of the worm either with a computer mouse, or – more intuitively – by moving a hand within the two antennae of a computer-monitored theremin, and the computer software shapes the performance accordingly in real time.[45] Since this interface is only able to control overall tempo and loudness, the template performances to be used for playing with the system are 'flattened' real performances with all the small-scale, local expression (chord asynchronies, dynamics of individual voices, etc.) still in them. Thus, the (lay-) user becomes a conductor in their own right with the help of computer software.

Appropriate and possibly interactive data visualization can be used in music education or for practising an instrument. There have been several attempts to provide feedback on expression in music performance. We refer the reader to a very elaborate educational system for the singing voice that is audio-based and involves fundamental pitch trackers,[46] and also to Chapter 5 by David Howard in this volume. For piano performances, the use of MIDI-based pianos makes data collection easy. Such instruments are not as widely available as conventional computers equipped with microphones are. Nevertheless, there are reports by piano teachers that computer-monitored acoustic pianos combined with simple piano-roll displays were used successfully in piano instruction.[47] A current research initiative is being carried out at the Piano Pedagogy Lab in Ottawa, Canada, where researchers are developing a software tool (the MIDIator)[48] that analyses and displays performance data relatively quickly after the performance

44 <http://www.ofai.at/~werner.goebl/animations/>, accessed 21 April 2009.

45 S. Dixon, W. Goebl and G. Widmer, 'The "Air Worm": An Interface for Real-time Manipulation of Expressive Music Performance', in *Proceedings of the 2005 International Computer Music Conference* (San Francisco: International Computer Music Association, 2005), pp. 614–17.

46 VOXed, G.F. Welch, E. Himonides, D.M. Howard and J. Brereton, 'VOXed: Technology as a Meaningful Teaching Aid in the Singing Studio', in R. Parncutt, A. Kessler and F. Zimmer (eds), *Conference on Interdisciplinary Musicology* (Graz: University of Graz, 2004).

47 E.g. K. Riley-Butler, 'Teaching Expressivity: An Aural–Visual Feedback-replication Model', in *ESCOM 10th Anniversary Conference on Musical Creativity* (Liège: Université de Liège, 2002), CD-ROM.

48 <http://www.piano.uottawa.ca/>, accessed 21 April 2009.

has been recorded.[49] This research initiative is especially promising as it is situated in an explicitly pedagogical environment where the impact and usefulness of such technologies can immediately be tested and evaluated in practice.[50] A similar path is taken by a European research consortium which developed an interactive multimedia music tuition system[51] that is aimed specifically at beginners. However, just like other computational teaching or visualization approaches,[52] the MIDIator and IMUTUS work offline – that is, the data can only be viewed after the performance is completed.

A real-time approach was taken by Goebl and Widmer.[53] The proposed interfaces, called Practice Tools, are designed to display performance as it comes from a MIDI piano, and to keep running and adapting automatically to the performer's needs without explicit interaction. They feature an extended ('acoustic') piano-roll display that incorporates all aspects of the piano sound, including the pedals, tone decay and their interaction. In addition to this, separate displays are provided that show special sub-features of the performance. For instance, a chord display shows the relative timing and dynamic differences between the tones of a chord whenever a chord occurs. With this tool, pianists can practise to balance the sound of their chords or train to bring out individual voices more deliberately.

Also operating in real time is PracticeSpace, a tool for drummers interactively to improve the timing of complex rhythms.[54] First assessments demonstrate improved learning with this visualization system.[55]

---

49 S. Shirmohammadi, A. Khanafar and G. Comeau, 'MIDIator: A Tool for Analysing Students' Piano Performance', *Recherche en Éducation Musicale*, 24 (2006): 35–48.

50 G. Comeau, 'Recherche scientifique et pédagogie du piano', *Recherche en Éducation Musicale*, 24 (2006): 1–11.

51 IMUTUS, see S. Raptis, A. Askenfelt, D. Fober et al., 'IMUTUS – An Effective Practicing Environment for Music Tuition', in *Proceedings of the 2005 International Computer Music Conference* (Barcelona, 2005), pp. 383–6.

52 As, for example, S.W. Smoliar, J.A. Waterworth and P.R. Kellock, 'pianoFORTE: A System for Piano Education beyond Notation Literacy', in *Proceedings of the ACM International Conference on Multimedia, San Francisco* (New York: ACM Press, 1995), pp. 457–65; R. Hiraga, and N. Matsuda, 'Visualization of Music Performance as an Aid to Listener's Comprehension', in *Proceedings of the Working Conference on Advanced Visual Interfaces* (Gallipoli: ACM Press, 2004), pp. 103–106.

53 W. Goebl and G. Widmer, 'Unobtrusive Practice Tools for Pianists', in *Proceedings of the 9th International Conference on Music Perception and Cognition* (Bologna, 2006), pp. 209–14.

54 A. Brandmeyer, D. Hoppe, M. Sadakata, R. Timmers and P. Desain, 'PracticeSpace: A Platform for Real-time Visual Feedback in Music Instruction', in *Proceedings of the 9th International Conference on Music Perception and Cognition* (Bologna, 2006).

55 D. Hoppe, A. Brandmeyer, M. Sadakata, R. Timmers and P. Desain, 'The Effect of Realtime Visual Feedback on the Training of Expressive Performance Skills', in *Proceedings of the 9th International Conference on Music Perception and Cognition* (Bologna, 2006).

With further advances in research on intelligent online music (audio) processing and the parallel growth in technological solutions, we may expect several of the approaches mentioned above to be combined into compact and lightweight software packages that will be available to everybody. In particular, improved audio processing algorithms will eliminate the need for costly computer-controlled musical instruments like the Disklavier. Readily and instantaneously available visualization tools will be crucial for the further spread and acceptance of advanced computational technology in music practice and research.

3. Modelling expressive performance

Data visualization can provide researchers with valuable insights, and practitioners (musicians) with useful feedback. But if the goal of music performance research is to build a thorough understanding of the phenomenon, quantitative analyses and studies must be performed, with verifiable results. Naturally, computers also play an important role in this.

An obvious first step is statistical analysis of the measurement data, which permits the researcher to verify or falsify various hypotheses about the data, and to ascertain the significance of the findings. However, in this chapter we are interested in more sophisticated uses of computers, viz. as the carriers or embodiments of computational models of (aspects of) expressive performance. As discussed elsewhere by Widmer and Goebl,[56] the purpose of computational performance models is 'to specify precisely the physical parameters defining a performance (e.g. onset timing, inter-onset intervals, loudness levels, note durations, etc.), and to postulate (quasi)systematic relationships between certain properties of the musical score, the performance context, and an actual performance of a given piece' – in short, to represent a hypothesis about music performance in the form of an operational computer program. Computational models are predictive in the sense that they can be made to produce 'expressive' performances, which opens up new possibilities for directly testing hypotheses via listening and quantitative comparison between model predictions and real measured performances.

Widmer and Goebl[57] reference a substantial number of computational modelling approaches and describe four of them in more detail. In the context of the present chapter, we focus on two of these, in order to highlight two ways in which computers can play a central role in performance analysis, beyond pure statistical data analysis.

Example 1 – the system of performance rules developed over decades at the Royal Institute of Technology (KTH) in Stockholm, by Johan Sundberg and co-workers – illustrates how computational models can be used actively to explore hypotheses via simulation and analysis. Example 2 – a massively data-driven,

---

56 Widmer and Goebl, 'Computational Models of Expressive Music Performance'.
57 Ibid.

bottom-up approach based on artificial intelligence and machine learning developed at our own institute in Vienna – shows how the computer can play a much more active role in the research process, as an active, autonomous discoverer. Both of these projects have been published extensively in the literature. In this section, we merely want to highlight those aspects that demonstrate the specific advantages of computer-based approaches to performance research.

The KTH rule system was developed over more than twenty years of research, starting with Sundberg et al.[58] Over the years, it has been extended in many ways. A fairly comprehensive description is given in Friberg[59] and more recently in Friberg et al.[60] The KTH model consists of a set of performance rules, each of which predicts, or prescribes, a specific aspect of timing, dynamics or articulation based on the local musical context. For instance, one particular rule ('Duration Contrast') is concerned with modifying the duration ratio of two successive notes; another ('Harmonic Charge') with changing the dynamics of a note depending on the harmonic context, etc. All rules are parameterized with a varying number of parameters.

Here, the computer plays the role of an interpreter of performance rules. Rules – that is, individual, partial hypotheses about some aspect of performance – can be formulated and added to the system one by one, and their impact on performances generated by the model can be analysed by listening tests, or by comparing the computer performances to real ones. Information from these tests then feeds back into the modelling process, prompting the researchers to modify rules, change parameter settings, etc. This incremental, iterative modelling process has been termed analysis by synthesis by Sundberg and colleagues[61] and is made possible by the modular nature of the model: rules produce their effects independently of other rules in the system. While modularity offers practical advantages in the modelling process, the deeper question of whether it adequately reflects the nature of the phenomenon under study – the factors governing expressive performance decisions – is more difficult to answer.

Modularity does, however, have undeniable advantages when it comes to practical applications of such models. The KTH rules have been implemented in the program Director Musices[62] that comes with different predefined rule

58 J. Sundberg, A. Askenfelt and L. Frydén, 'Musical Performance. A Synthesis-by-Rule Approach', *Computer Music Journal*, 7 (1983): 37–43.

59 A. Friberg, 'A Quantitative Rule System for Musical Performance', Doctoral dissertation, Department of Speech, Music and Hearing, Royal Institute of Technology, Stockholm, 1995.

60 A. Friberg, R. Bresin and J. Sundberg, 'Overview of the KTH Rule System for Musical Performance', *Advances in Cognitive Psychology*, 2/2–3 (2006): 145–61.

61 J. Sundberg, L. Frydèn and A. Askenfelt, 'What Tells You the Player is Musical? An Analysis-by-Synthesis Study of Music Performance', in J. Sundberg (ed.), *Studies of Music Performance* (Stockholm: Royal Swedish Academy of Music, 1983b), vol. 39, 61–75.

62 <http://www.speech.kth.se/music/performance/download/>, accessed 21 April 2009.

sets and parameter settings ('rule palettes') that are intended to model different basic emotions, for example fear, anger, happiness, sadness, tenderness, and solemnity.[63] Director Musices has recently been combined with an interactive real-time conducting system based on the Radio Baton,[64] which has been used in numerous public performances. More recently, Friberg[65] has provided a system that allows manipulation of the rule parameters in real time. There have also been efforts to combine Director Musices with computational research on expressive intentions performed at the University of Padova;[66] the resulting computer system, Expressive Director,[67] permits real-time control of music performance synthesis, in particular regarding expressive and emotional aspects.

The increasing interest of the KTH group in modelling emotional aspects of performance via the rule system has even led to practical, commercial applications: 'emotional' ring tones ('moodies') for mobile phones produced with the help of some expression rules[68] are now being sold by a Swedish company.

The second approach to performance modelling that we want to discuss briefly here takes the role of the computer one step further, from a modelling machine to an autonomous discovery machine. This is a new approach to performance research that was developed at the Austrian Research Institute for Artificial Intelligence in Vienna.[69] The basic idea is to start from large amounts of measurement data and to develop computer programs that autonomously discover significant regularities and patterns in the data, via machine-learning and data-mining techniques. In other words, the predictive performance model is built by the machine in such a way that it 'explains' the given data as well as possible. The potential advantages of this approach are that it is firmly rooted in large amounts of empirical data and that, in principle, the machine, free from human biases, may discover truly novel and

---

63 R. Bresin and A. Friberg, 'Emotional Coloring of Computer-controlled Music Performances', *Computer Music Journal*, 24/4 (2000): 44–63.

64 M.V. Mathews, A. Friberg, G. Bennett et al., 'A Marriage of the Director Musices Program and the Conductor Program', in R. Bresin (ed.), *Proceedings of the Stockholm Music Acoustics Conference* (Stockholm: Department of Speech, Music, and Hearing, Royal Institute of Technology, 2003), vol. 1, pp. 13–15.

65 A. Friberg, 'pDM: An Expressive Sequencer with Realtime Control of the KTH Music Performance Rules', *Computer Music Journal*, 30/1 (2005): 37–48.

66 E.g., S. Canazza, G. De Poli, C. Drioli, A. Rod'a and A. Vidolin, 'An Abstract Control Space for Communication of Sensory Expressive Intentions in Music Performance', *Journal of New Music Research*, 32/3 (2003a): 281–94.

67 S. Canazza, A. Rodá, P. Zanon and A. Friberg, 'Expressive Director: A System for the Realtime Control of Music Performance Synthesis', in R. Bresin (ed.), *Proceedings of the Stockholm Music Acoustics Conference*, 2nd edn (Department of Speech, Music, and Hearing, Royal Institute of Technology, Stockholm, 2003), vol. 2, pp. 521–4.

68 R. Bresin and A. Friberg, 'Expressive Musical Icons', in *Proceedings of the 2001 International Conference on Auditory Display* (Espoo, 2001).

69 G. Widmer, 'Studying a Creative Act with Computers: Music Performance Studies with Automated Discovery Methods', *Musicae Scientiae*, 9/1 (2005): 11–30.

unexpected things. On the other hand, it is not that straightforward to incorporate musicological knowledge and hypotheses into the discovery and model building process.

In numerous studies, we have demonstrated that machine-learning algorithms do have the potential to make interesting discoveries. For instance, in a set of experiments based on a very large set of performance data (recordings of 13 complete Mozart piano sonatas by a Viennese concert pianist), the computer discovered a small set of 17 quite simple and succinct rules that predict certain aspects of local timing and articulation surprisingly well. The complete set of rules is analysed in great detail by Widmer,[70] where also the generality of the rules is quantified, based on independent reference performances. Indeed, it was shown that some of the rules seem to describe very general (if simple) performance principles, as they carried over, with little loss in predictive accuracy, to performances by other pianists and even music of a different style. One of the interesting aspects is that some of the rules discovered by the machine turned out to bear a strong resemblance to some rules in the KTH model. In this way, the machine-learning approach provides further circumstantial evidence for the relevance and validity of the KTH model.

This rule model was later extended to a multilevel model of expressive timing and dynamics, again via machine learning. Widmer and Tobudic[71] describe how the computer learns to apply extended expressive tempo and dynamics gestures to entire musical phrases, at several levels of the structural hierarchy, via a kind of case-based reasoning. In other words, the computer learns to transfer, in a suitable way, appropriate timing and dynamics patterns from reference performances to new pieces. An 'expressive' Mozart performance generated by this model won second prize at the International Performance Rendering Contest (RENCON 2002) in Kyoto.[72] Again, this shows that computers can, in principle, extract musically relevant patterns from performance data. Unfortunately, the structure-level model is not readily amenable to interpretation, being based as it is on the direct transfer of expressive patterns between performances based on a measure of phrase similarity. Developing algorithms for learning human-interpretable high-level models remains a challenge.

Recent research has also produced first indications that machine learning may help in getting a first grasp on the elusive notion of individual artistic performance

---

70 G. Widmer, 'Machine Discoveries: A Few Simple, Robust Local Expression Principles', *Journal of New Music Research*, 31/1 (2002): 37–50.

71 G. Widmer and A. Tobudic, 'Playing Mozart by Analogy: Learning Multilevel Timing and Dynamics Strategies', *Journal of New Music Research*, 32/3 (2003): 259–68.

72 G. Widmer and A. Tobudic, 'Playing Mozart by Analogy: Learning Multilevel Timing and Dynamics Strategies', in R. Hiraga (ed.), *Proceedings of the ICAD 2002 Rencon Workshop on Performance Rendering Systems* (Kyoto: Rencon Steering Group, 2002), pp. 28–35.

style. Stamatatos and Widmer[73] and Saunders et al.[74] managed to show that computers can learn to identify different concert pianists, based only on timing and dynamics patterns extracted from their performances. A machine-learning study presented by Tobudic and Widmer,[75] demonstrated, in precise quantitative terms, that to a certain extent, learning algorithms seem to be able to learn artist-specific performance strategies from recordings of famous pianists. And Madsen and Widmer[76] describe a computational study where, using string-matching algorithms and evolutionary computing methods, computers could compute a quantitative measure of something like the relative stylistic consistency of famous pianists.

Other researchers have also experimented with machine learning as a tool for expressive performance research. For instance, in the context of jazz standards, Arcos and López de Mántaras[77] describe a system that transforms saxophone phrases in expressive ways, also by analogy to a corpus of known performed phrases, and Grachten et al.[78] present a system named TempoExpress that learns to transform expressively played jazz phrases to different tempi in musically meaningful ways.

In the field of machine learning, there is currently a strong trend towards probabilistic models. This is also reflected by some recent work on music performance analysis. For instance, Grindlay and Helmbold[79] use Hierarchical Hidden Markov Models (HH-MMs) empirically to model statistical relationships between musical scores and expressive timing. Probabilistic models (such as Bayesian Networks, Hidden Markov Models, Conditional Random Fields, etc.), along with new powerful learning algorithms, promise to become very useful for performance research, provided that they can be extended not just to reveal probabilistic patterns, but also to yield intelligible descriptions that can be readily understood by musicologists. That is one of the challenges we will be working on in a new research project.

---

73 E. Stamatatos and G. Widmer, 'Automatic Identification of Music Performers with Learning Ensembles', *Artificial Intelligence*, 165/1 (2005): 37–56.

74 C. Saunders, D.R. Hardoon, J. ShaweTaylor and G. Widmer, 'Using String Kernels to Identify Famous Performers from their Playing Style', in *Proceedings of the 15th European Conference on Machine Learning (ECML) and the 8th European Conference on Principles and Practice of Knowledge Discovery in Databases* (Pisa, 2004).

75 A. Tobudic and G. Widmer, 'Learning to Play like the Great Pianists', in *Proceedings of the 19th Joint International Conference in Artificial Intelligence* (Edinburgh, 2005).

76 T.S. Madsen and G. Widmer, 'Exploring Pianistic Performance Styles with Evolutionary String Matching', *International Journal of Artificial Intelligence Tools*, 15/4 (2006): 495–514.

77 J.L. Arcos and R. López de Mántaras, 'An Interactive CBR Approach for Generating Expressive Music', *Applied Intelligence* 14/1 (2001): 115–29.

78 M. Grachten, J.L. Arcos, and R. López de Mántaras, 'A Case Based Approach to Expressivity Aware Tempo Transformation', *Machine Learning*, 65/2–3 (2006): 411–37.

79 G. Grindlay and D. Helmbold, 'Modeling, Analyzing, and Synthesizing Expressive Piano Performance with Graphical Models', *Machine Learning*, 65/2–3(2006): 361–87.

What all this is intended to illustrate is that computers are becoming much more than mere computation assistants – in music performance research as in many other fields of scientific investigation. Combined with refined and more efficient methods for extracting performance information from real recordings (see section 2 above), computational modelling and learning will contribute to a growing trend towards large-scale quantitative, data-based investigations in performance research (as exemplified, for example, by the Mazurka project[80] in the context of the CHARM Research Centre in the UK[81]).

4. Final remarks

We have reviewed recent computational methods for data retrieval, display and modelling of expressive music performance, mainly for two purposes: first, to point the technically interested scholar and musician to potentially useful technology, and second, to encourage the computer researcher and developer to contribute algorithms or software solutions that might help enhance our access to, and understanding of, phenomena connected with music performance.

As the application of computational technology in the wide field ranging from music education to quantitative music research is relatively young, one might speculate about its future. In what domains will the use of such technology be fruitful, where will it make less sense?

One promising domain where the use of computational methods and technologies will and should play an increasingly important role is in music education. As reported in section 3, a number of steps have already been taken to explore this field of application. However, there are limitations as to where and when technology can be applied. Probably the most important aspect is that the widespread application of computers in music education will only be possible and successful when computer programs are well designed and easy to use, do not require complex hardware and are freely available. If information on a performance can be sensibly assessed while playing or immediately afterwards with a relatively short amount of interaction, the performer can still relate the information to an experience that is still fresh in their mind. So, computer programs should reach a level where they can handle arbitrary performance data autonomously in order to provide appropriate, usually visual feedback. While visualization can enhance cognition and help in reasoning regarding the subject under discussion (and also in teacher–student interaction), the fundamental mode of learning in music will always be based on an auditory feedback loop, not a visual one. Any technological tools should therefore be used with care and knowledge, and certainly cannot replace conventional methods of teaching and practice. But they could assist occasionally when needed in order to enhance awareness – just as a metronome

80 <http://www.mazurka.org.uk/>, accessed 21 April 2009.
81 <http://www.charm.rhul.ac.uk/>, accessed 21 April 2009.

should not be switched on the whole time during a practice day, but can help a great deal in certain selected situations.

Another domain of promising applications is real-time interaction systems that allow interactive manipulation and control of music performances and recordings, as we have sketched briefly in section 3. A new generation of researchers are working on novel interfaces for controlling musical expression, for example by using optical gesture trackers based on simple webcam setups. With such technology, one may even be able to manipulate recordings of great performers with intuitive gestural interaction according to personal taste. This would contribute to redefining the notion of music 'consumption' from one of passive exposure to a more active, and perhaps creative, process.

With respect to the role of computers in performance research, here there is also still ample room for further work. Current work in computational performance modelling – interesting results though it may have produced – is severely limited by some of the basic assumptions it makes (or must make, given the data it has gathered and the methods it uses). One serious problem is the tacit assumption of a deterministic (or at least probabilistic) mapping from musical structure to performance, which is certainly not the case in real life. A performer may well choose different dynamics, phrasing or other variations to shape a repeat of the same part of the music in a different way. Such variability often manifests itself in rather subtle nuances, which are, nevertheless, clearly discernible and understandable for an informed audience. As David Huron (2006) puts it, it is the micro-emotions that make music interesting and not so much the bold, big emotions (fear, anger, sadness) that are the topic of much of the current research on musical emotion. Here, one would have to gather very precise data in rather subtle experimental setups in order to get at the fine-grained level of these phenomena.

Another source of new opportunities might be the emerging alliance between musicology and the field of music information retrieval. Musicologists are beginning to make substantial efforts to digitize and put online large amounts of historical material (e.g. the entire works of Mozart[82]). Such enormous databases could be fertile sources for musical data mining, which might lead to even more well-founded and significant empirical findings than the results reported above. One initiative to gather together the diverse research approaches on computational modelling of music performance is the RENCON initiative,[83] which organizes annual workshops on performance rendering research, including a competition to determine the 'best' artificially performed piece of music. However, the goal (as stated on the RENCON web page) to win the Chopin competition in 2050 with a computer program is, if not intended to be tongue-in-cheek, simply a misleading

---

82 <http://dme.mozarteum.at/>, accessed 21 April 2009.

83 R. Hiraga, R. Bresin, K. Hirata and H. Katayose, 'Rencon 2004: Turing Test for Musical Expression', in *Proceedings of the 2004 Conference on New Interfaces for Musical Expression* (Hamamatsu, 2004), pp. 120–23; <http://shouchan.ei.tuat.ac.jp/~rencon/>, accessed 21 April 2009.

approach. The aim of modelling expressive artistic behaviour should not be to replace or compete with a human in this domain, but to create models with which the complex nature of expressive performance can be better investigated and understood.

Finally, it is challenging to probe the limits of quantifiability in expressive music performance. What aspects of it cannot be modelled at all? Even if research into expression of movement, motor control and biomechanics advances, how would it ever be possible to measure, quantify and finally model the performer's 'mind and body in the "heroic struggle" to express and communicate'?[84]

Acknowledgements

This work is supported by the Austrian Science Fund (the Erwin Schrödinger Fellowship J2526 and the research project P19349N15) and the Vienna Science and Technology Fund ('Interfaces to Music', I2M, CI010). The Austrian Research Institute for Artificial Intelligence acknowledges basic support by the Austrian Federal Ministries BMBWK and BMVIT.

---

84 As so aptly described by E.F. Clarke, 'Listening to Performance', in J. Rink (ed.), *Musical Performance: A Guide to Understanding* (Cambridge: Cambridge University Press, 2002), pp. 185–96.

Chapter 8

Understanding the Capabilities of ICT Tools for Searching, Annotation and Analysis of Audio-visual Media

Adam T. Lindsay

1. Introduction

This chapter outlines the 'ICT Tools for Searching, Annotation and Analysis of Audio-visual Media' (hereafter, ICT4AV) technology consultation project, results relevant to music, and other thoughts gained from experience in the area of applying information and communication technology (ICT) tools and activities to music research.

The ICT4AV project's goal was to survey the tools, technologies and research being explored by technologists, and to collect the needs and requirements of humanities researchers. The domains are time-based multimedia: primarily music, speech and video. Much of the project's dissemination was performed in the open; we collected interesting projects and immediately published via a weblog, which had some interesting side-effects. Phase 2 of the project moved from the blog towards researchers, with directed interviews about their research needs.

The partners in the project were the Phonetics Laboratory at the University of Oxford and the Institute for Cultural Research and Lancaster Institute for Contemporary Arts, incorporating Music, at Lancaster University.

We foresee a few challenges in communicating about ICT with those who have not incorporated it into their research. There may be resistance to ICT tools in general, or the tendency to ascribe magical properties to ICT. It is hard to explain how computer technology may really affect humanities research in a neutral way, without sounding as if one is 'selling' a specific technology. As a result, we will spend some time highlighting some specific research tools, then some relevant research communities likely to produce such tools, and finally end with a meditation upon what ICT is good *at* and good *for* (and conversely, where ICT can fail a researcher).

2. Project methodology: first phase

Before launching into a description of the project's findings, it is worthwhile to explore the weblog methodology, as it has been an interesting and productive collaboration tool for the project. A weblog ('blog') is a website, in 'log' format, characteristically with new items on top, and past items listed in reverse chronological order. This format has evolved to encourage readers to visit the site repeatedly, as last-read items are easy to find, and old items are displaced off the bottom of the page. The format has readily adapted to political discussion, technical news, personal journals and special interests of all types. Many free and for-pay hosting services and software packages have developed blogging into a minor industry.

The high quality of free hosting software enables easy on-line collaboration. My colleagues and I post new items at any hour, comment upon them at leisure, and closely monitor the blog for new developments. The method is part research, part reaction and serendipity. Although we contributors will seek out news or summarize known events, research or communities, the lifeblood of a blog is news and commentary on current events. As such, much of the discussion is orientated towards the events and interests of the last six months. While this is helpful for the purposes of the project (the trends of the past year offer a good clue as to what will happen the following year), it can be somewhat limiting in painting a full picture of a field. Long-lived research programmes (such as music information retrieval with symbolic music) may not produce any headlining results in a given time period, but those pursuits are surely important to the field covered by the blog.

There are many regular readers of the blog from around the world. With regular site visits from Europe, North America and the Far East, the weblog peaked at thousands of hits a day, and regularly gets visitors directed from the top search engines.

3. Trends in ICT tools for a digital workflow

During the initial phases of the ICT4AV weblog,[1] we have observed a few patterns in the progression of the field. On a broad level, one can distinguish between technologies and research issues arising from simply moving to a digital workflow on the one hand, and specialist audio-visual tools, often derived from contemporary research intended as aids in musical data analysis, on the other. Figure 8.1 illustrates a few topic keywords in relation to music articles.

There are several sub-issues that are of active interest within the digital workflow rubric. Perhaps most fundamental is access and availability of digital corpora. The musical case is thrown into contrast by the other media types within the project: from our interviews, many visual culture researchers' 'new' methods are being influenced heavily by serendipity and the raw availability of materials on the world wide web. Finding such materials may well result in further scholarship,

---

1 A.T. Lindsay et al., 'AV Tools for Humanities Research', Lancaster University, 2006, now continued at <http://mediadescri.be/>, accessed 21 April 2009.

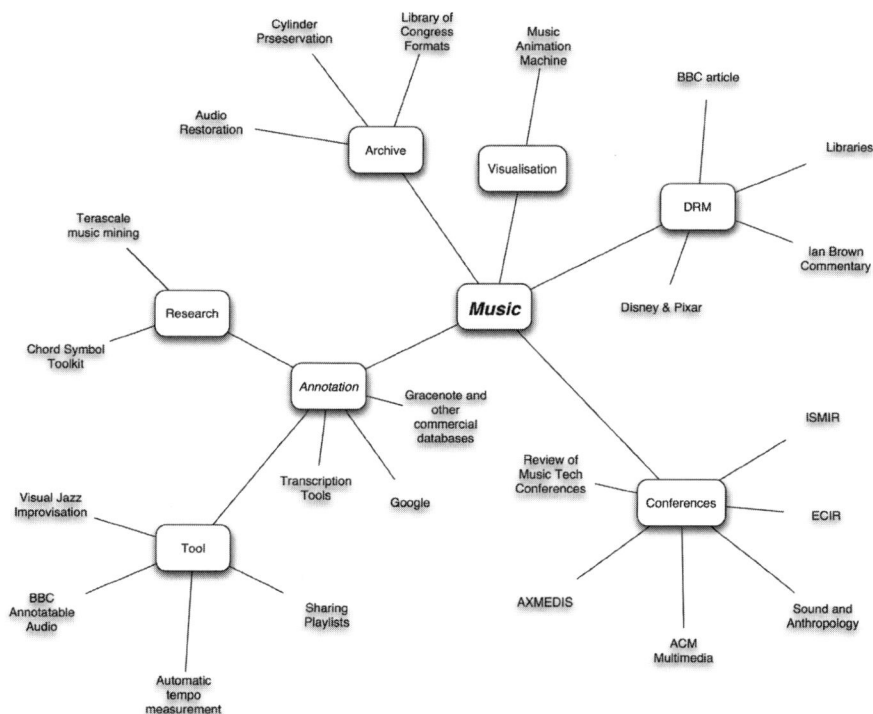

Figure 8.1   A rough visualization of keywords (in boxes) and article titles (shadowed text) from the ICT4AV weblog

often based in the library, but the fact remains that there is a new strand of research influenced heavily by what is readily available on the web as popular cultural artefacts.

The ready availability of commercially sourced music is a distraction from the fact that many materials are not commercially viable, and that there is still a public good in providing public archives of such audio sources. Another issue with regard to digital workflow is in digitization of audio materials, which includes concerns with audio restoration when necessary. In order to support people creating archives, appropriate tools for digitization and for making the audio of acceptable quality are needed. Fortunately, the Arts and Humanities Data Service made good practice guides readily available.[2]

---

2 Arts and Humanities Data Service, *AHDS Guides to Good Practice* (AHDS, 2004). Available online at <http://ahds.ac.uk/creating/guides/index.htm#performing-arts>, accessed 21 April 2009.

3.1 The spectre of digital rights management

Looming large over both issues is the fact of digital rights management (DRM): multimedia content owners want to protect their content and profits, and for distribution of digital-only content, insist upon some form of anti-copying technology. When it comes to research, especially as aided by the data analysis tools below, this becomes a grave concern and a major roadblock.

DRM is the general term for a variety of technical solutions (reinforced by legislation) designed to allow the rights owner of content to determine how a consumer may use it. In the case of digital audio, rights often extend to listening to the content (on a limited number of computers and/or associated compatible portable devices), burning the content to compact disc and backing up the audio file. In some cases, the rights may be time-limited, such as when the rights to listen are tied to a monthly subscription. The status of DRMed content (that is, content protected by some digital rights management system) paid for by consumers now no longer resembles the ownership that people have been accustomed to in the case of physical media. DRMed content, lacking any tangible form, is now licensed or leased, ultimately subject to the will of the rights owner.

The general technical method for implementing DRM is to encrypt a (typically) compressed audio file, tying the encryption key to the content purchaser, the computer and/or the date. A specialized application on the computer or portable device has the ability to decrypt the file and play it. No other applications may do so.

When it comes to DRMed content's compatibility with data analysis methods, it is this final point that causes difficulties. No applications other than those blessed by the DRM scheme provider may have access to the decrypted content: it is unknown what they would do with the data, and therefore they cannot be trusted. As a result, data analysis programmes are shut out of working with DRMed content directly. Cumbersome, legal work-arounds are possible (e.g. by writing the content to a compact disc and then re-importing it to the computer), but unrealistic for large amounts of content.

It is worth noting that after the course of the ICT4AV project's lifetime, at least two major events in the DRM world opened up some hope for researchers working with digital music. First, the Gowers Review was released in December 2006, which advocated clarifying a research extension, provisions for 'orphaned works' and better rights for libraries with regards to copyright. Second, EMI, in partnership with Apple, made moves to make DRM-free digital music downloads available, a first for the major labels.

3.2 Metadata management

Of ultimate interest within digital workflow concerns is metadata management. Metadata is literally data about data, but in this case covers all sorts of card-catalogue-type information to help mark and label digital files for easy access.

Controlling large numbers of digital assets is not trivial, and there are few satisfactory tools for such things, especially with respect to researchers' needs.

It is a topic that has presented itself with our initial interviews, especially with researchers who are already engaging strongly with digital media. Their current systems are approaching a breaking point: so much asset retrieval is dependent on the researcher's memory of their personal archive. The most typical digital asset systems readily available to researchers are the folder hierarchy of a normal file system and common, consumer-orientated media collection managers, like iTunes and iPhoto. Without careful, principled archive discipline, consumer-grade applications are insufficient for providing a path from personal organization to a publishable archive – or even to an order of magnitude increase in the capacity of the personal archive.

A secondary issue associated with metadata management is reliable referencing of digital resources. The standard unit of internet reference, the URL (uniform resource locator), is fragile. It can only be guaranteed to be valid at one point in time. It is too-common practice for an online resource to move after time, no longer accessible from the original URL. Even with the best will and best efforts of the linked resource owner, it is clear that the ephemeral nature of the world wide web makes long-lived scholarly reference to online resources a difficult issue.

4. Background issues informing ICT tools for multimedia

4.1 High- and low-level feature understanding

Throughout this chapter, a distinction is made between low-level and high-level features. In order to create terms of reference, low-level features are features that lie close to what the computer understands as elemental – in this case, signal processing. Given an input, there is a mathematical formula (or algorithm) that can be written to yield some parameters representing the feature. A high-level feature is idealized as what an informed human might say about the content. It should not be surprising that there is often a tremendous gulf between these two. That gulf reveals differences in the approach to computing, as in the following stereotypes:

Machine perception typically begins from a low-level, signal-processing approach, and then builds up from there. From observed features, higher-level features are generated through the combination of low-level features and assumptions on how the world works. The assumptions on how the world works are often generated by observations from other data sets, and applying pattern recognition to them.

Symbolic approaches have a different starting point: they typically deal exclusively with high-level features in order to draw even higher-level conclusions about the content. This is an outgrowth of traditional artificial intelligence techniques. A drawback is that one must find a way of inputting the high-level information, which is often not trivial manual labour. Score processing in order to test hypotheses about a composition is a typical application. In some cases, researchers do work to connect the high-level features with low-level features, such as the precise timing of the note events in the Chopin Mazurka project.[3]

Hybrid approaches combine some aspects of the bottom-up signal processing and top-down symbolic approaches. One approach is to use high-level symbolic approaches as a form of evolving model, moderating expectations of how the world is, based on low-level observations. By feeding back and forth between these models, the computer itself can generate hypotheses about the world, and test them from observations.

4.2 On MPEG-7

MPEG-7 is an ISO standard, conceived in 1996, and finalized (in its first versions) in 2001–2002. It is intended to be a comprehensive multimedia content description framework, enabling detailed metadata description aimed at multiple levels within the content. It is worthwhile going into a little detail on the standard and what it might offer to humanities researchers.

A key to understanding MPEG-7 is appreciating the goals that shaped its conception and the environment in which it was born. It was conceived at a time when the world wide web was just showing its potential to be a massively interconnected (multi)media resource. Text search on the web was beginning, and throwing into relief the opacity of multimedia files: there was then no reliable way of giving human or computer access 'inside' a multimedia resource without a human viewing it in its entirety. Spurred on by developments in the general area of query by example (including query by image content and query by humming), it was thought that MPEG could bring its considerable signal processing prowess to bear on those problems.

Along the way to the standard, people discovered that the problem of multimedia content description was not all that trivial, nor could it rely wholly upon signal processing. It had to bring in higher-level concerns, such as knowledge representation, and digital library and archivist expertise. In doing so, the nascent standard became much more complex, but had the potential to be much more complete.

The standard, as delivered, has a blend of high- and low-level approaches. The visual part of the standard kept closest to MPEG's old guard, concentrating on features unambiguously based upon signal processing and very compact representations. The newly created Multimedia Description Schemes subgroup (MDS) brought in a very rich, often-complex set of description structures that

---

3 C. Sapp, *The Mazurka Project*, The AHRC Research Centre for the History and Analysis of Recorded Music, Royal Holloway, University of London, 2006–9. Available online at <http://mazurka.org.uk/>, accessed 21 April 2009.

could be adopted for many different applications. MPEG-7 Audio[4] took a middle path, offering both generic, signal processing inspired feature descriptors and high-level description schemes geared towards specific applications.

Technically, MPEG-7 offers a description representation framework expressible in XML. Data validation is offered by the computationally rich, but somewhat complex, XML Schema standard. Users and application providers may customize the precise schema via a variety of methods. There are numerous descriptive elements available throughout the standard, which can be mixed and matched as appropriate, a sampling of which is as follows:

- Hierarchical segmentation of time-based media: a single audio file of an opera performance may be divided into acts, scenes and individual arias. Each of these segments may then have fully detailed descriptions associated with them.
- Fine-grained, detailed, content-neutral low-level audio descriptors. These descriptors can accommodate any sampling rate, and 'fold up' on themselves for increased compactness. Example features described are:
  - audio power (akin to instantaneous loudness);
  - audio spectrum (a constant-Q spectrogram);
  - fundamental frequency (correlates with pitch);
  - spectral centroid (akin to brightness);
  - spectral spread;
  - spectral flatness;
  - spectral basis and projection (ways of decomposing a sound).
- Descriptors geared towards describing the timbre of isolated musical instrument sounds.
- Descriptors for comparing input with possibly matching 'fingerprints' in a known database of songs.
- A description scheme for general audio indexing which can be adapted to developing data-derived models of a musical selection, used to show internal similarity.
- Description schemes for coarse or fine representations of the notes in a melody, intended for quick and compact query-by-humming.
- Description schemes for describing high-level metadata, such as title, author and year of a given work. The vocabulary used in these schemes is extensible via the flexible 'classification scheme' mechanism provided by MPEG-7.

Industrial take-up of MPEG-7 has been inconsistent at best so far. The representation format offered by MPEG-7, however, seems to be one that would serve arts and

---

4 A.T. Lindsay, I. Burnett, S. Quackenbush and M. Jackson, 'Fundamentals of Audio Descriptions', in B.S. Manjunath, P. Salembier and T. Sikora, *Introduction to MPEG-7: Multimedia Content Description Interface* (Chichester, John Wiley and Sons, 2002).

humanities research very well. It is agnostic to media type and format. It is very general, and can be adapted to serve a variety of different applications. Despite its flexibility, it is far more than a 'guideline' standard: it has very specific rules for ensuring compatibility and interoperability. If someone were to invent a framework serving the arts and humanities research community for its metadata needs, it would resemble MPEG-7, at least conceptually.

5. Trends in ICT tools for a musical data analysis

There are many strands of technical research that can conceivably aid music researchers, but chief amongst the musical data analysis sub-disciplines is music information retrieval (MIR). It is a lively research community, largely represented by the yearly ISMIR conference. Early in the community's life, the major perceived goal was to enable query by humming, in which a user would hum a tune, and the computer would respond with the song itself. Since then, the community has expanded to include analysis of musical information for harmony, rhythm and genre (and other classification or organization), not just melody.

Analysis of symbolic music (i.e. as represented by MIDI or other direct note/ score-like representations) has diminished in relation to signal-based approaches, but remains a vital part of the field. All of these areas hold the potential to help answer music researchers' questions, but there have to be some compromises for the researcher: very few tools are of production quality, and most require some special care in terms of framing the question in a way appropriate to the tool. The classic tool in this area is the Humdrum Toolkit,[5] which offers a very powerful level of genericity that is well suited to a research environment. Unfortunately, the genericity is presented in a way that can be very daunting to the uninitiated, and is often left ignored or under-used.

One potentially very useful tool that wraps together some degree of metadata creation and basic management (notably metadata within a single sound) with low-level feature analysis is MUCOSA,[6] a music content semantic annotator, which combines signal processing with user-added annotations. Plate 8.1 shows a typical case of annotation use.

Beyond MIR, there are some tools that may aid researchers, such as general, low-level signal processing tools for generic audio information retrieval. The general low-level descriptors and segmentation tools from the MPEG-7 standard are typical of this. There are also tools for music and audio visualization that may be of use. Visualization tools do not necessarily enable one directly to ask a

---

5 D. Huron, 'Humdrum and Kern: Selective Feature Encoding', in E. Selfridge-Field, *Beyond MIDI: The Handbook of Musical Codes* (Cambridge, MA: MIT Press, 1997).

6 P. Herrera, Ò. Celma, J. Massaguer et al., 'MUCOSA: A Music Content Semantic Annotator', *Proceedings of the 6th International Conference on Music Information Retrieval* (2005), pp. 77–83.

question of a data set, but may provide a way of seeing patterns in the data that are not necessarily obvious by other means. The ICAD conference and community serve this area of enquiry.

A recent example of very effective visualization and analysis is the MATCH[7] temporal alignment analysis software presented at the 2005 ISMIR conference. It analyses two renditions of the same musical piece for temporal alignment. Its chief output method is a graph that wiggles and varies from a simple, straight line as one source rendition varies in tempo from the other. See Plate 8.2 for an illustration of MATCH at work.

6. Challenges in communication about ICT tools

One early result from the project was that in interviews with (non-music) humanities researchers, a colleague discovered that when it comes to preconceptions about ICT tools that aid data analysis, as the researcher summarized, 'any automated technology is perfect in performance'. In other words, a computer always gives a definitive, correct answer. To a technologist, this perception may be risible, but it clearly has a logical basis: computers are portrayed as not dealing with uncertainty, so all answers must be correct with absolute confidence. Furthermore, researchers not immersed in technology culture are subject to being deceived by the *demo effect*, in which any demonstration of a technology is surely cooked up to show the technology in the best possible light. Real-life deployment will contrast strongly with the demonstration. Finally, for researchers truly naive about technology there is this 'law' from Arthur C. Clarke: 'Any sufficiently advanced technology is indistinguishable from magic.'[8]

In actuality, computers are stupid. Any appearance of cleverness is the product of good programming (or good marketing). There are no shortcuts in computer perception of multimedia: a computer does not have an innate understanding of notes, of music or even of hearing. Everything is data to a computer, and every bit of knowledge about a data stream is hard-won.

When communicating with colleagues about tools that we eventually propose they use, we, as technologists, clearly need to do some work in 'managing expectations'. What, one might ask, are ICT tools – or computers – good at, after all, if they are so stupid? One observation is that ICT tools work much better than people at very small or very large scales. Automated tools can outperform human perception with tasks such as measuring micro-timing, micro-tuning or comparing features across huge corpora of music. This may well be more of an effect of human perception working best at scales between these two extremes: human cognition

---

7 S. Dixon and G. Widmer, 'MATCH: A Music Alignment Tool Chest', *Proceedings of the 6th International Conference on Music Information Retrieval* (2005), pp. 492–7.

8 A.C. Clarke, *Profiles of The Future* (New York: Holt, Rinehart and Winston, 1984; repr. of 1962 edn).

has its limits based on our experiential world; computer cognition typically has no such bias towards the 'human scale', and so can extend its capabilities arbitrarily.

With regard to our earlier discussion of machine perception, symbolic and hybrid processing, notice that there are only three main sources of information to the computer: the input multimedia itself, a human observer operating the computer, or the knowledge provided by the programmer who created the system. When considering what computers might be capable of, it is best to consider the deficiencies of knowledge with each of those information sources. For example:

- Statistical methods are a very powerful way of discriminating patterns in data. Unfortunately, as they are commonly used, such bottom-up methods are just as likely to reveal biases and limitations in their training data when applied to other problems.
- Top-down methods, such as expert systems and knowledge-based symbolic manipulations, carry the limitations of the algorithm author: there are limits to how many special cases or classes of data can be foreseen.

A classic observation from artificial intelligence pioneer Marvin Minsky is that 'easy things are hard'[9] for computers, while so-called hard tasks can often be easier. Tasks that we humans think of as easy, such as gross genre judgements or comparison of *forte* and *piano*, generally embody a lot of cultural and/or implicit knowledge. Such knowledge is very hard to capture and represent in a computational form. On the other hand, tasks that we think of as hard tend to require conscious thought, which is actually a decision-making process that can be broken down and introspected, and potentially converted into a computational process.

7. Conclusion

This chapter has detailed some of the concerns and methods of the recently completed ICT4AV project. Collaborating and collecting much data via blogging, the project aimed to gather data regarding technology aiding arts and humanities researchers in their data analysis and management. From the early stages in the project, it was clear that digital rights management and metadata management were major issues of the day, and will greatly influence the effectiveness of all related content analysis tools in the future: pervasive DRM threatens all forms of research with digital content, and without effective metadata management, tools that perform content analysis will be useless.

The chapter spends some time elucidating what different sorts of approach are commonly used for content analysis, and on the possibilities offered by MPEG-7, a framework for metadata potentially appropriate for humanities research. Some

9 M. Minsky, *The Society of Mind* (New York: Simon & Schuster, 1986), p. 29.

potentially effective content analysis tools for music researchers are then noted. Finally, the chapter ends with a discussion of challenges found in the meeting of humanities and computing cultures, both challenges in communication and challenges in computation. When giving over some expertise to ICT tools in order to let them aid one's research, it is best to have a clear idea of their general advantages and weaknesses.

Chapter 9

Audio Tools for Music Discovery

Michael Casey

1. Introduction

An open problem in music research is to discover musical relationships between compositional works, or performances, either by a single artist or by many artists. This chapter examines a package of new tools for retrieving similar polyphonic music sequences from audio collections. As with all complex tools, many parameters need tuning for each specific application. This chapter outlines a successful arrangement of tools for experiments on two contrasting musical tasks. Both tasks were applied to a large collection of 2,741 recordings of Chopin's Mazurkas.

2. Overview

This chapter examines the processes for discovering specific, but not identical, occurrences of a polyphonic audio query from large audio collections – approximate audio matching. Examples of the queries posed are: *sampling history* (find literal quotations of a musical fragment identifying its earliest use), *chord sequence* (find musical passages built upon a given chord sequence, for example passages consisting of canonical secondary sevenths IV7-vii7-iii7-vi7-ii7-V7-I) and *leitmotif identification* (find all occurrences of Siegfried's theme in recordings of *The Ring*). To make automatic tools that can pose such queries to a collection of recorded music, it is first necessary to define algorithms to (a) extract specific musical features and (b) retrieve nearest-neighbour matches from a large collection given a query sequence.

The complexity of these retrieval tasks demands algorithms that perform efficiently as well as accurately. This chapter examines high performance methods for feature extraction and nearest-neighbour retrieval for polyphonic audio recordings. These methods build on research into computational auditory modelling, music modelling and information retrieval in large databases. What follows is a summary of the key literature and an overview of some experimental results in passage-level music retrieval by approximate audio matching.

3. Audio similarity

In the spectrum of applications of *machine listening* there is a wide range of audio matching problems. At the most detailed level, audio fingerprinting is the process of finding exact matches to a target waveform.[1] The problem is not trivial because the signal to be identified may be subject to distortions and noise, for example in a mobile channel as with *Shazam*'s mobile-phone song identification application.[2] Fingerprinting treats two different recordings of the same song as different entities; their audio signals are not similar in detail. The degree of specificity is high for fingerprinting applications because the concept of similarity has a narrow definition. Music genre recognition,[3] artist recognition,[4] musical key identification[5] and speaker identification,[6] in contrast, aim to classify unknown music into broad target concepts, such as *rap* and *disco*. The specificity is low because these applications require a very broad definition of similarity.

Between the above extremes of audio similarity applications is approximate audio matching. Here the sense of similarity is limited to selected attributes of music, and the unspecified attributes are allowed to vary without restriction in the retrieval results. This requires employing a similarity measure that finds in the sequences of features being searched the maximum correlation to the query sequence. An intuitively appealing approach might be to attempt to isolate a 'melody' from a query and find other 'melodies' using symbolic sequence matching methods. But it is widely recognized that extracting even simple melodies from polyphonic textures is a hard problem, and errors introduced in the extraction make the problem of matching exponentially difficult. It is important to seek methods that are robust to small encoding errors, such as audio feature encoding, rather than forcing robustness at the highest levels of abstraction. My chosen approach is to make the entire process statistical without hard decision boundaries.[7]

---

1 J. Herre, E. Allamanche, O. Hellmuth and T. Kastner, 'Robust Identification/ Fingerprinting of Audio Signals Using Spectral Flatness Features', *Journal of the Acoustical Society of America*, 111/5 (2002): 2417.

2 <http://www.shazam.com>, accessed 26 March 2009.

3 G. Tzanetakis and P. Cook, 'Musical Genre Classification of Audio Signals', *IEEE Transactions on Speech and Audio Processing*, 10/5 (2002): 293–302.

4 D. Ellis, B. Whitman, A. Berenzweig and S. Lawrence, 'The Quest for Ground Truth in Musical Artist Similarity', *Proceedings of the International Symposium on Music Information Retrieval* (Paris, 2002), pp. 170–77.

5 S. Pauws, 'Musical Key Extraction from Audio', in *Proceedings of the International Symposium on Music Information Retrieval* (Barcelona, 2004), pp. 96–9.

6 D.A. Reynolds, 'Speaker Identification and Verification using Gaussian Mixture Speaker Models', *Speech Communication*, 17/1–2 (1995): 91–108.

7 J.P. Bello and J.A. Pickens, 'A Robust Mid-level Representation for Harmonic Content in Music Signals', *Proceedings of the 6th International Conference on Music Information Retrieval* (London, 2005).

One aim is to find musical passages that are similar to a query passage based on the audio information. In one type of study, passages are regarded as being equivalent if a human listener judges them similar, even if they are acoustically distinct. For example, a leitmotif query application might look for the thematic repeats (recurring melodies) in classical works or popular music tracks, while being robust to changes in the lyrics, instrumentation, tempo, rhythm, voicing and so forth.

Inherent in this problem is the need to measure distances in a perceptually relevant manner and quickly find similar matches without an exhaustive search through the entire database. This is unsuccessful if every signal needs to be examined to decide which are the closest to the query because the search would take too long for a large database consisting of hundreds or thousands of musical works. Instead, we can use a new, efficient retrieval technique for feature vectors called locality sensitive hashing (LSH). This method has already found application in visual multimedia retrieval problems.[8]

To extract musically salient features we use a tool called FFTextract. This creates low-level audio descriptions conforming to the MPEG-7 International Standard for multimedia content description (ISO 15938). Following previous research, features that roughly measure timbre and harmony were chosen, namely Log Frequency Cepstral Coefficients (LFCC) and the pitch class profile (PCP).[9] Sequences of these features, sampled at 100 ms intervals, preserve the temporal information.

Finding similar passages in a large collection requires an enormous amount of computation. For collections greater than a few works, this computation becomes intractable because of the combinatorial bottleneck that grows rapidly as the database becomes large. The second tool, which is described below, performs efficient retrieval using audio hashing; AudioDB is a tool for similarity retrieval from large databases that avoids exhaustive comparisons between the query and the database. Based on LSH, the tool statistically divides a feature space into regions of similarity, and exhaustive searching occurs only within those narrow regions. Audio hashing speeds up similarity computations by several orders of magnitude, thereby making the methods usable for research on large audio collections.

8 A.Z. Broder, S.C. Glassman, M.S. Manasse and G. Zweig, 'Syntactic Clustering of the Web', in *Proceedings of 6th Word Wide Web Conference, '97* (Oxford: Elsevier Science, 1997), pp. 391–404.

9 M. Casey and M. Slaney, 'The Importance of Sequences in Musical Similarity', in *Proceedings of the International Conference on Acoustics, Speech and Signal Processing* (ICASSP'06), Toulouse, France, 2006, pp. v, 5, 8.

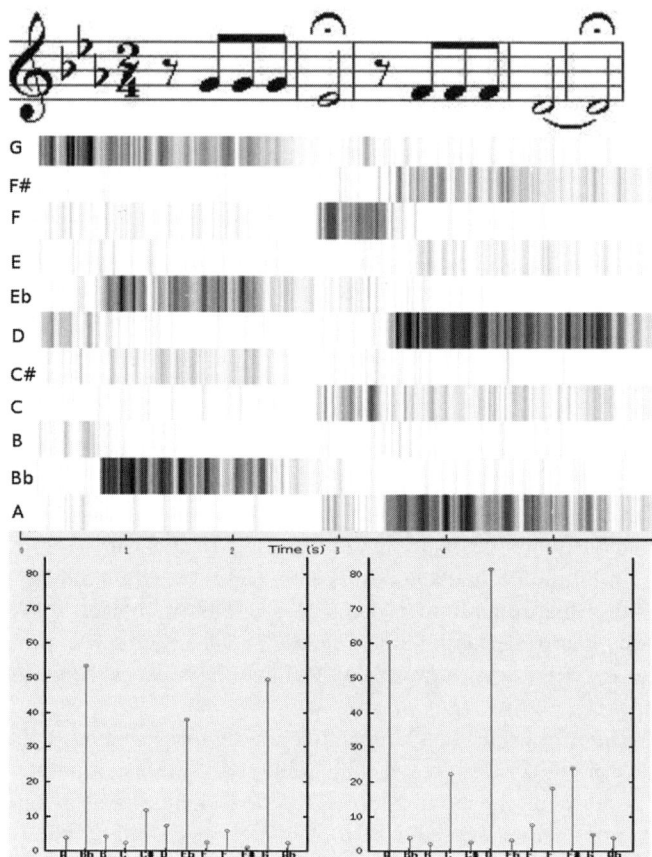

Figure 9.1   The chroma profile of the opening of Beethoven's Symphony No. 5 in C minor

4. Features

Most of the literature on audio similarity adopts a 'bag-of-features' approach, such as that used successfully by genre-recognition systems.[10] This approach was designed for tasks that are insensitive to the specific content of the music; they are low-specificity tasks. In contrast, high-specificity tasks, such as audio fingerprinting systems,[11] find key salient aspects of the audio signal and then match the signal using robust measures. The tasks that are described above exhibit

---

10 B. Logan and S. Chu, 'Music Summarization Using Key Phrases', in *Proceedings of IEEE International Conference on Acoustics, Speech, and Signal Processing* (Turkey, 2000).

11 Herre et al., 'Robust Identification/Fingerprinting of Audio Signals'.

mid-level specificity. Here the specific musical content is important, but the highly specific values of the signal are not important.

Two audio representations in this work were investigated in the experiments described below. LFCC (log-frequency cepstral coefficients) are a simplification of MFCC (mel-frequency cepstral coefficients), widely used to represent timbre in speech recognition and some music tasks.[12] The chromagram representation (i.e. PCP) captures the harmony in the audio by accumulating the energies associated with a given pitch chroma.

Features were extracted using overlapping 372-ms long frames every 100 ms. A constant-Q power spectrum[13] was used with 1/12th octave resolution, aligned with and corresponding to notes (equal-tempered semitones) in Western tonal music. Each element of this spectrum is compressed to approximate loudness perception using a logarithm. The resulting high-dimensional spectrum was collapsed to a low-dimensional representation using one of our two chosen methods: LFCC and chromagram. In LFCC, the shape of the spectrum is approximated with a discrete cosine transform in the same way that MFCC models the approximate shape of the spectrum and reduces the dimensionality of the auditory spectrum. The result is a 13-dimensional representation as a function of time. In the chromagram, the spectral representation is collapsed to the base octave, A1-G#2 (55 Hz–104 Hz), to give an octave-independent measure of the pitch use profile of the music. The result is a 12-dimensional representation of chroma (or note) as a function of time (see Figure 9.1).

The upper figure shows the sequence of chroma energies for the opening phrase of Beethoven's Fifth Symphony. The lower two figures show the time-averaged chromagrams of each sub-motif of the opening; they have similar peak profiles with the transposed motif shifted along the chroma axis.

5. Efficient nearest-neighbour retrieval

Having established features that were desirable to use to characterize thematic material, a method to locate similar themes, or sequences of features, in a collection of sequences is defined. To do this, nearest-neighbour retrieval is used, which treats the collection of sequences as points in the high-dimensional feature-sequence space. The aim is to discover points that are closest to a query point in this space. Hence, a novel type of distance measure that operates over sequences of frames is required.

To consider a sequence as a point, the feature values for each time point in the sequence are simply concatenated into one long array (or vector). If the

---

12 Logan and Chu, 'Music Summarization Using Key Phrases'.

13 J.C. Brown and M.S. Puckette, 'An Efficient Algorithm for the Calculation of a Constant Q Transform.' *Journal of the Acoustical Society of America*, 92 (1992): 2698–701.

sequence were 50 frames (5 s) each with 12 chroma features, then there would be 600 dimensions in the concatenated feature-sequence vector, compared with 12 dimensions for the single-frame case.

The distance metric that is used is the Euclidean distance (L2-norm) in the high-dimensional feature space; this is simply the sum of squares of differences between query and target vector values. In the simplest implementation of search, to find the closest neighbour to a query sequence, a linear scan is performed on the database of sequences of the same length. This involves computing the Euclidean distance between the query and all sequences in the database, sorting the resulting distances into ascending order and keeping the first N entries for N-nearest-neighbour searching.

The matched filter, and its cousin the Wiener filter,[14] is the optimal linear operator for matching a waveform. Whether this operation is done in the waveform or the cepstral domain, a matched filter looks for an exact match over the given temporal window. The matched filter cannot find an *exact* match in the presence of human-created variation, especially as longer windows are viewed. Therefore, the correlation value produced by the matched filter as a measure of similarity is used.

A matched filter is implemented using convolution. But this operation can also be thought of as an L2 norm; if first the energy is subtracted in the query with the signal window then the L2 norm gives a result that is proportional to the convolution. Andoni and Indyk describe a method for indexing and retrieving high-dimensional feature vectors very efficiently using hashing.[15] Their method, LSH, requires that a metric space is used such as that produced by the matched filter.

If the energy in the signal and the query are normalized, and independently of time and query, then the last term is proportional to a matched-filter implementation of the query operator. It is thus amenable to an implementation based on LSH.

6. Similarity-based audio retrieval experiments

I illustrate AudioDB with two contrasting examples of content-based audio retrieval tasks. The first is opus retrieval: given a query, find other performances of the same work: only the *musical* content is similar here, there is no audio in common between query and retrieved items. The second task is acoustic fingerprinting to detect mis-attributed recordings called *apocrypha*: where the retrieved audio recording is a transformed version of an original. The experiments were conducted

---

14 N. Wiener, *Extrapolation, Interpolation, and Smoothing of Stationary Time Series* (New York: Wiley, 1949).

15 A. Andoni and P. Indyk, 'Near-Optimal Hashing Algorithms for Approximate Nearest Neighbors in High Dimensions', *Communications of the ACM*, vol. 51, no. 1, 2008, pp. 117–122,

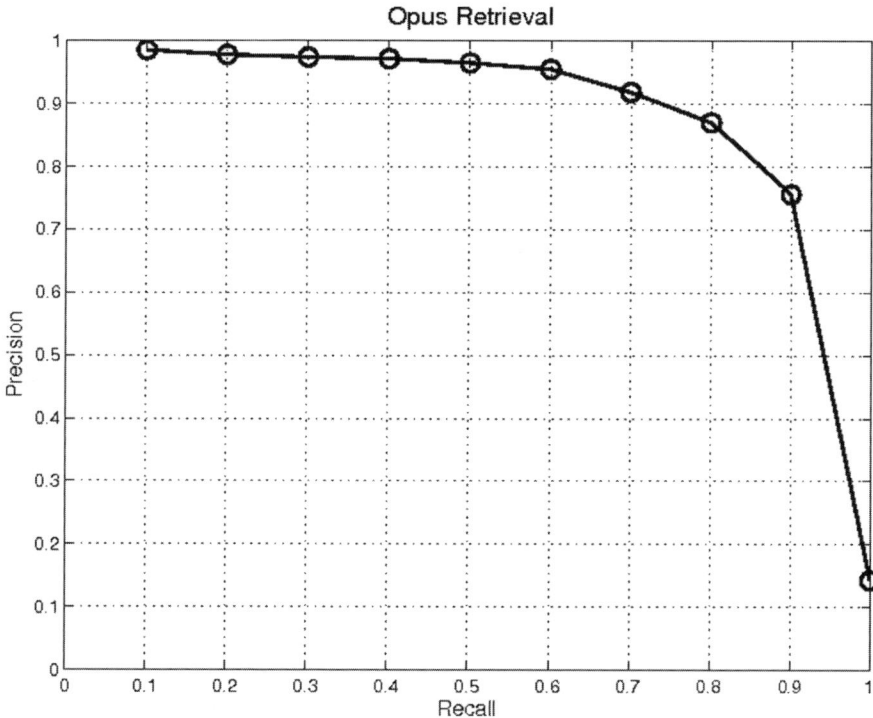

Figure 9.2   Precision-Recall graph for the opus retrieval task

Note: Each of the 49 works had between 31 and 65 relevant items out of a 2,741-track database. Results indicate 88% precision at 80% recall. The rapid falloff in precision is due to problems in dealing with historically early recordings

on a database of 2,741 recordings of the 49 Chopin Mazurkas by 125 different pianists.[16]

Opus retrieval starts with a query performance, in this case one of the Chopin Mazurka recordings, and attempts to retrieve all the performances of the same work from a large database, which includes the same work and different works performed by different artists. The task is difficult because performances by different artists show significant variation in the expressive interpretation of the music. Furthermore, each performance has a different structure due to the performers' choices whether to perform repeats and how many times to play them.

First, the database was sampled using 10 second segments drawn from 40 unrelated performances, i.e. different opuses performed by different artists. From this an estimate of the probability distribution of inter-sample distances

---

16 N. Cook, 'Performance Analysis and Chopin's Mazurkas', *Musicae Scientiae*, 11/2 (2007): 183–208.

was calculated. The next step was to calculate a minimum distance threshold for accepting features as being drawn from this background non-relevant distribution. Any distance below this threshold is then considered to be a close match; a high proportion of such matches between two recordings is interpreted as a 'hit' where the two performances are of the same work.

The results of the opus retrieval experiment (see Figure 9.2) show that the precision was very high for recall rates below 90%. For most of the 49 Mazurkas, there were two to three outliers in our database. On inspection, these were typically early recordings that were transferred from 78 rpm shellac media and contained a high degree of surface noise and extreme wide-band filtering; additionally, the cut-off frequency for these tracks was typically much lower than for the remaining tracks. These results suggest that a near-perfect score can be obtained for opus retrieval if such problematic recordings are first removed or pre-processed to make them compatible with the retrieval method.

Apocrypha in audio recordings are those recorded performances that are falsely attributed to an artist which are, in fact, performed or composed by an artist other than the person named in the documentation. A recent commercial example of this occurred during the 1990s in the classical music repertoire when a significant number of recordings (100 CDs) were released in the UK by the Concert Artists recording label falsely claiming to be new complete recordings of various repertories by classical composers (such as the Chopin Mazurkas). It was eventually discovered that these recordings were re-releases of decades-old performances by different artists which had previously been released on different labels.[17]

It took many years for experts to discover that these recordings were not authentic. This was in part due to some careful modifications that had been applied to disguise the sources: signal treatments such as filtering and time-compression/expansion were used. To understand why it took so long to discover them, consider that there are hundreds of recordings of the Chopin Mazurkas. Each is a performance of exactly the same set of works; the differences are not in the music content but in the acoustic environment, the instrument used and in the expressive interpretation of the performer. Pair-wise listening to detect apocrypha would take a prohibitive amount of time; for example, to compare 50 versions of one work requires listening closely to 1,225 pairs of recordings. It was by chance that the first of these recordings was uncovered; subsequently, sheer determination on the part of expert listeners has located the sources of many remaining apocrypha in the Concert Artists catalogue. The search continues today.

In our second experiment, AudioDB automatically identifies apocrypha using similarity analysis on a large collection of recordings of the same works (this task of pre-selection can be achieved using the opus retrieval task, above). A similarity matrix is first constructed by measuring features and computing a similarity between

---

17 N. Cook and C. Sapp, 'Purely Coincidental? Joyce Hatto and Chopin's Mazurkas', <http://www.charm.rhul.ac.uk/content/contact/hatto_article.html>, accessed 21 April 2009.

tracks based on those features. Those recordings with a large proportion of features falling within a predetermined distance threshold, obtained by measuring known non-apocrypha recordings, are then considered apocrypha. The specificity of this task is similar to that of audio fingerprinting: to establish whether two recordings are acoustically identical, allowing for some degree of signal transformation and distortion such as filtering or time compression/expansion.

In this experiment AudioDB was able to retrieve 60 recordings that are known, or suspected, to be apocrypha. The misattributions were to pianists Joyce Hatto and Sergei Fiorentino. The former were already widely known when we conducted the experiments; but the latter case contained new apocryphal recordings that were previously not known other than to the originator of the misattributions.

Conclusion

This chapter has examined low-level audio tools conforming to the MPEG-7 International Standard for extracting musically salient information from audio signals. Evidence for the utility of the tools was presented in the form of opus retrieval and apocrypha detection experiments, as well as through insight into the way in which tools will scale to very large collections using new audio hashing methods. It is hoped that the public release of these tools will contribute significantly to the development of new methods in humanities research.[18]

---

18 See <http://omras2.org>, accessed 26 March 2009, for more information on these and other tools.

Chapter 10
'What was the question?':
Music Analysis and the Computer

Alan Marsden

1. A 'gulf'?

> In spite of the ever-increasing use and acceptance of modern data processing
> equipment for humanistic research, there would appear to be ... a widening gulf
> between scholars who pursue the traditional methods of historical musicology
> and those who have adopted the computer as their chief research tool. This
> unfortunate and unnecessary division stems largely from a misunderstanding
> of the nature and limits of computer-aided scholarship by the former group;
> however, the situation is hardly assuaged by members of the other camp who are
> often unwilling to discuss their work in terms intelligible to the uninitiated.

These are the opening sentences of an article on 'Music Analysis and the Computer'
written nearly forty years ago.[1] I was surprised to find how apt they are to opening
my own contribution on the topic: little has changed, it would appear. We can now
strike out the word 'widening', but there is little evidence that the gulf between
'traditional' analysts and those who use the computer 'as their chief research tool'
is narrowing. The publication of *Empirical Musicology*[2] and the establishment of
the online journal *Empirical Musicology Review* in 2006 provide some evidence,
but books and journals come and go. The journal *Computers in Music Research*,
for example, seems to have ceased publication in 1999.

Certainly the pages of the journal *Music Analysis* do not provide evidence of the
widespread use of computers in analysis. Out of 221 articles, I have found only six
which report or refer to the explicit use of computers, and they are spread evenly
throughout the journal's issues. Two are concerned mostly with matters of theory
(Baroni's article on musical grammar,[3] and Temperley's on the 'Line of Fifths'[4])

---

1 R. Erickson, 'Music Analysis and the Computer', *Journal of Music Theory*, 12/2
(1968): 240–63, 240–41.

2 E. Clarke and N. Cook (eds), *Empirical Musicology: Aims, Methods, Prospects*
(Oxford: Oxford University Press, 2004).

3 M. Baroni, 'The Concept of Musical Grammar', trans. S. Maguire with W. Drabkin,
Music Analysis, 2/2 (1983): 175–208.

4 D. Temperley, 'The Line of Fifths', *Music Analysis*, 19/3 (2000): 289–319.

but do give examples or refer to applications of software to particular pieces or a particular repertoire. Another two linked articles also principally concern theory, but in this case theory which is of such a degree of complexity that a computer is required for its application: Pople's exposition of his Tonalities project,[5] and Russ's account of analytical examples applying the theory and software.[6] (In truth, traditional tonal-harmonic theory is similarly complex – Pople intended his theory very much as an extension of existing theory – but we learn to apply it without a computer only through years of practice. The essential role of the computer in Pople's theory is to enable the assumptions which remain tacit in our application 'by hand' of traditional tonal theory to be made explicit in the application of the software.) The author of the fifth article[7] does not use a computer himself but makes a comparison with another study of the same piece in which the use of a computer was essential.[8] Tenney's use of the computer is similar to Pople's: as a means both for making discoveries and for testing and making assumptions explicit, though about segmentation rather than about harmony and tonality. It is only in Cook's analysis of performances of a Bach prelude[9] that the principal focus is on what can be discovered about the music rather than on the development of new theory, and the computer is an incidental tool, in this case for discovering the timings of notes in audio recordings.

Probably the computer has also been an incidental but unreported tool in other studies published in *Music Analysis*. The journal contains two brief comments by Forte on the use of computers in pitch-class-set analysis. In one he seems to look forward to an all-encompassing analytical tool: 'one can envision … a powerful set-complex analyser with artificial intelligence aspects'.[10] Thirteen years later, the computer is mentioned not as an intelligent analysis tool, but as a kind of calculator: 'you really need a computer program to generate matrices'.[11] Certainly, computers must have been used in the preparation of a number of the contributions concerning pitch-class-set genera in that issue of *Music Analysis*, some quoting figures to four decimal places! Probably it is as a calculator and collator of pitch-class sets that computers are most widely used by music analysts (if we discount

---

5 A. Pople, 'Using Complex Set Theory for Tonal Analysis: An Introduction to the *Tonalities* Project', *Music Analysis*, 23/2–3 (2004): 153–94.

6 M. Russ, '"Fishing in the Right Place": Analytical Examples from the *Tonalities* Project', *Music Analysis*, 23/2–3 (2004): 195–244.

7 J.-J. Nattiez, 'Varèse's "Density 21.5": A Study in Semiological Analysis', trans. Anna Barry, *Music Analysis*, 1/3 (1982): 243–340.

8 J. Tenney, 'Temporal Gestalt Perception in Music', *Journal of Music Theory*, 24/2 (1980), pp. 205–41.

9 N. Cook, 'Structure and Performance Timing in Bach's C Major Prelude (WTC I): An Empirical Study', *Music Analysis*, 6/3 (1987): 257–72.

10 A. Forte, 'Pitch-class Set Analysis Today', *Music Analysis*, 4/1–2 (1985): 29–58, 54–6.

11 C. Ayrey (ed.), 'Pitch-class Set Genera: A Symposium', *Music Analysis*, 17/2 (1998): 161–244, 231.

the widespread and equally not-worth-mentioning use of computers in preparing music examples and writing papers). Among software specifically intended for music analysis, programs for pitch-class-set analysis are the most common: a number are readily available, and there are even online tools to work out pitch-class-set membership. Though unreported, the impact of this use of computer as quasi-calculator is not to be underestimated. It leads to greater productivity, and perhaps we should take this silent use of computers as evidence against the gulf Erickson saw forty years ago. On the other hand, this kind of use of computers is not worth mentioning in articles, and not worth discussing further here, because the actual *analytical* step in making pitch-class-set analyses is the segmentation – everything else is trivial calculation and collation – and it is precisely in this step that computers are *not* used.

2. Examples of music analysis by computer

A recent volume of the series *Computing in Musicology* is dedicated to music analysis,[12] but even here actual analysis of pieces of music is found only in a minority of the contributions: four out of thirteen. The remainder are principally about issues of representation and software design. (One of the four does not actually mention computers, but we must presume, since it is in this volume, that computers have been used.) What is interesting about these four, however, is that they provide examples of the three kinds of non-trivial contribution computers can make in analysis. One, like the uses reflected in the articles by Pople, Temperley and Tenney mentioned above, is to use the computer as a means for developing and testing a theory. The task the computer performs is one a human could do, but the computer can be relied upon to be accurate and, above all, impartial. An analyst approaching a piece of music brings with her or him a richness of experience of this and other pieces, which inevitably influences judgements. One way to make explicit the reasons for one analysis of a piece rather than another is to do so through a theory which does not rely on personal experience, and one way to lay aside personal experience in the application of a theory is to delegate it to a computer which has no personal experience. Mavromatis[13] uses a Hidden Markov Model to model the structure of Greek church chants. (This is a formalism well established in computer science and so one about which there is a wealth of knowledge on which to draw.) An added bonus is that the computer can do some of the work in theory formation, in that a Hidden Markov Model can 'learn' from a set of examples. The resulting model is able to generate new chants in a similar style to the given examples, and from the internal structure of the model

---

12 W.B. Hewlett and E. Selfridge-Field, *Music Analysis East and West: Computing in Musicology 14* (Cambridge, MA: MIT Press, 2006).

13 P. Mavromatis, 'A Hidden Markov Model of Melody Production in Greek Church Chant', in Hewlett and Selfridge-Field, *Music Analysis East and West*, pp. 93–112.

Mavromatis is able to draw conclusions about the stability of cadential formulas in this repertoire, in comparison to the variability of opening gestures. (Machine-learning research has become quite common in the field of music information retrieval – see below – but often there is no focus on *what* has been learned, and so no direct music-theoretic or analytical benefit.)

A second kind of computer application also uses the computer to do something humans can already do, but not because the computer is more accurate and neutral, rather because it is very much quicker. This kind of research typically analyses a body of data larger than a researcher could hope to deal with, and two examples are found in *Music Analysis East and West*. Veltman[14] demonstrates that hierarchical metre can be found in sixteenth-century vocal polyphony by counting the occurrences of stressed syllables in notionally stronger and weaker positions in specific rhythmic patterns. Deguchi and Shirai[15] count the occurrence of three- and four-note pitch sequences in the melismatic and non-melismatic sections of Japanese koto songs, concluding that the melismas use a more restricted range of patterns but are more variable. Neither of these studies uses particularly large datasets (seven motets in the first case and six songs in two versions each in the second case). It would have been possible to complete both pieces of research by hand, though extremely time-consuming. Computer-based studies do exist, however, which have used larger datasets than a single researcher could study in an entire lifetime. Meredith[16] tested five classes of pitch-spelling algorithm on a corpus of 216 movements, testing several, and sometimes many, different versions of each algorithm. (A pitch-spelling algorithm converts pitches designated in a twelve-note chromatic scale to pitches with a specific letter-name plus accidental.) Pople's software also falls into this category of enabling research which would otherwise be rendered impossible by the sheer quantity of data. In his case it is not the number of pieces which is at issue (Pople's software could be applied to a corpus of many pieces, but the design of adjustable parameters is intended more for studies of single pieces); it is the number and complexity of interpretations within a single piece which would swamp the analyst trying to follow the same analytical procedures by hand. To return to pitch-class-set analysis, if one wanted to list all the Fortean set classes found in all possible segmentations of a melody of a hundred notes, one would have to determine the classes for approximately seven hundred sets. In a polyphonic piece where sets can be found also by combining notes from more than one voice, the number increases rapidly. Thorough and systematic analysis of even single pieces thus often involves larger quantities of data than can reasonably be dealt with by hand. If one needs to consider not just

14 J. Veltman, 'Syllable Placement and Metrical Hierarchy in Sixteenth-century Motets', in Hewlett and Selfridge-Field, *Music Analysis East and West*, pp. 73–89.

15 S. Deguchi and K. Shirai, 'An Analysis of Melismatic Patterns in Koto Songs', in Hewlett and Selfridge-Field, *Music Analysis East and West*, pp. 159–70.

16 D. Meredith, 'Computing Pitch Names in Tonal Music: A Comparative Analysis of Pitch Spelling Algorithms', D.Phil. thesis, University of Oxford, 2007.

all the possibilities at each point in a piece but also the different combinations of possibilities, the quantities can become larger even than a computer can handle. Imagine, for example, that each bar in a piece of music can be interpreted in one of two ways. The number of different combinations of interpretations for n bars is then 2^n, and a piece of just 64 bars would have more than 18 million million million different interpretations. The most powerful computers in the world might just about deal with all of these combinations within a century! Thus while a computer *can* make possible kinds of analysis which would otherwise be impossible, one must not think of it as a machine which makes possible *any* kind of analysis we can think of.

The third class of computer-based analyses also uses the computer to achieve something otherwise impossible: to extract data from sound at a level of detail too small or too precise to achieve by ear. Krishnaswamy[17] examines pitch-time traces of Indian classical singing to argue that pitch in this music is based on twelve tones, and notes claimed by others (on the basis of assessments by ear) to be microtonal are actually distinguished not by their tuning but by their articulation or ornamentation. Cook's measurements of timing referred to above, more precise than could be easily achieved by ear, and similar studies based on timing extracted from MIDI or other performance data also fall into this category. Computer tools for the analysis of audio are now extremely sophisticated, and increasingly easy to use with the development of software such as Sonic Visualiser.[18] This opens a large and very significant potential field of research in analysis of music-from-sound rather than music-from-score.

3. Tools for analysis by computer

In considering the lack of use of computers in music analysis, Erickson commented that 'there are as yet no standards for the encoding of music, no generally available musical analysis programs ... and no comprehensive theoretical system for computer-aided analysis'.[19] In our postmodern world, it is no surprise to find that we have many encodings for music, but no single standard, many music analysis programs, but few that are generally available, and – of course – many theoretical systems but none that is comprehensive.

Early efforts in music research with computers spent considerable amounts of time on designing a representation, and then on encoding music in that representation. A number of representations designed since then are described

---

17 A. Krishnaswamy, 'Melodic Atoms, Ornamentation, Tuning and Intonation in Classical Indian Music', in W.B. Hewlett and E. Selfridge-Field, *Music Analysis East and West* (Cambridge, MA: MIT Press, 2006), pp. 139–51.

18 Queen Mary, University of London, 'Sonic Visualiser' (n.d.). Available online at <http://www.sonicvisualiser.org>, accessed 21 April 2009.

19 Erickson, 'Music Analysis and the Computer', p. 242.

in *Beyond MIDI*,[20] but new ones are still arising, among them the increasingly significant MusicXML.[21] Representation is only an issue for those who need specific information not already contained in existing schemes. Furthermore, large quantities of music are now freely available encoded in MIDI, MuseData or **kern formats in the MuseData and KernScores databases,[22] so there is a reasonable chance that a researcher will be spared the work of encoding as well. This, at least, has changed in the past forty years. Unfortunately, the promise of software able to derive encodings by scanning printed scores does not seem yet to have been realized. Researchers do need to be aware of what an encoding does and does not represent, and they should be concerned about accuracy also: the issues of interpretation of sources which apply to score-based studies do not disappear in the digital domain.

Some music analysis programs are now generally available. Pople's Tonalities software has already been mentioned, and is available for download.[23] To describe what it achieves in a single sentence is not easy, but broadly speaking it allows one to see the consequences in analysis of considering a piece of music to use a particular vocabulary of chords and scales. Apart from Russ's article, I am not aware of published cases of use of the software, however. Software by Sleator and Temperley,[24] which produces analyses of metre, grouping, key and harmony (though not always with a high degree of accuracy), may be downloaded as source code. Some published studies have used this software, usually as a quick means of determining harmony.[25] By far the most widely used analysis software, however, is Huron's Humdrum.[26] Its beauty is its flexibility. It consists of many components, each of which performs a small task, but which may be strung together to perform complex analytical tasks. The framework of representation is specifically designed to allow new representations to be incorporated, both to represent novel kinds of music and to add previously unrepresented detail to existing encodings. New tools can be written by those with the appropriate programming expertise and used along with existing components. As might be guessed from this description, however, it is not the sort of software that one can pick up and start using after just

---

20 E. Selfridge-Field (ed.), *Beyond MIDI: The Handbook of Musical Codes* (Cambridge MA: MIT Press, 1997).

21 Recordare, 'MusicXML Definition, V.2.0'. Available online at <http://www.recordare.com/xml.html>, accessed 21 April 2009.

22 <http://www.musedata.org> and <http://kern.humdrum.net>, respectively, both accessed 21 April 2009.

23 R. Adlington, 'The Pople *Tonalities* Project' (2007). Available online at <http://www.nottingham.ac.uk/music/tonalities/> accessed 21 April 2009.

24 D. Sleator and D. Temperley, 'The Melisma Music Analyzer' (n.d.). Available online at <http://www.link.cs.cmu.edu/music-analysis/>, accessed 21 April 2009.

25 E.g., B. Aarden and P.T. von Hippel, 'Rules for Chord Doubling (and Spacing): Which Ones Do We Need?', *Music Theory Online*, 10/2 (2004).

26 D. Huron, 'The Humdrum Toolkit: Software for Music Research' (n.d.). Available online at <http://dactyl.som.ohio-state.edu/Humdrum/>, accessed 21 April 2009.

a few minutes' perusal. Some indication of the flexibility is given by the fact that Veltman[27] used Humdrum for his study of stress and metre, while Aarden and von Hippel[28] used Humdrum to study doubling in chords.

4. New analytical directions

If we now have the benefit of examples such as those listed in section 2, and the tools listed in section 3, why does Erickson's 40-year-old gulf still exist? Certainly humans are capable of extreme ignorance, arrogance and stupidity, but surely those cannot be the only causes of the lack of interest on one side and failure to communicate on the other that Erickson lamented. One answer has already been adumbrated in the discussion of the capabilities of the computer: its ability to be neutral and impersonal, to deal with large quantities of music, and to reveal what cannot be heard by the ear. Yet the most common preoccupations of music analysis are to deal with what the ear *can* hear, to examine single pieces, and to expound and influence the personal listening experience. This does not mean that the computer is useless or irrelevant for analysis (the examples above demonstrate otherwise) but it is important to realize that an extra step is needed after the computer has done its work to make the connections back to the world of personal listening experience, to illustrate how conclusions drawn from a study of a many pieces influence our understanding of individual pieces, and to explain how the imperceptible details of tuning or timing do nevertheless have an impact on what we hear.

Often to take this extra step would be premature, though, because even after 40 years computer-based analysis is still largely experimental and conclusions of a traditional analytical kind can only be tentative. Erickson warned in 1968 that 'there is a danger ... that the System may become the end in itself',[29] and this remains the case today. (Indeed, I have fallen victim to it myself, when what began as a simple consideration of how to represent information about temporal relations in music became an entire book.[30]) But this is only a danger from the perspective of traditional analysis. Scholars frequently pursue ends in themselves, and the application of computers in music has opened paths to many such ends. I commented above that instead of the comprehensive theoretical system for computer-aided analysis which Erickson hoped for, we now have a plethora of theories.[31] The concepts of traditional music analysis are not entirely systematic

---

27 Veltmann, 'Syllable Placement and Metrical Hierarchy'.

28 Aarden and von Hippel, 'Rules for Chord Doubling (and Spacing)'.

29 Erickson, 'Music Analysis and the Computer', p. 260.

30 A. Marsden, *Representing Musical Time: A Temporal-logic Approach* (Lisse: Swets & Zeitlinger, 2000).

31 See, for example, A. Marsden, 'Musical Informatics: An Emerging Discipline?', *Revue Informatique et Statistique dans les Sciences humaines*, 29 (1993): 77–90.

and precise (their power is specifically in their allowance for expert knowledge and experience), so those who apply computers to analytical problems must redefine concepts for the impersonal, digital domain. What does it mean, for example, for a passage of music to be in a particular key?[32]

Perhaps *Music Analysis* was the wrong journal in which to look for examples of analysis by computer. A similar survey of a journal where use of computers is the norm, *Journal of New Music Research* (JNMR formerly *Interface*), turns up, among 365 articles since volume 18 (1989) (a slightly shorter period than the 25 years of *Music Analysis*), 18 articles which use a computer in the explicit analysis of a single piece of music or collection of pieces, and furthermore these occur with increasing frequency in more recent years. It must be said though, that five of these are by a single author[33] who makes comparative analyses of collections of folksongs. Four others[34] could be described as analyses by synthesis, where a piece is 'reconstructed' in a systematic manner using a computer tool. Two[35] apply systems to extract motives from scores. Issues of rhythm and metre connected with performance are examined in two others.[36] Two analyse performance, in one

---

32 A. Marsden, 'Computers and the Concept of Tonality', in J.T. Coppock (ed.), *Information Technology and Scholarly Disciplines* (Oxford: Oxford University Press, for the British Academy, 1999), pp. 33–52.

33 Z. Juhász, 'Contour Analysis of Hungarian Folk Music in a Multidimensional Metric-Space', *Journal of New Music Research*, 29/1 (2000a): 71–83; Z. Juhász, 'A Model of Variation in the Music of a Hungarian Ethnic Group', *Journal of New Music Research*, 29/2 (2000b): 159–72; Z. Juhász, 'The Structure of an Oral Tradition – Mapping of Hungarian Folk Music to a Metric Space', *Journal of New Music Research*, 31/4 (2002): 295–310; Z. Juhász, 'Segmentation of Hungarian Fold Songs Using an Entropy-based Learning System', *Journal of New Music Research*, 33/1 (2004): 5–15; Z. Juhász, 'A Systematic Comparison of Different European Folk Music Traditions Using Self-organizing Maps', *Journal of New Music Research*, 35/2 (2006): 95–112.

34 A. De Matteis and G. Haus, 'Formalization of Generative Structures within Stravinsky's "The Rite of Spring"', *Journal of New Music Research*, 25/1 (1996): 47–76; C. Agon, A. Moreno, G. Assayag and S. Schaub, 'Formal Aspects of Iannis Xenakis' "Symbolic Music": A Computer-aided Exploration of Compositional Processes', *Journal of New Music Research*, 33/2 (2004): 145–59; P. Hoffmann, '"Something Rich and Strange": Exploring the Pitch Structure of *GENDY3*', *Journal of New Music Research*, 33/2 (2004): 137–44; Keller, D. and Ferneyhough, B., 'Analysis by Modeling: Xenakis's *ST/10-1 080262*', *Journal of New Music Research*, 33/2 (2004): 161–71.

35 E. Cambouropoulos and G. Widmer, 'Automated Motivic Analysis via Melodic Clustering', *Journal of New Music Research*, 29/4 (2000): 303–17; Lartillot, O., 'Multi-dimensional Motivic Pattern Extraction Founded on Adaptive Redundancy Filtering', *Journal of New Music Research*, 34/4 (2005): 375–93.

36 D. Moelants, 'Statistical Analysis of Written and Performed Music. A Study of Compositional Principles and Problems of Coordination and Expression in "Punctional" Serial Music', *Journal of New Music Research*, 29/1 (2000): 37–60; A. Fleischer and T. Noll, 'Analytical Coherence and Performance Regulation', *Journal of New Music Research*, 31/3 (2002): 239–47.

case from recordings[37] and in the other in a live set-up.[38] Nettheim[39] tests a theory of 1/f distribution of pitches by application to pieces by a number of classical composers. Guigue[40] demonstrates software that extracts 'sonic' properties from configurations of notes and allows those configurations to be compared. Chew[41] examines automatic segmentations in two pieces by Messiaen. As the occurrence in the titles of terms such as 'adaptive redundancy filtering' and 'entropy-based learning system' implies, most of these are not expressed in language 'intelligible to the uninitiated' (to quote Erickson); the readership of *Journal of New Music Research* is presumably not considered uninitiated. Furthermore, all of these to some degree concern exposition and development of method rather than focusing on analytical conclusions (not surprising in what is still a largely experimental field). Indeed, many other articles contain data drawn from individual pieces or segments of pieces, but which do not focus sufficiently on the analysis to be counted in this survey.

Besides its different methodology, all of this research has rather different objectives from traditional music analysis. While some familiar themes can be found in the articles referred to above – segmentation and motives, for example – even here the focus is different. The conclusion is not a single segmentation, but that if one measures in this way this segmentation follows, whereas if one measures in that way that segmentation follows. Similarly it is not a single motivic analysis that is presented, but an array of possible motives of different strengths. Thus the analytical result of such studies is often not an interpretation of the piece in question but a mapping of the terrain of possible interpretations. While the analysis is undoubtedly therefore shallower in one sense, it is richer in another.

Even greater difference is found in the objectives which underlie the field of music information retrieval (MIR), which has increased markedly since 2000, and is now probably the most productive field of music research with computers. The driving forces here are commercial: companies would like to be able to process musical content in a manner to produce the most desirable services in a digital music marketplace. Nevertheless, interesting and imaginative research is being conducted with relevance wider than these narrow commercial interests. The

---

37 Rapoport, E., 'Schoenberg-Hartleben's Pierrot Lunaire: Speech – Poem – Melody – Vocal Performance', *Journal of New Music Research*, 33/1 (2004): 71–111.

38 R.D. Kopiez, M. Bangert, W. Goebl and E. Altenmüller, 'Tempo and Loudness Analysis of a Continuous 28-hour Performance of Erik Satie's Composition "*Vexations*"', *Journal of New Music Research*, 32/2 (2003): 243–58.

39 N. Nettheim, 'On the Spectral Analysis of Melody', *Interface*, 21/2 (1992): 135–48.

40 D. Guigue, 'Sonic Object: A Model for Twentieth-century Music Analysis', *Journal of New Music Research*, 26/4 (1997): 346–75.

41 E. Chew, 'Regards on Two Regards by Messiaen: Post-tonal Music Segmentation Using Pitch Context Distances in the Spiral Array', *Journal of New Music Research*, 34/4 (2005): 341–54.

MIREX competition associated with the ISMIR 2005 conference[42] included an evaluation of 13 different systems for automatic genre classification. A database of audio recordings, labelled 'ambient', 'blues', 'classical', 'electronic', 'ethnic', 'folk', 'jazz', 'new age', 'punk' or 'rock' was used, and each system had to determine, from the sound alone, into which of these ten genres to classify each item. The best-performing system classified with an accuracy of 69–78 per cent (depending on how it was measured).[43] Looking more closely at the detailed results for all tested systems, we find that 'punk' and 'classical' were most often correctly classified (90 per cent of cases), but 'punk' more consistently so (i.e. some systems performed badly at identifying 'classical'). At the other extreme, 'new age' music was correctly classified only in 25 per cent of cases, and it was just as frequently mis-classified as 'ethnic'. However, music that was labelled as 'ethnic' was only infrequently mis-classified as 'new age'. Furthermore, there was considerable variation between the systems in how often 'new age' music was mis-classified as 'ethnic'. The objectives in this research were not explicitly analytical, but analytical conclusions can be drawn. Specifically, 'punk' music appears to have the most distinctive sonic characteristics; 'new age' music has some characteristics which are similar to 'ethnic' music, causing some systems to mis-classify, but other characteristics which are distinctive.

5. A gulf

The gulf seems wider than Erickson thought: it is not one of understanding only but one of objectives also. This is probably inevitable. Artificial intelligence has not enabled computers to behave just like humans, and I suspect that if it did we would lose the benefits which computers bring to research. If we want to use computers in music research, we cannot escape translating fuzzy musical concepts into precise computational terms: the language is bound to be different and so incomprehensible to some. Furthermore, we should not be surprised that the different capabilities of computers have influenced researchers to pursue different objectives. Like explorers who set off to find one thing but discover another, those using computers for research in music have inevitably forsaken the original questions of music analysis and pursued novel lines of enquiry.

Though the gulf is perhaps inevitable, we should not allow it to impede research. Three particular kinds of bridge are possible. First, training programmes, especially at postgraduate level, could increase the number of individuals

---

42 J.S. Downie, K. West, A. Ehmann and E. Vincent, 'The 2005 Music Information Retrieval Evaluation Exchange (MIREX 2005): Preliminary Overview', *Proceedings of the 6th International Conference on Music Information Retrieval* (London, 2005), pp. 320–23.

43 Full results can be accessed from <http://www.music-ir.org/evaluation/mirex-results/audio-genre/index.html>, accessed 21 April 2009.

with expertise in both music analysis and computing. I suspect it is easier for a musician to learn the necessary computing skills and concepts, because these are more circumscribed, than it is for a computer scientist to learn the subtleties of music analysis. Second, interdisciplinary research teams with both musicians and computer scientists could achieve the same degree of productivity in music analysis as seen in the field of computer music at centres such as IRCAM in Paris and CCRMA in California. Finally, more could be done to effect the step I outlined above of drawing out music-analytic conclusions from computer-based work. This requires both greater effort from those who work with computers to relate their work to the preoccupations of musicology and music analysis, and greater vision on the part of music analysts to see the new horizons being exposed by computer-based research.

Bibliography

The place of publication is presumed as London, unless otherwise stated.

Aarden, B. and von Hippel, P.T., 'Rules for Chord Doubling (and Spacing): Which Ones Do We Need?', *Music Theory Online*, 10/2 (2004).

Abberton, E.R.M., Howard, D.M. and Fourcin, A.J., 'Laryngographic Assessment of Normal Voice: A Tutorial', *Clinical Linguistics and Phonetics*, 3 (1989): 281–96.

Abdallah, S., Raimond, Y. and Sandler, M., 'An Ontology-based Approach to Information Management for Music Analysis Systems', in *Proceedings of the 120th AES Convention, Toulouse, France*, 2006.

Adlington, R.. 'The Pople *Tonalities* Project' (2007). Available online at <http://www.nottingham.ac.uk/music/tonalities/> accessed 30 May 2007.

Agawu, K., 'Schenkerian Notation in Theory and Practice', *Music Analysis*, 8/3 (1989): 275–301.

Agon, C., Andreatta, M., Assayag, G. and Schaub, S., 'Formal Aspects of Iannis Xenakis' "Symbolic Music": A Computer-aided Exploration of Compositional Processes', *JNMR*, 33/2 (2004): 145–59.

Amatriain, X., Massaguer, J., Garcia, D. and Mosquera, I., 'The CLAM Annotator: A Crossplatform Audio Descriptors Editing Tool', in *Proceedings of the 6th International Conference on Music Information Retrieval* (London, UK, 2005): 426–9.

Andoni, A. and Indyk, P., 'Near Optimal Hashing Algorithms for Approximate Nearest Neighbors in High Dimensions', *Communications of the ACM*, vol. 51, no. 1, 2008, p. 117–122.

Arcos, J.L. and López de Mántaras, R., 'An Interactive CBR Approach for Generating Expressive Music', *Applied Intelligence*, 14/1 (2001): 115–29.

Arts and Humanities Data Service, *AHDS Guides to Good Practice* (AHDS, 2004). Available online at <http://ahds.ac.uk/creating/guides/index.htm#performing-arts>.

Audi, R. (ed.), *The Cambridge Dictionary of Philosophy*, 2nd edn (Cambridge: Cambridge University Press, 1999).

Ayrey, C. (ed.), 'Pitch-class Set Genera: A Symposium', *Music Analysis*, 17/2 (1998): 161–244, 231.

Babbitt, M. 'The Use of Computers in Musicological Research', *Perspectives of New Music*, 3/2 (1965): 74–83. Available online at <http://www.jstor.org>.

Bach, J.S., *Messe in h-Moll*, ed. C. Wolff (Frankfurt: Peters, 1997).

Bach, J.S., *Messe in h-Moll*, ed. J. Rifkin (Wiesbaden: Breitkopf & Härtel, 2006).

Baken, R.J., *Clinical Measurement of Speech and Voice* (Boston, MA: Little Brown, 1987).

Balaban, M., 'Music Structures: Interleaving the Temporal and Hierarchical Aspects in Music', in O. Laske, M. Balaban and K. Ebcioğlu (eds), *Understanding Music with A: Perspectives on Music Cognition* (Cambridge, MA: MIT Press, 1992), pp. 110–39.

Barlow, C.A. and Howard, D.M., 'Voice Source Changes of Child and Adolescent Subjects Undergoing Singing Training', *Logopedics Phoniatrics Vocology*, 27 (2002): 66–73.

Barlow, C.A. and Howard, D.M., 'Electrolaryngographically Derived Voice Source Changes of Child and Adolescent Singers', *Logopedics Phoniatrics Vocology*, 30, 3/4 (2005): 147–57.

Baroni, M., 'The Concept of Musical Grammar', trans. S. Maguire with W. Drabkin, *Music Analysis*, 2/2 (1983): 175–208.

Bartsch, M.A. and Wakefield, G.H., 'To Catch a Chorus: Using Chroma-based Representations for Audio Thumbnailing', in *Proceedings of the Workshop on Applications of Signal Processing to Audio and Acoustics* (2001).

Behne, K.E. '"Blicken Sie auf die Pianisten?!" Zur bildbeeinflußten Beurteilung von Klaviermusik im Fernsehen', *Medienpsychologie*, 2/2 (1990): 115–31.

Bellegarda, J.R. and Nahamoo, D., 'Tied Mixture Continuous Parameter Models for Large Vocabulary Isolated Speech Recognition', in *Proceedings of the IEEE International Conference on Acoustics, Speech, Signal Processing* (1990), pp. 13–16.

Bello, J.P. and Pickens, J.A., 'A Robust Mid-level Representation for Harmonic Content in Music Signals', *Proceedings of the 6th International Conference on Music Information Retrieval*, (London, 2005).

Bishop, C.M., *Neural Networks for Pattern Recognition* (Oxford: Oxford University Press, 1995), section 1.4.

Bonardi, A., 'Information Retrieval for Contemporary Music: What the Musicologist Needs', *Proceedings of the [First] International Symposium on Music Information Retrieval*, Plymouth, MA, October 2000. Available online from <http://mediatheque.ircam.fr/articles/textes/Bonardi00a/>.

Brachman, R.J. and Levesque, H.J. (eds), *Readings in Knowledge Representation* (Los Altos, CA: Morgan Kaufmann, 1985).

Brandmeyer, A., Hoppe, D., Sadakata, M., Timmers, R. and Desain, P., 'PracticeSpace: A Platform for Real-time Visual Feedback in Music Instruction', in *Proceedings of the 9th International Conference on Music Perception and Cognition* (Bologna, 2006).

Bresin, R. and Friberg, A., 'Expressive Musical Icons', in *Proceedings of the 2001 International Conference on Auditory Display* (Espoo, 2001).

Bresin, R. and Friberg, A., 'Emotional Coloring of Computer-controlled Music Performances', *Computer Music Journal*, 24/4 (2000): 44–63.

Bresson, J., Agon, C. and Assayag, G., 'OpenMusic 5: A Cross-Platform Release of the Computer-assisted Composition Environment', *10th Brazilian Symposium on Computer Music*, Belo Horizonte, October 2005. Available online from <http://mediatheque.ircam.fr/articles/textes/Bresson05b/>.

Brett, P., 'Text, Context, and the Early Music Editor', in N. Kenyon (ed.), *Authenticity and Early Music: A Symposium* (Oxford: Oxford University Press, 1988), pp. 83–114.

Breure, L., Boonstra, O. and Doorn, P.K., *Past, Present and Future of Historical Information Science* (Amsterdam: NIWI-KNAW, 2004).

Broder, A.Z., Glassman, S.C., Manasse, M.S. and Zweig, G., 'Syntactic Clustering of the Web', in *Proceedings of 6th World Wide Web Conference, '97* (Oxford: Elsevier Science, 1997), pp. 391–404.

Brown, J.C. and Puckette, M.S., 'An Efficient Algorithm for the Calculation of a Constant Q Transform,' *Journal of the Acoustical Society of America*, 92 (1992): 2698–701.

Butt, J., *Bach: Mass in B Minor* (Cambridge: Cambridge University Press, 1991).

Byrd, D. and Fingerhut, M. 'The History of ISMIR – A Short Happy Tale', *D-Lib Magazine*, 8/11 (2002). Available online from <http://www.ismir.net/texts/Byrd02.html>.

Cambouropoulos, E. and Widmer, G., 'Automated Motivic Analysis via Melodic Clustering', *JNMR*, 29/4 (2000): 303–17.

Camurri, A., Volpe, G., De Poli, G. and Leman, M., 'Communicating Expressiveness and Affect in Multimodal Interactive Systems', *IEEE Multimedia*, 12/1 (2005): 43–53.

Canazza, S., De Poli, G., Drioli, C., Rod'a, A. and Vidolin, A., 'An Abstract Control Space for Communication of Sensory Expressive Intentions in Music Performance', *JNMR*, 32/3 (2003): 281–94.

Canazza, S., Rodá, A., Zanon, P. and Friberg, A., 'Expressive Director: A System for the Realtime Control of Music Performance Synthesis', in R. Bresin (ed.), *Proceedings of the Stockholm Music Acoustics Conference*, 2nd edn (Department of Speech, Music, and Hearing, Royal Institute of Technology, Stockholm, 2003b), vol. 2, 521–4.

Casey, M. and Slaney, M., 'The Importance of Sequences in Musical Similarity', *Proceedings of the International Conference on Acoustics, Speech and Signal Processing*, v. 5, 8 (Toulouse, 2006).

Channam, C., Landone, C., Sandler, M. and Bello, J.P., 'The Sonic Visualiser: A Visualisation Platform for Semantic Descriptors of Musical Signals', in *Proceedings of the 7th International Conference on Music Information Retrieval* (Victoria, 2006).

Chemillier, M. and Timis, D., 'Towards a Theory of Formal Musical Languages', in C. Lischka and J. Fritsch (eds), *Proceedings of the 14th International Computer Music Conference*, 1988, 175–83.

Clarke, A.C., *Profiles of The Future* (New York: Holt, Rinehart and Winston, 1984; repr. of 1962 edn).

Clarke, E.F., 'Empirical Methods in the Study of Performance', in E.F. Clarke and N. Cook (eds), *Empirical Musicology: Aims, Methods, and Prospects* (Oxford: Oxford University Press, 2004), pp. 77–102.

Clarke, E.F. and Cook, N., *Empirical Musicology: Aims, Methods, and Prospects* (Oxford: Oxford University Press, 2004).

Comeau, G., 'Recherche scientifique et pédagogie du piano', *Recherche en Éducation Musicale*, 24 (2006): 1–11.

Conklin, D. and Anagnostopolou, C., 'Representation and Discovery of Multiple Viewpoint Patterns', on *Proceedings of the 2001 International Computer Music Conference*, ICMA, October 2001.

Conklin, D. and Witten, I.H., 'Multiple Viewpoint Systems for Music Prediction', *JNMR*, 24 (1995): 51–73.

Cook, N., 'Performance Analysis and Chopin's Mazurkas', *Musicae Scientiae*, 11/2 (2007): 183–208.

Cook, N., 'Structure and Performance Timing in Bach's C Major Prelude (WTC I): An Empirical Study', *Music Analysis*, 6/3 (1987): 257–72.

Cook, N., *Towards the Compleat Musicologist?*, invited talk at ISMIR 2005. Available online at <http://ismir2005.ismir.net/documents/Cook-CompleatMusicologist.pdf>.

Cook, N. and Sapp, C., 'Purely Coincidental? Joyce Hatto and Chopin's Mazurkas', <http:// www.charm-rhul.ac.uk/content/contact/hatto_article.html>, accessed 20 April 2009.

Cooke, P., *On the Feasibility of a Scottish Music Performance Resource Centre as a Research Facility Principally Aimed at Performers and Composers*, RSAMD, 2003, unpublished report.

Crawford, T., 'Applications Involving Tablatures: *TabCode* for Lute Repertories', *Computing in Musicology* 7 (1991): 57–9.

Dannenberg, R., 'An Online Algorithm for Real-time Accompaniment', in *Proceedings of the 1984 International Computer Music Conference* (San Francisco: International Computer Music Association, 1984), pp. 193–8.

Dannenberg, R.B. and Hu, N., 'Polyphonic Audio Matching for Score Following and Intelligent Audio Editors', in *Proceedings of the International Computer Music Conference 2003* (Singapore, 2003).

Darnton, R., 'Old Books and E-Books. The Gutenberg Prize Acceptance Speech of 2004', *Gutenberg-Jahrbuch* (2005): 17–20.

Datar, M., Indyk, P., Immorlica, N. and Mirrokni, V., 'Locality-sensitive Hashing Scheme Based on p-stable Distributions', in *Proceedings of the Symposium on Computational Geometry* (2004).

Davidson, J.W., 'What Type of Information is Conveyed in the Body Movements of Solo Musician Performers?', *Journal of Human Movement Studies*, 26/6 (1994): 279–301.

Davidson, J.W. and Correia, J.S., 'Body Movement', in R. Parncutt and G. McPherson (eds), *The Science and Psychology of Music Performance:*

Creating Strategies for Teaching and Learning (Oxford: Oxford University Press, 2002), pp. 237–50.

Davies, M. and Plumbley, M., 'Beat Tracking with a Two State Model', in *Proceedings of the IEEE International Conference on Acoustics, Speech, and Signal Processing* (Philadelphia, 2005), vol. 3, pp. 241–4.

Deguchi, S. and Shirai, K., 'An Analysis of Melismatic Patterns in Koto Songs', in W.B. Hewlett and E. Selfridge-Field, *Music Analysis East and West* (Cambridge, MA: MIT Press, 2006), pp. 159–70.

Dempster, S., 'Report on the British Library and Joint Information Systems Committee Usability Evaluation Workshop, 20 October 2004', JISC Moving Pictures and Sound Working Group, London, 20 October 2004.

De Matteis, A. and Haus, G., 'Formalization of Generative Structures within Stravinsky's "The Rite of Spring"', *JNMR*, 25/1 (1996): 47–76.

De Poli, G., 'Methodologies for Expressiveness Modelling of and for Music Performance', *JNMR*, 33/3 (2004): 189–202.

DeRose, D., 'Markup Overview: A Review and a Horse', *interChange*, March (2005).

Dixon, S., 'An Interactive Beat Tracking and Visualisation System', in A. Schloss, R. Dannenberg and P. Driessen (eds), *Proceedings of the 2001 International Computer Music Conference* (San Francisco: International Computer Music Association, 2001), pp. 215–18.

Dixon, S., 'Automatic Extraction of Tempo and Beat from Expressive Performances', *JNMR*, 30/1 (2001): 39–58.

Dixon, S., 'An Online Time Warping Algorithm for Tracking Musical Performances', in *Proceedings of the International Joint Conference on Artificial Intelligence* (Edinburgh, 2005), pp. 1727–8.

Dixon, S., 'Live Tracking of Musical Performances Using Online Time Warping', in *Proceedings of the 8th International Conference on Digital Audio Effects* (Madrid, 2005), p. 92–7.

Dixon, S., 'MIREX 2006 Audio Beat Tracking Evaluation: BeatRoot' (2006). Available online at <http://www. music-ir.org/mirex2006>.

Dixon, S., 'Onset Detection Revisited', in *Proceedings of the 9th International Conference on Digital Audio Effects* (Montreal, 2006), pp. 133–7.

Dixon, S. and Widmer, G., 'MATCH: A Music Alignment Tool Chest', in *Proceedings of the 6th International Conference on Music Information Retrieval* (2005), pp. 492–7.

Dixon, S., Goebl, W. and Widmer, G., 'Real Time Tracking and Visualisation of Musical Expression', in C. Anagnostopoulou, M. Ferrand, and A. Smaill (eds), *Proceedings of the Second International Conference on Music and Artificial Intelligence* (Berlin: Springer, 2002), Lecture Notes in Artificial Intelligence 2445, pp. 58–68.

Dixon, S., Goebl, W. and Widmer, G., 'The Performance Worm: Real Time Visualisation Based on Langner's Representation', in M. Nordahl (ed.),

Proceedings of the 2002 International Computer Music Conference (San Francisco: International Computer Music Association, 2002), pp. 361–4.

Dixon, S., Goebl, W. and Widmer, G., 'The "Air Worm": An Interface for Real-time Manipulation of Expressive Music Performance', in *Proceedings of the 2005 International Computer Music Conference* (San Francisco: International Computer Music Association, 2005), pp. 614–17.

Donin, N., 'Problèmes d'analyse de l'interprétation. Un essai de comparaison assistée par ordinateur d'enregistrements du Premier prélude du *Clavier bien tempéré*', *Musurgia, Analyse et pratique musicales*, 12/4 (2005), pp. 19–43.

Donin, N., Goldszmidt, S. and Theureau, J., 'De *Voi(rex)* à *Apocalypsis*, fragments d'une genèse. Exploration multimédia du travail de composition de Philippe Leroux' (DVD-ROM), in *L'Inouï. Revue de l'Ircam*, 2 (2006).

Downie, J.S., West, K., Ehmann, A. and Vincent, E., 'The 2005 Music Information Retrieval Evaluation Exchange (MIREX 2005): Preliminary Overview', *Proceedings of the 6th International Conference on Music Information Retrieval (ISMIR 2005)* (London: 2005), pp. 320–23.

Dumitrescu, T., *Corpus Mensurabilis Musicae 'Electronicum'*: Toward a Flexible Electronic Representation of Music in Mensural Notation', *Computing in Musicology* 12 (2001): 3–18.

Ellis, D., Whitman, B., Berenzweig, A. and Lawrence, S., 'The Quest for Ground Truth in Musical Artist Similarity', *Proceedings of the International Symposium on Music Information Retrieval* (Paris, 2002), pp. 170–77.

Emmerson, S. (ed.), *Music, Electronic Media and Culture* (Aldershot: Ashgate, 2000).

Erickson, R., 'Music Analysis and the Computer', *Journal of Music Theory*, 12/2 (1968): 240–63.

Erickson, R.F., 'The DARMS Project: A Status Report', *Computing and the Humanities*, 9/6 (1975): 291–8.

Evans, M. and Howard, D.M., 'Larynx Closed Quotient in Female Belt and Opera Qualities: A Case Study', *Voice*, 2/1 (1993): 7-14.

Fant, G., *Acoustic Theory of Speech Production* (The Hague: Mouton: 1960).

Fingerhut, M., 'Music Information Retrieval, or How to Search for (and Maybe Find) Music and Do Away with Incipits', IAML-IASA 2004 Congress, Oslo, 8–13 August 2004. Available online from <http://mediatheque.ircam.fr/articles/textes/Fingerhut04b>.

Fleischer, A. and Noll, T., 'Analytical Coherence and Performance Regulation', *JNMR*, 31/3 (2002): 239–47.

Foote, J., 'Visualizing Music and Audio Using Self-similarity', in *ACM Multimedia*, 1 (1999): 77–80.

Forte, A., 'Pitch-class Set Analysis Today', *Music Analysis*, 4/1–2 (1985): 29–58, 54–6.

Friberg, A., 'A Quantitative Rule System for Musical Performance', Doctoral dissertation, Department of Speech, Music and Hearing, Royal Institute of Technology, Stockholm, 1995.

Friberg, A., 'pDM: An Expressive Sequencer with Realtime Control of the KTH Music Performance Rules', *Computer Music Journal*, 30/1 (2005): 37–48.

Friberg, A., Bresin, R. and Sundberg, J., 'Overview of the KTH Rule System for Musical Performance', *Advances in Cognitive Psychology*, 2/2–3 (2006): 145–61.

Gabrielsson, A., 'Music Performance', in D. Deutsch (ed.), *Psychology of Music*, 2nd edn (San Diego: Academic Press, 1999), pp. 501–602.

Gabrielsson, A., 'Music Performance Research at the Millennium', *Psychology of Music*, 31/3 (2003): 221–72.

Galilei, V., *Fronimo dialogo ... sopra l'arte del bene intavolare* (Venice: Scotto, 1568).

Gionis, A., Indyk, P. and Motwani, R., 'Similarity Search in High Dimensions via Hashing'. *The VLDB Journal* (1999): 518–29.

Goebl, W. and Bresin, R., 'Measurement and Reproduction Accuracy of Computer Controlled Grand Pianos', *Journal of the Acoustical Society of America*, 114/4 (2003): 2273–83.

Goebl, W. and Palmer, C., 'Anticipatory Motion in Piano Performance', *Journal of the Acoustical Society of America*, 120/5 (2006): 3002.

Goebl, W. and Widmer, G., 'Unobtrusive Practice Tools for Pianists', in *Proceedings of the 9th International Conference on Music Perception and Cognition* (Bologna, 2006), 209–14.

Goebl, W., Pampalk, E. and Widmer, G., 'Exploring Expressive Performance Trajectories: Six Famous Pianists Play Six Chopin Pieces', in S.D. Lipscomp, R. Ashley, R.O. Gjerdingen, and P. Webster (eds), *Proceedings of the 8th International Conference on Music Perception and Cognition*, CD-ROM (Adelaide: Causal Productions, 2004), pp. 505–509.

Good, M., 'MusicXML for Notation and Analysis', *Computing in Musicology* 12 (2001): 113–24.

Gouyon, F., Wack, N. and Dixon, S., 'An Open Source Tool for Semiautomatic Rhythmic Annotation', in *Proceedings of the 7th International Conference on Digital Audio Effects* (Naples, 2004), pp. 193–6.

Grachten, M., Arcos, J.L. and López de Mántaras, R., 'A Case Based Approach to Expressivity Aware Tempo Transformation', *Machine Learning*, 65/2–3 (2006): 411–37.

Grier, J., 'Editing', in S. Sadie and J. Tyrrell (eds), *The New Grove Dictionary of Music and Musicians* (London: Macmillan 2001), vol. 7, pp. 885–95.

Grindlay, G. and Helmbold, D., 'Modeling, Analyzing, and Synthesizing Expressive Piano Performance with Graphical Models', *Machine Learning*, 65/2–3 (2006): 361–87.

Guigue, D., 'Sonic Object: A Model for Twentieth-century Music Analysis', *JNMR*, 26/4 (1997): 346–75.

Hall, T., 'Some Computer Aids for the Preparation of Critical Editions of Renaissance Music', *Tijdschrift van de Vereniging voor Nederlandse Muziekgeschiedenis* 25 (1975): 38–53.

Heijink, H., Windsor, L. and Desain, P., 'Data Processing in Music Performance Research: Using Structural Information to Improve Score-performance Matching', *Behavior Research Methods, Instruments and Computers*, 32/4 (2000): 546–54.

Heijink, H., Desain, P., Honing, H. and Windsor, L., 'Make Me a Match: An Evaluation of Different Approaches to Score-performance Matching', *Computer Music Journal* 24/1 (2000): 43–56.

Herre, J., Allamanche, E., Hellmuth, O. and Kastner, T., 'Robust Identification/ Fingerprinting of Audio Signals Using Spectral Flatness Features', *Journal of the Acoustical Society of America*, 111/5 (2002): 2417.

Herrera, P., Celma, Ò., Massaguer, J. et al., 'MUCOSA: A Music Content Semantic Annotator', *Proceedings of the 6th International Conference on Music Information Retrieval* (2005), pp. 77–83.

Herz, G., 'Der lombardische Rhythmus im "Domine Deus" der h-Moll-Messe J.S. Bachs', *Bach-Jahrbuch*, 60 (1975): 90–97.

Hess, W., *Pitch Determination of Speech Signals* (Berlin: Springer Verlag, 1983).

Hewlett, W.B. and Selfridge-Field, E., *Music Analysis East and West: Computing in Musicology 14* (Cambridge, MA: MIT Press, 2006).

Hiraga, R. and Matsuda, N., 'Visualization of Music Performance as an Aid to Listener's Comprehension', in *Proceedings of the Working Conference on Advanced Visual Interfaces* (Gallipoli: ACM Press, 2004), pp. 103–106.

Hiraga, R., Bresin, R., Hirata, K. and Katayose, H., 'Rencon 2004: Turing Test for Musical Expression', in *Proceedings of the 2004 Conference on New Interfaces for Musical Expression* (Hamamatsu, 2004), pp. 120–23.

Hoffmann, P., '"Something Rich and Strange": Exploring the Pitch Structure of *GENDY3*', *JNMR*, 33/2 (2004): 137–44.

Hoppe, D., Brandmeyer, A., Sadakata, M., Timmers, R. and Desain, P., 'The effect of realtime visual feedback on the training of expressive performance skills', in *Proceedings of the 9th International Conference on Music Perception and Cognition* (Bologna, 2006).

Howard, D.M., 'Quantifiable Aspects of Different Singing Styles: A Case Study, *Voice*, 1/1 (1992): 47-62.

Howard, D.M., 'Variation of Electrolaryngographically Derived Closed Quotient for Trained and Untrained Adult Singers', *Journal of Voice*, 9/2 (1995): 163–72.

Howard, D.M., 'Practical Voice Measurement', in T. Harris, S. Harris, J.S. Rubin and D.M. Howard (eds), *The Voice Clinic Handbook* (Whurr Publishers, 1998).

Howard, D.M., 'A Capella SATB Quartet In-tune Singing: Evidence of Intonation Shift', *Proceedings of the Stockholm Music Acoustics Conference*, 2 (2003): 462–6.

Howard, D.M., 'Human Hearing Modelling Real-time Spectrography for Visual Feedback in Singing Training', *Folia Phoniatrica et Logopaedica*, 57, 5/6 (2005): 328–41.

Howard, D.M., 'Intonation Drift in a Capella SATB Quartet Singing with Key Modulation', *Journal of Voice* (in press).

Howard, D.M. and Angus, J.A.S., 'A Comparison between Singing Pitching Strategies of 8 to 11 Year Olds and Trained Adult Singers', *Logopedics Phoniatrics Vocology*, 22/4 (1997): 169–76.

Howard D.M. and Angus J.A.S., *Acoustics and Psychoacoustics*, 3rd edn (Oxford: Focal Press, 2006).

Howard, D.M. and Fourcin, A.J., 'Instantaneous Voice Period Measurement for Cochlear Stimulation', *Electronic Letters*, 19 (1983): 776–9.

Howard, D.M. and Lindsey, G.A., 'New Laryngograms of the Singing Voice', *Proceedings of the 11th International Congress of Phonetic Sciences*, 5 (1987): 166-9.

Howard, D.M. and Welch, G.F., 'Microcomputer-based Singing Ability Assessment and Development', *Applied Acoustics*, 27/2 (1989): 89-102.

Howard, D.M. and Welch, G.F., 'Real-time Visual Displays for Singing Development', *Journal of the Indian Musicological Society*, 34 (2003): 7–23.

Howard, D.M., Lindsey, G.A. and Allen, B. 'Towards the Quantification of Vocal Efficiency', *Journal of Voice*, 4/ 3 (1990): 205-12. (See also errata, *Journal of Voice*, 5/1 (1991): 93-5.)

Howard, D.M., Barlow, C., Szymanski, J.E. and Welch, G.F., 'Vocal Production and Listener Perception of Trained English Cathedral Girl and Boy Choristers', *Bulletin of the Council for Research in Music Education*, 147 (2000): 81–6.

Howard, D.M., Brereton, J., Welch, G.F., Himonides, E., DeCosta, M., Williams, J., and Howard, A.W., 'Are Real-time Displays of Benefit in the Singing Studio? An Exploratory Study, *Journal of Voice* (in press).

Howard, D.M., Welch, G.F., Brereton, J., Himonides, E., DeCosta, M., Williams, J. and Howard, A.W., 'WinSingad: A Real-time Display for the Singing Studio', *Logopedics Phoniatrics Vocology*, 29/3 (2004): 135–44.

Huron, D. 'Humdrum and Kern: Selective Feature Encoding', in E. Selfridge-Field (ed.), *Beyond MIDI: The Handbook of Musical Codes* (Cambridge, MA: MIT Press, 1997), pp. 375–401.

Huron, D., 'The Humdrum Toolkit: Software for Music Research' (n.d.). Available online at <http://dactyl.som.ohio-state.edu/Humdrum/>.

Huron, D., 'Humdrum and Kern: Selective Feature Encoding', in E. Selfridge-Field, *Beyond MIDI: The Handbook of Musical Codes* (Cambridge, MA: MIT Press, 1997).

Huron, D.B., *Sweet Anticipation: Music and the Psychology of Expectation* (Cambridge, MA: MIT Press, 2006).

International Standards Organization, 'Coding of Moving Pictures and Audio, 15938-4 (Audio)' (ISO, 2002).

ISMIR Proceedings, Online Proceedings of the ISMIR Series of Conferences (2000–). Available online from <http://www.ismir.net/all-papers.html>.

Johnson, P., '"Expressive Intonation" in String Performance: Problems of Analysis and Interpretation', in J. Davison, *The Music Practitioner: Research for the*

Music Performer, Teacher and Listener (Aldershot UK and Burlington, VT: Ashgate, 2004), pp. 79–90.

Juhász, Z., 'Contour Analysis of Hungarian Folk Music in a Multidimensional Metric-Space', *JNMR*, 29/1 (2000): 71–83.

Juhász, Z., 'A Model of Variation in the Music of a Hungarian Ethnic Group', *JNMR*, 29/2 (2000): 159–72.

Juhász, Z., 'The Structure of an Oral Tradition – Mapping of Hungarian Folk Music to a Metric Space', *JNMR*, 31/4 (2002): 295–310.

Juhász, Z.. 'Segmentation of Hungarian Folk Songs Using an Entropy-based Learning System', *JNMR*, 33/1 (2004): 5–15.

Juhász, Z., 'A Systematic Comparison of Different European Folk Music Traditions Using Self-organizing Maps', *JNMR*, 35/2 (2006): 95–112.

Ke, Y., Sukthankar, R., Huston, L., 'An Efficient Near-duplicate and Sub-image Retrieval System', *ACM Multimedia* (2004): 869–76.

Keller, D. and Ferneyhough, B., 'Analysis by Modeling: Xenakis's *ST/10-1 080262*', *JNMR*, 33/2 (2004): 161–71.

Kopiez, R., 'Interpretationsforschung mit Hilfe des Computerflügels. Eine Studie zur Wahrnehmung von Interpretationsmerkmalen [Interpretation Research with the Help of Computer Pianos: An Analysis of the Perception of Features of Music Interpretation]', in K.E. Behne, G. Kleinen and H. d. la MotteHaber (eds), *Musikpsychologie. Empirische Forschungen, ästhetische Experimente*, vol. 10, *Jahrbuch der Deutschen Gesellschaft für Musikpsychologie* (Wilhelmshaven: Noetzel, 1994), pp. 7–23.

Kopiez, R.D, Bangert, M., Goebl, W. and Altenmüller, E., 'Tempo and Loudness Analysis of a Continuous 28-hour Performance of Erik Satie's Composition "Vexations"', *JNMR*, 32/2 (2003): 243–58.

Kress, G., *Reading Images: Multimodality, Representation and New Media* (2004). Available online from <http://www.knowledgepresentation.org/BuildingTheFuture/Kress2/Kress2.html>.

Krishnaswamy, A., 'Melodic Atoms, Ornamentation, Tuning and Intonation in Classical Indian Music', in W.B. Hewlett and E. Selfridge-Field, *Music Analysis East and West* (Cambridge, MA: MIT Press, 2006), pp. 139–51.

Krumhansl, C.L., *Cognitive Foundations of Musical Pitch* (New York and Oxford: Oxford University Press, 1990).

Langner, J. and Goebl, W., 'Visualizing Expressive Performance in Tempo–Loudness Space', *Computer Music Journal*, 27/4 (2003): 69–83.

Large, E.W., 'Dynamic Programming for the Analysis of Serial Behaviors', *Behavior Research Methods, Instruments and Computers*, 25/2 (1993): 238–41.

Lartillot, O., 'Multi-dimensional Motivic Pattern Extraction Founded on Adaptive Redundancy Filtering', *JNMR*, 34/4 (2005): 375–93.

Lazzaro, J. and Wawrzynek, J., *The MPEG-4 Structured Audio Book* (1999). Available online at <http://www.cs.berkeley.edu/~lazzaro/sa/book/index.html>, accessed 30 August 2007.

Lerdahl, F. and Jackendoff, R., *A Generative Theory of Tonal Music* (Cambridge, MA: MIT Press, 1983).

Levenshtein, V.I., 'A Binary Code Capable of Correcting Spurious Insertions and Deletions of Ones', *Cybernetics and Control Theory*, 10/8 (1966): 707–710

Lewin, D., *Generalized Musical Intervals and Transformations* (New Haven and London: Yale University Press, 1987).

Lindsay, A.T., Burnett, I., Quackenbush, S. and Jackson, M., 'Fundamentals of Audio Descriptions', in B.S. Manjunath, P. Salembier and T. Sikora, *Introduction to MPEG-7: Multimedia Content Description Interface* (Chichester, John Wiley and Sons, 2002).

Logan, B. and Chu, S., 'Music Summarization Using Key Phrases', in *Proceedings of IEEE International Conference on Acoustics, Speech, and Signal Processing* (Turkey, 2000).

McCarty, W. and Short, H., 'A Rough Intellectual Map for Humanities Computing', in *Mapping the Field* (Pisa: Association for Literary and Linguistic Computing, 2002). Available online at <http://www.allc.org/reports/map/mapping.html>.

McGann, J.J., 'The Rationale of HyperText' (1995). Available online at <http://jefferson.village.virginia.edu/public/jjm2f/rationale.html>.

McGann, J.J., 'The Rationale of HyperText', in K. Sutherland (ed.), *Electronic Text, Investigations in Method and Theory* (Oxford: Oxford University Press, 1997), pp. 19–46.

Madsen, T.S. and Widmer, G., 'Exploring Pianist Performance Styles with Evolutionary String Matching', *International Journal of Artificial Intelligence Tools*, 15/4 (2006): 495–514.

Marsden, A., 'Musical Informatics: An Emerging Discipline?', *Revue Informatique et Statistique dans les Sciences humaines*, 29 (1993): 77–90.

Marsden, A., 'Computers and the Concept of Tonality', in J.T. Coppock (ed.), *Information Technology and Scholarly Disciplines* (Oxford: Oxford University Press, for the British Academy, 1999), pp. 33–52.

Marsden, A., *Representing Musical Time: A Temporal-Logic Approach* (Lisse: Swets & Zeitlinger, 2000).

Mathews, M.V., Friberg, A., Bennett, G., Sapp, C. and Sundberg, J., 'A Marriage of the Director Musices Program and the Conductor Program', in R. Bresin (ed.), *Proceedings of the Stockholm Music Acoustics Conference* (Stockholm: Department of Speech, Music, and Hearing, Royal Institute of Technology, 2003), vol. 1, pp. 13–15.

Mavromatis, P., 'A Hidden Markov Model of Melody Production in Greek Church Chant', in W.B. Hewlett and E. Selfridge-Field, *Music Analysis East and West* (Cambridge, MA: MIT Press, 2006), pp. 93–112.

Meredith, D., 'Rapporteur's Report' on AHRC ICT Methods Network Expert Seminar on 'Modern Methods for Musicology: Prospects, Proposals and Realities', Royal Holloway, University of London, 3 March 2006. Available online at <http://www.methodsnetwork.ac.uk/redist/pdf/es2rappreport.pdf>.

Meredith, D., 'Computing Pitch Names in Tonal Music: A Comparative Analysis of Pitch Spelling Algorithms', D.Phil. thesis, University of Oxford, 2007.

Minsky, M., *The Society of Mind* (New York: Simon & Schuster, 1986).

Moelants, D., 'Statistical Analysis of Written and Performed Music. A Study of Compositional Principles and Problems of Coordination and Expression in "Punctional" Serial Music', *JNMR*, 29/1 (2000): 37–60.

Nair, G., *Voice: Tradition and Technology* (San Diego: Singular Publishing Company, 1999).

Nattiez, J.-J., *Fondements d'une sémiologie de la musique* (Paris: Union Générale d'Editions, 1975).

Nattiez, J.-J., 'Varèse's "Density 21.5": A Study in Semiological Analysis', trans. Anna Barry, *Music Analysis*, 1/3 (1982): 243–340.

Nettheim, N., 'On the Spectral Analysis of Melody', *Interface*, 21/2 (1992): 135–48.

Newcomb, S.R., 'Standard Music Description Language Complies with Hypermedia Standard', *Computer*, 24/7 (1991): 76–9.

Ockeghem, J., *Motets and chansons, Collected Works*, vol. 3, ed. Richard Wexler with Dragan Plamenac (Urbana, IL: American Musicological Society, 1992).

Olive, K., 'The Anonymous *Missa Ma bouche rit*, Vienna, Österreichische Nationalbibliothek, Ms. 11883: A Study and Modern Edition', undergraduate thesis, University of Manchester, 2003.

Orio, N. and Déchelle, F., 'Score Following Using Spectral Analysis and Hidden Markov Models', in *Proceedings of the 2001 International Computer Music Conference* (Havana: International Computer Music Association, 2001), 151–4.

Pachet, F. and Addessi, A.R., 'When Children Reflect on their Own Playing Style: Experiments with Continuator and Children', *Computers in Education*, 2/1 (2004): 14.

Palmer, C., 'Music Performance', *Annual Review of Psychology*, 48 (1997): 115–38.

Parncutt, R., 'Systematic Musicology and the History and Future of Western Musical Scholarship', *Journal of Interdisciplinary Music Studies, 1* (2007): 1–32. Available online at <http://www-gewi.uni-graz.at/staff/parncutt/SMW. HTM>.

Parncutt, R. and McPherson, G. (eds), *The Science and Psychology of Music Performance. Creating Strategies for Teaching and Learning* (New York: Oxford University Press, 2002).

Pauws, S. 'Musical Key Extraction from Audio', in *Proceedings of the International Symposium on Music Information Retrieval* (Barcelona, 2004), pp. 96–9.

Peeters, G., 'A Large Set of Audio Features for Sound Description (Similarity and Classification)', internal report (IRCAM, 2004).

Peeters, G., La Burthe, A. and Rodet, X., 'Toward Automatic Music Audio Summary Generation from Signal Analysis', *Proceedings of the Third International Conference on Music Information Retrieval* (ISMIR), Paris, 13–17 October 2002. Available online from <http://ismir2002.ismir.net/proceedings/02-FP03-3.pdf>.

Plato, *The Republic*, trans. J.L. Davies and D.J. Vaughan (Ware: Wordsworth Editions, 1997).

PLATO, 'PLATO reports, PLATO documents, and CERL progress reports, 1958–1993' (1993). Computer-based Education Research Laboratory, University of Illinois at Urbana-Champaign. Available online from <http://www.cbi.umn.edu/collections/inv/cbi00133.html>.

Pople, A., 'Using Complex Set Theory for Tonal Analysis: An Introduction to the *Tonalities* Project', *Music Analysis*, 23/2–3 (2004): 153–94.

Potter, R., Kopp, G. and Green, H., *Visible Speech* (New York: Van Nostrand Company, 1947).

Puig, V., Guédy, F., Fingerhut, M. et al., 'Musique Lab 2: A Three Level Approach for Music Education at School', *Conference Proceedings International Computer Music Conference* (ICMC), Barcelona, 4–10 September 2005, pp. 419–422.

Puzicha, J., Hofmann, T. and Buhmann, J.M., 'Histogram Clustering for Unsupervised Image Segmentation', in *Proceedings of the Conference on Computer Vision and Pattern Recognition* (1999).

Queen Mary, University of London, 'Sonic Visualiser' (n.d.). Available online at <http://www.sonicvisualiser.org>.

Raphael, C., 'A Hybrid Graphical Model for Aligning Polyphonic Audio with Musical Scores', in *Proceedings of the 5th International Conference on Music Information Retrieval* (Barcelona, 2004), 387–94.

Raphael, C., 'Aligning Music Audio with Symbolic Scores Using a Hybrid Graphical Model', *Machine Learning*, 65/2–3 (2006): 389–409.

Rapoport, E., 'Schoenberg-Hartleben's Pierrot Lunaire: Speech – Poem – Melody – Vocal Performance', *JNMR*, 33/1 (2004): 71–111.

Raptis, S., Askenfelt, A., Fober, D. et al., 'IMUTUS – An Effective Practicing Environment for Music Tuition', in *Proceedings of the 2005 International Computer Music Conference* (Barcelona, 2005), pp. 383–6.

Recordare, 'MusicXML Definition, v. 2.0' (2005). Available online at <http://www.recordare.com/xml.html>.

Reynolds, D.A., 'Speaker Identification and Verification using Gaussian Mixture Speaker Models', *Speech Communication*, 17/1–2 (1995): 91–108.

van Rijsbergen, C.J., *Information Retrieval* (London: Butterworth, 1979).

Riley-Butler, K., 'Teaching Expressivity: An Aural–Visual Feedback-replication Model', in *ESCOM 10th Anniversary Conference on Musical Creativity* (Liège: Université de Liège, 2002), CD-ROM.

Rink, J. (ed.), *The Practice of Performance: Studies in Musical Interpretation* (Cambridge: Cambridge University Press, 1995).

Rink, J. (ed.), *Musical Performance. A Guide to Understanding* (Cambridge: Cambridge University Press, 2002).

Rink, J., Online Chopin Variorum Edition (OCVE), funded by the Andrew W. Mellon Foundation (2006). Available online from <http://www.ocve.org.uk>.

Robinson, P., 'Where We Are with Electronic Scholarly Editions, and Where We Want to Be', *Jahrbuch für Computerphilologie* (2002): 4. Available online from <http://www.computerphilologie.uni-muenchen.de/jg03/robinson.html>.

Roland, P., 'Design Patterns in XML Music Representation', in *Proceedings of ISMIR 2003*, Baltimore, Maryland, 2003. Available online at <http://www.ismir.net>, accessed 30 August 2007.

Roland, P., 'The Music Encoding Initiative (MEI)' (2005). Available online from <http://www.lib.virginia.edu/digital/resndev/mei/>, accessed 1 September 2007.

Rossiter, D. and Howard, D.M. 'ALBERT: A Real-time Visual Feedback Computer Tool for Professional Vocal Development', *Journal of Voice*, 10/4 (1996): 321–36.

Rossiter, D.P., Howard, D.M. and Comins, R., 'Objective Measurement of Voice Source and Acoustic Output Change with a Short Period of Vocal Tuition', *Voice* 4/1 (1995): 16-31.

Russ, M., '"Fishing in the Right Place": Analytical Examples from the *Tonalities* Project', *Music Analysis*, 23/2–3 (2004): 195–244.

Ruwet, N., *Language, musique, poésie* (Paris: Editions du Seuil, 1972).

Sankoff, D. and Kruskal, J. *Time Warps, String Edits and Macromolecules: The Theory and Practice of Sequence Comparison* (Reading, MA: Addison-Wesley, 1983).

Sapp, C., *The Mazurka Project*, The AHRC Research Centre for the History and Analysis of Recorded Music, Royal Holloway, University of London, 2006. Available online at <http://mazurka.org.uk/>

Saunders, C., Hardoon, D.R., ShaweTaylor, J. and Widmer, G., 'Using String Kernels to Identify Famous Performers from their Playing Style', in *Proceedings of the 15th European Conference on Machine Learning (ECML) and the 8th European Conference on Principles and Practice of Knowledge Discovery in Databases* (Pisa, 2004).

Scheirer, E. and Slaney, M., 'Construction and Evaluation of a Robust Multifeatures Speech/Music Discriminator', in *IEEE Transactions on Acoustics, Speech, and Signal Processing* (1997): 1331–4.

Schwartz, D., 'The Caterpillar System for Concatenative Sound Synthesis', in *Proceedings of Digital Audio Effects Conference* (2003).

Seashore, C.E. (ed.), *Objective Analysis of Musical Performance, University of Iowa Studies in the Psychology of Music*, vol. 4 (Iowa City: Iowa University Press, 1936).

Selfridge-Field, E. (ed.), *Beyond MIDI: The Handbook of Musical Codes* (Cambridge, MA: MIT Press, 1997).

Shaffer, L.H., 'Analysing Piano Performance', in G.E. Stelmach and J. Requin (eds), *Tutorials in Motor Behavior* (Amsterdam: North Holland, 1980).

Shaffer, L.H., 'Performances of Chopin, Bach and Bartòk: Studies in Motor Programming', *Cognitive Psychology*, 13/3 (1981): 326–76.

Shirmohammadi, S., Khanafar, A. and Comeau, G., 'MIDIator: A Tool for Analysing Students' Piano Performance', *Recherche en Éducation Musicale*, 24 (2006): 35–48.

Sjölander, K. and Beskow, J., 'WaveSurfer – An Open Source Speech Tool', in B. Yuan, T. Huang, and X. Tang (eds), *Proceedings of the International Conference on Spoken Language Processing* (Bejing, 2000), pp. 464–7.

Sleator, D. and Temperley, D., 'The Melisma Music Analyzer' (n.d.). Available online at <http://www.link.cs.cmu.edu/music-analysis/>, accessed 30 May 2007.

Smaill, A., Wiggins, G.A. and Harris, M., 'Hierarchical Music Representation for Analysis and Composition', *Computers and the Humanities*, 27 (1993): 7–17. Also available as Edinburgh DAI Research Paper no. 511.

Smoliar, S.W., Waterworth, J.A. and Kellock, P.R., 'pianoFORTE: A System for Piano Education beyond Notation Literacy', in *Proceedings of the ACM International Conference on Multimedia, San Francisco* (New York: ACM Press, 1995), pp. 457–65.

Stamatatos, E. and Widmer, G., 'Automatic Identification of Music Performers with Learning Ensembles', *Artificial Intelligence*, 165/1 (2005): 37–56.

Sundberg, J., *The Science of the Singing Voice* (Dekalb, IL: Northern Illinois University Press, 1987).

Sundberg, J., Askenfelt, A. and Frydén, L., 'Musical Performance. A Synthesis-by-Rule Approach', *Computer Music Journal*, 7 (1983): 37–43.

Sundberg, J., Frydén, L. and Askenfelt, A., 'What Tells You the Player is Musical? An Analysis-by-Synthesis Study of Music Performance', in J. Sundberg (ed.), *Studies of Music Performance* (Stockholm: Royal Swedish Academy of Music, 1983b), vol. 39, 61–75.

Szabo, M., 'Enhancing the Interactive Classroom through Computer Based Instruction: Some Examples from Plato', *Computer-Mediated Communications and the Online Classroom*, vol. 1 (New Jersey: Hampton Press, 1994). Available online from <http://www.quasar.ualberta.ca/edmedia/readingsnc/cmc/cmc.html>.

Taylor, T., *Strange Sounds. Music, Technology and Culture* (New York and London: Routledge, 2001).

Temperley, D., 'The Line of Fifths', *Music Analysis*, 19/3 (2000): 289–319.

Tenney, J., 'Temporal Gestalt Perception in Music', *Journal of Music Theory*, 24/2 (1980), pp. 205–41.

Thorpe, C.W., Callaghan, J. and van Doorn, J., 'Visual Feedback of Acoustic Voice Features for the Teaching of Singing', *Australian Voice*, 5 (1999): 32–39.

Tobudic, A. and Widmer, G., 'Learning to Play like the Great Pianists', in *Proceedings of the 19th International Joint Conference on Artificial Intelligence* (Edinburgh, 2005).

Tomita, Y. and Fujinami, T., 'Managing a Large Text-critical Database of J.S. Bach's Well-tempered Clavier II with XML and Relational Database', in I. Asselman and B. Bouckaert (eds), *International Musicological Society: 17th*

International Conference, 1–7 August 2002, Leuven (Leuven: Alamire, 2002), pp. 256–7.

Turing, A., 'On computable Numbers, with an Application to the Entscheidungsproblem', *Proceedings of the London Mathematical Society*, 2 /42 (1936): 230–65.

Tzanetakis, G. and Cook, P., 'Musical Genre Classification of Audio Signals', *IEEE Transactions on Speech and Audio Processing*, 10/5 (2002): 293–302.

Veltman, J., 'Syllable Placement and Metrical Hierarchy in Sixteenth-century Motets', in W.B. Hewlett and E. Selfridge-Field, *Music Analysis East and West* (Cambridge, MA: MIT Press, 2006), pp. 73–89.

Wanderley, M.M., Vines, B., Middleton, N., McKay, C. and Hatch, W., 'The Musical Significance of Clarinetists' Ancillary Gestures: An Exploration of the Field', *JNMR*, 34/1 (2005): 97–113.

Welch, G.F. and Howard, D.M., 'Gendered Voice in the Cathedral Choir', *Psychology of Music*, 30/1 (2002): 102–20.

Welch, G.F., Howard, D.M. and Rush, C., 'Real-time Visual Feedback in the Development of Vocal Pitch Accuracy in Singing', *Psychology of Music*, 17 (1989): 146-57.

Welch, G.F., Rush, C. and Howard, D.M., 'A Developmental Continuum of Singing Ability: Evidence from a Study of Five-year-old Developing Singers', *Early Child Development and Care*, 69 (1991): 107-19.

Welch, G.F., Himonides, E., Howard, D.M. and Brereton, J., 'VOXed: Technology as a Meaningful Teaching Aid in the Singing Studio', in R. Parncutt, A. Kessler and F. Zimmer (eds), *Conference on Interdisciplinary Musicology* (Graz: University of Graz, 2004).

Widmer, G., 'Machine Discoveries: A Few Simple, Robust Local Expression Principles', *JNMR*, 31/1 (2002): 37–50.

Widmer, G., 'Studying a Creative Act with Computers: Music Performance Studies with Automated Discovery Methods', *Musicae Scientiae*, 9/1 (2005): 11–30.

Widmer, G. and Goebl, W., 'Computational Models of Expressive Music Performance: The State of the Art', *JNMR*, 33/3 (2004): 203–16.

Widmer, G. and Tobudic, A., 'Playing Mozart by Analogy: Learning Multilevel Timing and Dynamics Strategies', *JNMR*, 32/3 (2003): 259–68.

Widmer, G. and Tobudic, A., 'Playing Mozart by Analogy: Learning Multilevel Timing and Dynamics Strategies', in R. Hiraga (ed.), *Proceedings of the ICAD 2002 Rencon Workshop on Performance Rendering Systems* (Kyoto: Rencon Steering Group, 2002), pp. 28–35.

Widmer, G. and Tobudic, A., 'Playing Mozart by Analogy: Learning Multilevel Timing and Dynamics Strategies', *JNMR*, 32/3 (2003): 259–68.

Widmer, G., Dixon, S., Goebl, W., Pampalk, E. and Tobudic, A., 'In Search of the Horowitz Factor', *AI Magazine*, 24/3 (2003): 111–30.

Wiener, N., *Extrapolation, Interpolation, and Smoothing of Stationary Time Series* (New York: Wiley, 1949).

Wiering, F., Crawford, T. and Lewis, D., 'Creating an XML Vocabulary for Encoding Lute Music', in *Humanities, Computers and Cultural Heritage: Proceedings of the XVIth International Conference of the Association for History and Computing, 14–17 September 2005* (Amsterdam. Amsterdam: Royal Netherlands Academy of Arts and Sciences, 2005), pp. 279–87.

Wiering, F., Crawford, T. and Lewis, D., 'Fretting with the Computer: Designing a Markup Strategy for Digital Critical Editions of Lute Tablatures', presentation held at MedRen2005, Tours (2005). Available online from <http://people. cs.uu.nl/fransw/presentations/WieringMedRen2005.pdf>.

Wiggins, G.A., Harris, M. and Smaill, A., 'Representing Music for Analysis and Composition', in M. Balaban, K. Ebcioglu, O. Laske, C. Lischka and L. Sorisio (eds), *Proceedings of the 2nd IJCAI AI/Music Workshop* (Detroit, Michigan, 1989), pp. 63–71. Also available as Edinburgh DAI Research Paper no. 504.

Wiggins, G.A., Miranda, E., Smaill, A. and Harris, M., 'A Framework for the Evaluation of Music Representation Systems', *Computer Music Journal*, 17/3 (1993): 31–42. Also available as Edinburgh DAI Research Paper no. 658.

Williamon, A. (ed.), *Musical Excellence: Strategies and Techniques to Enhance Performance* (Oxford: Oxford University Press, 2004).

Williams, J., Welch, G. and Howard, D.M., 'An Exploratory Baseline Study of Boy Chorister Vocal Behaviour and Development in an Intensive Professional Context', *Logopedics Phoniatrics Vocology*, 30, 3/4 (2005): 158–62.

Wishart, T., *On Sonic Art*, rev. edn (Routledge, 1996).

Zoia, G., Nesi, P., Barthelemy, J., Crombie, D., Fuschi, D., Spadoni, F., Ng, K., Schmucker, M. and Bellini, P., 'Proposal for Music Notation Modelling and Its Integration within MPEG-4 and MPEG-7 (2003). ISO/IEC JTCI/SC29/WG11.

Other online resources

British Library's Archival Sound Recordings Project <http://sounds.bl.uk/>.
Chopin's First Editions Online (CFEO) <http://www.cfeo.org.uk/>.
HOTBED system <http://www.hotbed.ac.uk/index.php>.
Humdrum <http://www.music-cog.ohio-state.edu/Humdrum/>.
ICT4AV <http://ict4av.lancs.ac.uk/report/body/>.
ISMIR conferences <http://www.ismir.net>.
Locality sensitive hashing <http://www.mit.edu/~andoni/LSH/>.
MakeMusic's *SmartMusic* software <http://www.smartmusic.com/>.
MPEG7 <http://doc.gold.ac.uk/~mas01mc/mpeg7/>.
Music Lab 2 <http://musiquelab.ircam.fr/>.
MusicXML <http://www.recordare.com/xml.html>.
Online Chopin Variorum Edition (OCVE) <http://www.ocve.org.uk/>.
WinSingad software <http://www.winsingad.org/>.
(All accessed 30 August 2007.)

Index